Inflation and the Merchant Economy

90014

Inflation and the Merchant Economy
The Hamburg Mittelstand, 1914–1924

Peter J. Lyth

BERG
New York/Oxford/Munich
Distributed exclusively in the U.S. and Canada by
St. Martin's Press, New York

Published in 1990 by
Berg Publishers, Inc.
Editorial offices:
165 Taber Avenue, Providence, RI 02906, U.S.A.
150 Cowley Road, Oxford OX4 1JJ, UK
Westermühlstraße 26, 8000 München 5, FRG

Library of Congress Cataloging-in-Publication Data
Lyth, Peter J.
  Inflation in the merchant economy: the Hamburg Mittelstand,
1914–1924 / Peter J. Lyth.
      p.   cm.
  Includes bibliographical references (p.)
  ISBN 0–85496–592–0
  1. Hamburg (Germany)—Economic conditions. 2. Inflation
(Finance)—Germany—Hamburg—History—20th century.
3. Hamburg (Germany)—Commerce—History—20th century.
4. Middle classes—Germany—Hamburg—History—20th century.
5. Small business—Germany—Hamburg—History—20th century.
I. Title.
HC289.H2L98 1990
330.943′515084—dc20   89–18118
                                                                             CIP

British Library Cataloguing in Publication Data
Lyth, Peter J.
Inflation and the merchant economy: the Hamburg Mittelstand,
1914–1924.
1. Germany. Finance. Inflation, history. Social aspects
I. Title
332.4′1

ISBN 0–85496–592–0

(000553024 T

Printed in Great Britain by
Billing & Sons Ltd, Worcester

Contents

List of Tables   vii

Preface   ix

Abbreviations   xi

1 Introduction   1

2 Hamburg   25

3 War, 1914–1918   52

4 Revolution and Inflation, 1918–1921   75

5 Into the Abyss, 1921–1922   109

6 Year of Turmoil, 1923   136

7 Aftermath, 1924–1925   162

Sources and Bibliography   187

Index

List of Tables

1. Ships and Trade Tonnage (Imports and Exports) through Hamburg, 1866–1926   29
2. The Ten Largest Cities in Germany, 1910 and 1925   35
3. Hamburg Working Population by Occupational Categories and Economic Sectors, 1907 and 1925   36
4. Distribution of White-Collar Workers in the Hamburg Economy, 1907 and 1925   36
5. Registered Enterprises in Hamburg, 1907 and 1925   38
6. Artisan Guilds in Hamburg, 1911–1926   60
7. Staff Salaries at the HEW, 1914–1919   67
8. Cost-of-Living Supplements for Married Civil Servants in Hamburg and Prussia, 1917–1918   70
9. Daily Journeyman's Wage in Selected Crafts in Hamburg, 1913 and 1920   86
10. Index of Exchange Rates and Domestic Food Prices in Germany, 1914–1923   91
11. Households and Dwellings in Hamburg, 1919–1925   103
12. Staff Salaries at the HHA, 1914–1924   120
13. Index of Real Earnings of Civil Servants, State Employees, and Skilled and Unskilled Workers in Hamburg, 1920–1925   128
14. Reich Cost-of-Living Index for Hamburg, 1921–1922   133
15. Trading at the Hamburger Sparkasse von 1827, 1913–1925   147
16. Index of HHA Salary Increments and the Cost of Living, 1923   150
17. Number of Civil Servants and State Employees in Hamburg, 1914–1924   155
18. Nominal and Real Value of Monthly Rents in Hamburg: Index of Increases, 1919–1923   158
19. Changes in Land Ownership in Hamburg, 1907–1926 (Voluntary Sales)   159
20. Bankruptcy Statistics in Hamburg and Germany, 1913–1924   165

Preface

The great German inflation was not a freak phenomenon limited in time to the latter half of 1923, but a ten-year process beginning with the First World War in 1914. This book is about that process and the changing impact it had on a single locality. In probing the experience of different occupational groups, it aims to show that the middle stratum or Mittelstand within German society lost more than its savings in the inflation; it lost an era of relative security, recognition, and participation in the governmental process. More important for Germany, it lost its sense of identification with the state and the institutions that had been nurtured in the Wilhemine Empire.

The choice of a local format is intended to add more subtle and differentiated tones to the picture of the inflation normally acquired through the generalized observations of the national study. Indeed it is fair to say that it is only at the local level that the inflation's complex intertwining of cause and effect between the economic, social, and political life of a community can be properly understood.

In preparing the dissertation upon which the study is based, I received help from a number of people and institutions. I would like to thank the Social Science Research Council of Great Britain and the German Historical Institute in London for the financial backing that enabled me to undertake the necessary research. I would also like to acknowledge the assistance of the staffs of the Hamburg Handelskammer and Staatsarchiv, who were patient with my many inquiries. I am grateful to the following individuals, both for guidance through the Hamburg archives and for hours of stimulating discussion: Ursula Büttner, Richard J. Evans, Harm and Verena Schröter, Bernd-Jürgen Wendt, and Peter-Christian Witt. Above all, I would like to express my gratitude to my dissertation supervisor, Alice Teichova, on whose wide experience and critical insight I drew constantly.

Lastly I must thank my wife, Ofra, without whose encouragement this book would never have seen the light of day. I dedicate it to her.

Abbreviations

ADB	Allgemeiner Deutscher Beamtenbund
ADGB	Allgemeiner Deutscher Gewerkschaftsbund
AfA-Bund	Allgemeiner freier Angestellten-Bund
AIGZ	*Allgemeine Industrie- und Gewerbezeitung*
DB	*Der Bureaubeamte* (later *Der Bürobeamte*)
DBB	Deutscher Beamtenbund
DDP	Deutsche Demokratische Partei
DHSG	Deputation für Handel, Schiffahrt und Gewerbe
DHV	Deutschnationale Handlungsgehilfenverband
DHW	*Deutsche Handels-Wacht*
DKWR	*Der Kaufmann in Wirtschaft und Recht*
DNVP	Deutschnationale Volkspartei
DVP	Deutsche Volkspartei
GBHS	Gewerkschaft der Bürobeamten des Hamburgischen Staates
GdA	Gewerkschaftsbund der Angestellten
GVH	Grundeigentümer-Verein Hamburg
HBZ	*Hamburgische Beamtenzeitung*
HEW	Hamburgische Electricitäts-Werke AG
HGZ	*Hamburger Grundeigentümer-Zeitung*
HHA	Hamburger Hochbahn AG
HKH	Archive of the Hamburg Handelskammer
KPD	Kommunistische Partei Deutschlands
MEA	*Mieteinigungsamt* (rent arbitration office)
PPS	*Preisprüfungsstelle* (price control office)
PRO	Public Record Office, London
RGBl.	*Reichsgesetzblatt*
RMG	*Reichsmietengesetz* (Reich rent law)
SPD	Sozialdemokratische Partei Deutschlands
StA.H	Hamburg Staatsarchiv
USPD	Unabhängige Sozialdemokratische Partei Deutschlands
ZdA	Zentralverband der Angestellten

1

Introduction

Throughout the Continent the pre-war savings of the middle class, so far as they were invested in bonds, mortgages or bank deposits, have been largely or entirely wiped out. Nor can it be doubted that this experience must modify social psychology towards the practice of saving and investment. What was deemed most secure has proved least so. He who neither spent nor "speculated," who made "proper provision for his family," who sang hymns to security and observed most straitly the morals of the edified and respectable injunctions of the worldly-wise – he, indeed, who gave fewest pledges to Fortune has yet suffered her heaviest visitations.

—John Maynard Keynes, 1923[1]

Im Rückblick wäre sogar zu fragen, ob nicht das eigentliche Wunder sei, daß die Weimarer Republik so lange gehalten hat. Die Inflation von 1922/23 enteignete das arbeitende, aus einem bescheidenen Kapitalstock von Erspartem begrenzte Unabhängigkeit gewinnende Bürgertum. Der Selbständige zum Beispiel, der ein Leben lang gearbeitet hatte, war durch die brutale Konfiskation seiner Ersparnisse proletarisiert. Selbst der Fachar-

1. *A Tract on Monetary Reform*, Collected Writings (London, 1971), p. 16.

1

beiter sah sich seiner paar tausend
Mark beraubt die er sich als Zusatz
zur Rente hart erspart hatte.
—*Frankfurter Allgemeine Zeitung,* 1985[2]

Among the various explanations put forward for the collapse of the
Weimar Republic and the rise of Nazism, the disaffection of the
German Mittelstand has always figured prominently. Both its
supposed "preindustrial" value system and the difficulty it experienced in adapting to the economic upheavals after the First World
War are cited as reasons for its hostility to democracy. Alienated
from the two driving forces of the age, liberalism and socialism,
and practically ignored by the leaders of the Republic after 1918, it
appears to have floated rudderless upon the stormy sea of Weimar
party politics, before being finally washed up on the beckoning
shore of National Socialism.[3]

The widely held view that the social composition of the Nazi
movement was predominantly Mittelstand or lower middle class
began in the 1930s with the works of Theodore Abel and has been
sustained in modern treatments of the Third Reich.[4] Certainly since
the early 1970s revisionist interpretations have cast some doubt on
the thesis by presenting support for the Nazis as more broad-based
and differentiated,[5] and regional studies have demonstrated that a
determined effort was made to attract workers to the party, at least
after 1925,[6] but the strong connection between the Mittelstand and
the National Socialist phenomenon has remained.

2. Editorial by Friedrich Karl Fromme, 22 March 1985, "Die Schuld und die
Fehler," protesting Allied celebrations at the time of the fortieth anniversary of the
end of the Second World War and describing the "failure" of the Weimar Republic.

3. A definitive exposition of this view, with particular reference to the old
Mittelstand of artisans and retailers, is found in Heinrich A. Winkler, *Mittelstand,
Demokratie und Nationalsozialismus. Die politische Entwicklung von Handwerk und
Kleinhandel in der Weimarer Republik* (Cologne, 1972).

4. Theodore Abel, *Why Hitler Came into Power,* foreword by Thomas Childers
(Cambridge, Mass., 1986). For modern accounts see, for example, Karl-Dietrich
Bracher, *The German Dictatorship: The Origins, Structure, and Effects of National
Socialism* (New York, 1970), pp. 152–60; Martin Broszat, *The Hitler State: The
Foundation and Development of the Internal Structure of the Third Reich* (London, 1981),
pp. 29–32.

5. See, for example, Peter H. Merkl, *Political Violence under the Swastika* (Princeton, 1975); Richard Hamilton, *Who Voted for Hitler?* (Princeton, 1982). Revisionist
literature is reviewed in Jürgen W. Falter, "Wählerbewegungen zur NSDAP,
1924–1933," in Otto Büsch, ed., *Wählerbewegungen in der europäischen Geschichte*
(Berlin, 1980), pp. 159–202.

6. E.g., Jeremy Noakes, *The Nazi Party in Lower Saxony, 1921–1933* (Oxford,
1971); Johnpeter Horst Grill, *The Nazi Movement in Baden, 1920–1945* (Chapel Hill,
1983).

The persistence of preindustrial or antimodern values amongst the Mittelstand is an intriguing explanatory approach to German fascism and one that has been developed by numerous writers. These values seemed to revolve around a nostalgic view of an ordered, essentially rural past, before large-scale industry and impersonal market forces replaced social harmony with class conflict. Barrington Moore presented his notion of Catonism, a reactionary doctrine for mobilizing the peasantry in which the "organic life of the countryside" is portrayed as "supposedly superior to the atomised and disintegrating world of modern science and modern urban civilization."[7] Employing similar imagery, Mack Walker has referred to a "ubiquitous yearning for organic wholeness" in his study of provincial German towns,[8] while more recently Jeffrey Herf has identified the deep fear of modernity amongst urban Mittelstand groups, which even as city dwellers shared vivid "memories of small-town life and less rationalized forms of production."[9]

The German historian Thomas Nipperdey has criticized the concept of political "modernity" in so far as it tends to contrast a "deviant" Germany with an idealized modern state such as the United States, but has nonetheless found it a useful methodological tool.[10] Everything came too fast for Germany: industrialization, liberalism, democracy, socialism, national unification – all within the space of three generations. The speed of the nation's economic modernization left a residue of premodern political characteristics that help to explain something about Weimar's failure, while not determining it. The paradox, as Nipperdey points out, is that the Nazi opposition to modernity was not traditional but radical and brutal. Indeed Nazi methods were thoroughly modern: propaganda,

---

7. Barrington Moore, Jr., *Social Origins of Dictatorship and Democracy* (Harmondsworth, 1973), p. 492.

8. Mack Walker, *German Home Towns: Community, State, and General Estate, 1648–1871* (Ithaca, 1971), p. 426.

9. Jeffrey Herf, *Reactionary Modernism: Technology, Culture, and Politics in Weimar and the Third Reich* (Cambridge, 1984), p. 22. For other examples of the "preindustrial" attributes of the Mittelstand, see Jürgen Kocka, *White-Collar Workers in America, 1890–1940: A Social and Political History in International Perspective* (London, Beverly Hills, 1980), pp. 265–66; or Heinrich A. Winkler, *Die Neue Linke, Revolution, Staat, Faschismus: Zur Revision des historischen Materialismus* (Göttingen, 1978), p. 116.

10. Thomas Nipperdey, "Probleme der Modernisierung in Deutschland," in *Nachdenken über die deutsche Geschichte: Essays* (Munich, 1986), p. 45. For a more strident critique, from a Marxist perspective, see Geoff Eley, "What Produces Fascism: Pre-Industrial Traditions or a Crisis of the Capitalist State?" in *From Unification to Nazism: Reinterpreting the German Past* (Boston, 1986), pp. 254–82.

organization, and the harnessing of youthful dynamism.[11]

The fact of preindustrial sentiment amongst the Mittelstand must be recognized, but it should also be seen within the context of Weimar's economic turmoil. As Gerald Feldman has put it, the Mittelstand's "archaism" after 1918 was "less a product of a pre-industrial past than a charge against the modernity of the present that addressed itself to the very real 20th century circumstances and to the pitiless manner in which decline was being imposed."[12] Of those twentieth-century circumstances, the major upheaval caused by the First World War, the revolution, and the inflation between 1914 and 1924 was the most unsettling. And, as the predominant economic reality of the early Weimar years, the inflation has always offered a fruitful line of inquiry for those seeking a catalyst for the destabilization of Weimar politics. The idea of a people reduced to exchanging baskets of banknotes for a few of life's barest necessities conjures up an atmosphere of chronic discontent, ripe for exploitation by someone like Adolf Hitler. "If the horrified people notice that they can starve on billions," he is reputed to have told an audience in 1923, "they must arrive at this conclusion: we will no longer submit to a state which is built on the swindling idea of the majority, we want dictatorship."[13]

The link between the depreciation and final destruction of the German currency in 1923 and the assumption of power by the Nazis a decade later is long established. The Marxist Arthur Rosenberg spoke of the inflation as "one of the greatest robberies known to history," while in 1937 the British economist Lionel Robbins described Hitler as "the foster-child of the Inflation."[14] Both of them saw the Mittelstand as its victim. Since the 1970s, however, the inflation and its aftermath have been investigated by a modern generation of historians who have brought a fresh range of analysis to its complexities, including its social and political consequences.[15]

11. Nipperdey, "Probleme," pp. 53–57.

12. Gerald D. Feldman, "The Weimar Republic: A Problem of Modernization?" *Archiv für Sozialgeschichte* 26 (1986): 5.

13. Konrad Heiden, *Der Führer: Hitler's Rise to Power* (Boston, 1944), p. 133.

14. Arthur Rosenberg, *Geschichte der Weimarer Republik*, 19th ed. (Frankfurt a.M., 1978), p. 129; Foreword to Costantino Bresciani-Turroni, *The Economics of Inflation: A Study of Currency Depreciation in Post-War Germany* (London, 1937).

15. The name which springs foremost to mind in this connection is Gerald D. Feldman, a member of the steering committee for the project "Inflation and Reconstruction in Europe, 1914–1924," under which title four major research collections have been published: Gerald D. Feldman and Otto Büsch, eds., *Historische Prozesse der deutschen Inflation, 1914–1924* (Berlin, 1978); Gerald D. Feldman, Carl-Ludwig Holtfrerich, Gerhard A. Ritter, and Peter-Christian Witt, eds., *Die deutsche Inflation: Eine Zwischenbilanz* (Berlin, 1982); Gerald D. Feldman, Carl-

The inflation is not studied simply for its role in Weimar's demise, for it is worthy of investigation in itself, as an extraordinary economic episode and an object lesson in monetary policymaking. But the relationship between it and the dominating political fact of modern German history – the Third Reich – is bound to exercise the minds of historians. One obvious connection between 1923 and 1933 is the way the former crisis produced a sort of collective neurosis about inflation, which virtually immobilized the nation's decision makers when Germany was faced with another, more serious economic disaster after 1929.[16] But unlike the depression, which brought misery to millions of working-class homes in Germany, the inflation struck at the very group whose loyalty to the new Republic might be deemed vital to its survival, the Mittelstand. The inflation more than obliterated its savings; it also undermined the ethical basis of Mittelstand existence by challenging the cherished belief that hard work and thrift bring rewards. As one writer has put it, "In terms of their psychological repercussions, neither the War nor the Depression matched the destructive impact which the Inflation had upon traditional middle class values."[17] It replaced the old certainties that had evolved in the Wilhemine Empire with confusion and resentment. "A decade before the seizure of power," notes Heinrich Winkler, "there was not only *Panik im Mittelstand* [panic in the Mittelstand], but an extensive readiness on the part of small business to swap democracy for some kind of authoritarian regime."[18]

Ludwig Holtfrerich, Gerhard A. Ritter, and Peter-Christian Witt, eds., *Die Erfahrung der Inflation im internationalen Zusammenhang und Vergleich* (Berlin, New York, 1984); and Gerald D. Feldman, Carl-Ludwig Holtfrerich, Gerhard A. Ritter, and Peter-Christian Witt, eds., *Die Anpassung an die Inflation* (Berlin, New York, 1986). See also Gerald D. Feldman, ed., *Die Nachwirkungen der Inflation auf die deutsche Geschichte, 1924–1933* (Munich, 1985). A valuable general text is Carl-Ludwig Holtfrerich, *Die deutsche Inflation, 1914–1923: Ursachen und Folgen in internationaler Perspektive* (Berlin, New York, 1980).

16. See for example, Knut Borchardt, "Das Gewicht der Inflationsangst in den wirtschaftlichen Entscheidungsprozessen während der Weltwirtschaftskrise," in Feldman, ed., *Nachwirkungen*, pp. 233–60, where the assumption that fear of inflation limited the freedom of action of economic policymakers is shown to be well founded.

17. Larry E. Jones, "Inflation, Revaluation, and the Crisis of Middle Class Politics: A Study in the Dissolution of the German Party System, 1923–1928," *Central European History* 12 (1979): 144.

18. Winkler, *Mittelstand*, p. 78.

Mittelstand and Mittelstandspolitik

The term *Mittelstand* approximates what in Anglo-Saxon usage would be called the middle class, but it is not identical because the idea of a social order composed of *Stände* (estates) predates and is incompatible with the modern class structure. Whereas a class implies conflict and change, a *Stand* suggests stability and content-ment with one's assigned role in life. And while class tends to be determined by objective, socio-economic factors such as the re-lationship to the means of production, the concept of *Stände* relies on more subjective criteria for classification, the key to which is self-estimation: those Germans who thought they belonged to the Mittelstand invariably did so.[19] It was this quality that gave the Mittelstand a collective identity apart from the opposing blocs of industrial society. In the words of one authority, it cut across the lines of conventional class conflict, its members "captured neither by the reckless spirit of laissez-faire capitalism, nor by the class hatred of the workers."[20]

It might be argued that there is little to choose between the terms *Mittelstand* and *Bürger*, which in its original sense denoted the legal status of urban citizen and carried with it certain rights and responsibilities in the town. But in the nineteenth century the *Bürgertum* came to include wealthy merchants, factory owners, and the growing ranks of university-educated bureaucrats and peda-gogues. This was the bourgeoisie of classic capitalist society and, particularly in towns like Hamburg, represented not so much the middle strata as the ruling elite.[21]

The size of the Mittelstand very much depended on how it was defined. At the turn of the century Gustav Schmoller told an assembly in Leipzig that it "still comprised more than half the population."[22] A good approximation of its dimensions in the Weimar Republic is given by Theodor Geiger, who reckoned that of the total German population in 1925 (approximately 62 million), around 26 percent belonged to the Mittelstand when it was defined

19. Ibid., pp. 21–25.
20. David Blackbourn, "The Mittelstand in German Society and Politics, 1871–1914," *Social History* 4 (1977): 412. See also his "Between Resignation and Volatility: The German petite bourgeoisie in the nineteenth century," in Geoffrey Crossick and Heinz-Gerhard Haupt, eds., *Shopkeepers and Master Artisans in Nineteenth-Century Europe* (London, New York, 1984), pp. 35–61.
21. Jürgen Kocka, "Bürgertum und Bürgerlichkeit als Probleme deutscher Ge-schichte vom späten 18. zum frühen 20. Jahrhundert," in Jürgen Kocka, ed., *Bürger und Bürgerlichkeit im 19. Jahrhundert* (Göttingen, 1987), pp. 21–25.
22. Quoted in Herman Lebovics, *Social Conservatism and the Middle Classes in Germany, 1914–1933* (Princeton, 1969), p. 10.

according to "objective economic" criteria such as income and education.[23] More revealing however is Geiger's "deep structure" analysis (*Tiefgliederung*), where the differentiating quality is not economic factors, but "social mentality." When this approach is utilized, he presents the Mittelstand in two subgroups – small entrepreneurs and skilled earners – which together comprise about 36 percent of the total population.[24]

These two subgroups correspond to what is known as the old and new Mittelstand, the former exemplified by farmers, artisans, and retailers, the latter by white-collar workers. This division between old and new remains amongst the most useful analytical approaches to this amorphous body. But the first category receives further subdivision: artisans and peasants lived in a family setting which merged economic and social interest in a single Weltanschauung, and their hostility to modernity and capitalism rose naturally out of the practice of their age-old skills. Retailers also viewed the family as a self-sustaining economic unit, but since they lacked the tradition of the artisans and peasants, their anticapitalism was more a feeling of inferiority and resentment at their position as a by-product of capitalist industry. By contrast the new Mittelstand of white-collar workers was modern rather than traditional and gave its allegiance not to the family, but to the employer.[25]

The term Mittelstand was not simply a conglomeration of occupations, but an ideological concept with roots in the political and economic structure of the Wilhemine Empire. As part of an attempt to counter the growing power of the organized working class and its political manifestation, the Social Democratic Party (SPD), the ruling coalition of agrarians and industrialists fostered a Mittelstand policy. Designed to create a social buffer between the opposing forces of the rapidly polarizing class society of industrial Germany, the *Mittelstandpolitik* (Mittelstand policy) was initially centered on the old Mittelstand of small independents, but by the end of the nineteenth century the expanding army of white-collar workers had also been enlisted.[26]

23. Theodor Geiger, *Die soziale Schichtung des deutschen Volkes* (Stuttgart, 1932), pp. 20–21, 24.
24. Ibid., pp. 22–23, 90.
25. Ibid., pp. 84–86, 98–105.
26. See Theodor Brauer, "Das soziale System des Kapitalismus: Mittelstandspolitik," in *Grundriß der Sozialökonomie*, chap. 7, sect. 9, pt. 2 (Tübingen, 1927), pp. 398–400; Emil Lederer and Jakob Marschak, "Der neue Mittelstand," in *Grundriß der Sozialökonomie*, chap. 7, sect. 9, pt. 1 (Tübingen, 1926), p. 121; Gustav Schmoller, *Was verstehen wir unter dem Mittelstand?* (Göttingen, 1897), pp. 25–26; J. Wernicke, *Kapitalismus und Mittelstandspolitik*, 2d ed. (Jena, 1922), p. 409.

The Mittelstand policy was of course a political strategy. It was believed that if the Mittelstand could be integrated into the political consensus, then it would serve to bolster the institutional status quo – an assertion of harmony by the Right against the social conflict threatened by the Left.[27] And it was not merely designed to ensure loyalty to the ruling regime of agrarians and industrialists; the Center party also encouraged it energetically in the predominantly Catholic areas of southern and western Germany.[28] However it is doubtful if it could ever have been a great success. It was based on the assumption that the Mittelstand could be forged into a unified bulwark of society, but as Geiger points out, the many divergent streams within its ranks made this impossible; indeed its very divisions were a source of German political instability right up until Hitler's seizure of power.[29] David Crew has shown in his revealing study of Bochum before 1914 how the Mittelstand was too divided there to provide industrialists with any kind of successful ally against the organized working class.[30]

The Corporatist Setting

Whether or not Germany deviated from the normal path of political development in following its own *Sonderweg* to modernity, the fact remains that the nature of its economy differed markedly from the general pattern of capitalist evolution in the West.[31] By contrast

27. Winkler, *Mittelstand*, p. 23. Also Hans-Ulrich Wehler, *The German Empire, 1871–1918,* trans Kim Traynor (Leamington Spa, 1985).

28. See David Blackbourn, *Class, Religion, and Local Politics in Wilhelmine Germany: The Centre Party in Württemberg before 1914* (New Haven, 1980), esp. chap. 5.

29. Geiger, *Die soziale Schichtung*, pp. 122–38.

30. David F. Crew, *Town in the Ruhr: A Social History of Bochum, 1860–1914* (New York, 1979), pp. 127–45.

31. The *Sonderweg* theory stresses the peculiarity of Germany's social and political development. In comparison with other Western nations, which experienced "normal" bourgeois revolutions in tandem with their economic modernization, Germany continued to be dominated by a preindustrial elite until 1918, if not 1945. The sociologist Ralf Dahrendorf added momentum to the theory by pursuing the deficiencies of German development in comparison with Britain's "classical democracy" in his seminal work, *Society and Democracy in Germany* (London, 1968). Examples of the *Sonderweg* model in historical writing would include Helmut Boehme, *Deutschlands Weg zur Großmacht* (Cologne, 1966); Hans Rosenberg, *Große Depression und Bismarckzeit* (Berlin, 1967); Dirk Stegmann, *Die Erben Bismarcks* (Cologne, 1970); and Hans-Ulrich Wehler, *Das deutsche Kaiserreich, 1871–1918* (Göttingen, 1973). Having become something of an orthodoxy in German historiography, the theory has recently been under challenge, in particular from the British historians David Blackbourn and Geoff Eley. They argue in *The Peculiarities of German History* (Oxford/New York, 1984) that the political development of

with the gradual pace of Britain's Industrial Revolution and its accompanying liberal economic ideology, Germany's rapid industrialization in the late nineteenth century produced a more organized species of capitalism, characterized by voluntary association between firms and the co-option of those groups into the process of government.[32]

It was a corporatist system, as defined in these terms: an economic and political structure in which the major interests subject themselves to self-regulation and are afforded institutional recognition and in which the reconciliation of their rival aims takes place not within a free market but within a kind of political cartel.[33] In other words it was a society with a preference for collusion rather than competition, a desire for harmony and the elimination of conflict. It has not always been achieved, but the pursuit of this ideal has been an enduring trait of successive German states right down to the Federal Republic.[34]

The origins of this social order probably lie in Germany's philo-

---

nineteenth-century Germany seems "immature" only because it has been commonly compared with idealized versions of the American or British past. Whatever weaknesses their attack may have revealed, the *Sonderweg* thesis remains a fruitful approach to modern German history with its inherent need for an explanation of Hitler's rise. For an overview of the controversy see Richard J. Evans, "Introduction: Wilhelm II's Germany and the Historians," in Richard J. Evans, ed., *Society and Politics in Wilhelmine Germany* (London, 1978), pp. 11–39, and Georg Iggers's informative Introduction to *The Social History of Politics: Critical Perspectives in West German Historical Writing since 1945* (Leamington Spa, 1985).

32. The term "organized capitalism" was coined by Rudolf Hilferding. See the collection edited by Heinrich A. Winkler, *Organisierter Kapitalismus: Voraussetzungen und Anfrage*, Kritische Studien zur Geschichtswissenschaft 9 (Göttingen, 1974). In an interesting contribution to the debate on corporatism Werner Abelshauser suggests a reconsideration of the tendency to judge modern German history according to pluralist, essentially Anglo-Saxon standards; in the light of experience in the twentieth century it may be that Germany is a more relevant model for the development of industrializing societies than was previously supposed. See Werner Abelshauser, "The First Post-Liberal Nation: Stages in the Development of Modern Corporatism in Germany," *European History Quarterly*, n.s. 3, 14 (July 1984): 285–317.

33. Corporatism has been treated by Philippe C. Schmitter. See, for example, "Still the Century of Corporatism?," *Review of Politics* 36 (1974): 85–131, or more recently Philippe C. Schmitter and Gerhard Lehmbrech, eds., *Consequences of Corporatist Policy-Making* (London, Beverly Hills, 1981). For its application to Germany, see Ulrich Nocken, "Korporatistische Theorien und Strukturen in der deutschen Geschichte des 19. und frühen 20. Jahrhunderts," in Ulrich v. Alemann, ed., *Neokorporatismus* (Frankfurt, New York, 1982).

34. The fact that Germans have traditionally disliked open conflict within their society and considered it beyond the bounds of a legitimate political system is one of the themes of Dahrendorf's *Society and Democracy in Germany*.

sophical traditions and the inclination towards assignment of greater moral worth to the state than to the individual; but whatever its source the corporatist model has proved its worth in analyzing German history.[35] Probably the best example with reference to the Weimar Republic is Charles Maier's *Recasting Bourgeois Europe*. According to Maier, Germany was restabilized after the upheaval of the inflation years not by "traditional elites or the aggregation of voters' preferences," but by political agreement between the major economic interest groups, that is, industry, labor, and agriculture. Indeed for Maier a defining characteristic of the corporatist system is the "blurring of the distinction between political and economic power."[36] However, the very stability that corporatist-style agreement brought about also contained the seeds of its own destruction. If the Mittelstand was excluded from the industrial alignment of the inflation years, then it was equally dissatisfied with the stabilization that followed. Unable to change the axis of industry and labor by economic means because of its diversity and weakness in the marketplace, the Mittelstand sought political solutions, the results of which combined "hostility to liberalism and organized labor with a vague rhetorical anticapitalism." Nazism was thus a "revolt against the corporatist state."[37]

Maier's model has been subject to some criticism for confusing the type of corporatism developed by the voluntary association of private interests with that imposed from above by the state.[38] In fact both varieties were displayed in the short life of the Weimar Republic, the latter being more obviously identified with reactionary and nationalist groups. Another area of weakness in Maier's approach, but one which nonetheless prompts the line of this analysis, is his treatment of corporatism in Weimar as something new in itself, which merely built upon the "etatist patterns of authority and economic organization that had survived the nineteenth century in Germany."[39] Not only was a corporatist system well entrenched in Germany before the outbreak of the First World War, but the Mittelstand was strongly associated with it; indeed the

35. Abelshauser, "The First Post-Liberal Nation," p. 292.
36. Charles S. Maier, *Recasting Bourgeois Europe: Stabilization in France, Germany, and Italy in the Decade after World War 1* (Princeton, 1975), pp. 580–82. See also Ulrich Nocken, "Corporatism and Pluralism in Modern German History," in Dirk Stegmann, Berndt-Jürgen Wendt, and Peter-Christian Witt, eds., *Industrielle Gesellschaft und politisches System* (Bonn, 1978), pp. 37–56.
37. Maier, *Recasting*, pp. 591–93.
38. Nocken, "Corporatism and Pluralism," pp. 40–46.
39. Maier, *Recasting*, pp. 13–14.

whole Mittelstandspolitik is scarcely conceivable outside such a system. The price for Mittelstand loyalty to the Empire's ruling elite was recognition of, or at least the payment of lip service to, "the ideology of the craft as a closed and self-regulating moral body."[40] The artisans, for example, petitioned successfully for political representation through their own chambers (*Handwerker-kammer* or *Gewerbekammer*), while the retailers sought protection against department stores and cooperatives on the grounds that Germany needed a strong independent stratum responsible for the nation's nourishment (*Nahrung*).[41]

Then came the war and the mobilization of the German economy which got under way after 1916. As Gerald Feldman has put it, the Mittelstand "went almost overnight from being the political darlings of the regime to being the whipping boys of the war economy."[42] It was the products of industry, not the artisan's workshop, the labor of blue-collar, not white-collar workers, which were needed to supply the front. Big business and organized labor began to develop associational structures within German industry and to secure their position close to government power. Within a few days of the armistice in November 1918, the alliance was cemented, at least until 1923, in the so-called *Zentralarbeitsgemeinschaft*. This agreement between the industrialist Hugo Stinnes and the trade union leader Carl Legien established the principle of collective bargaining in German labor relations. Industry recognized the trade unions and the eight-hour day, while labor relinquished any residual affection it might have had for a revolutionary overthrow of capitalism and conceded the right of private companies to manage their own affairs.[43] It was an alliance based upon full employment and relatively high wages and

40. Geoffrey Crossick and Heinz-Gerhard Haupt, "Shopkeepers, Master Artisans, and the Historian: The Petite Bourgeoisie in Comparative Focus," in Crossick and Haupt, eds., *Shopkeepers*, p. 24.

41. Brauer, "Mittelstandspolitik," pp. 389–90. Also Heinrich A. Winkler, "From Social Protectionism to National Socialism: The German Small Business Movement in Comparative Perspective," *Journal of Modern History* 48, no. 1 (1976): 1–18.

42. Feldman, "A Problem of Modernization," p. 5.

43. The term *Arbeitsgemeinschaft* connotes an organic social partnership or working community and thus goes beyond the type of labor-management negotiations and collective bargaining familiar to Anglo-Saxon experience. See Gerald D. Feldman, "Big Business and the Kapp Putsch," *Central European History* 4 (1971): 101, and his "German Business between War and Revolution: The Origins of the Stinnes-Legien Agreement," in Gerhard Ritter, ed., *Entstehung und Wandel der modernen Gesellschaft* (Berlin, 1970). Also valuable is his *Iron and Steel in the German Inflation, 1916–1923* (Princeton, 1977).

the continuation of industrial power and influence. It was also the first attempt at a corporatist solution to the conflict between capital and labor, but now the Mittelstand was excluded from the arrangement.[44]

In many ways its exclusion from the new structure within the economy was more critical than its lack of influence in the new republican government. Even with Social Democratic administrations in Berlin, the hand of industry was still to be detected, guiding the fate of the nation. As the hated *Zwangswirtschaft* (controlled economy) of the war years continued into the peace, some producers appeared to be bypassing its provisions, thus making them even more onerous for those too weakly organized to do likewise. Where once the political considerations of Mittelstandspolitik had been paramount, now the economic pressures of the postwar inflation period produced a "primacy of economics." Unable to break the new cartel of capital and labor with its modest economic power, the Mittelstand called for the restoration of the "primacy of politics."[45] It was a reaction wholly within character, petitioning for the same respect and security that were enjoyed by big business, agriculture, and organized labor. That its demand was largely ignored was partly a consequence of its political impotence in a state which no longer perceived its support as vital and partly because it viewed the bewildering array of party alternatives in Weimar, indeed parliamentary government altogether, as an obstacle instead of a means of attaining its goals.[46]

Unable to deliver itself in mass support of one of the established parties of the bourgeois "middle," it allowed the economic conditions, and particularly the inflation, to force its divergent elements apart. Whatever potential it had to build a united pillar of the Republican order degenerated in its pursuit of feeble special interest parties with no goals beyond the satisfaction of limited economic objectives. Particularly within that quadrant of the Weimar party spectrum between the Democrats (DDP) and the Nationalists (DNVP), the Mittelstand's loyalty was fickle and ineffective. Of all the parties the DDP was worst hit by the inflation, but even the DNVP, which made temporary gains in 1924 by portraying itself as the party of the small, dispossessed saver, could not hold the Mittelstand's support. Only the National Socialists, with their

44. Abelshauser, "The First Post-Liberal Nation," p. 286. The corporatist truce between labor and industry collapsed as the mutual benefits gained from the inflation vanished after 1923.

45. Ibid., pp. 300–301.

46. Winkler, "The German Small Business Movement," p. 7.

appeals to narrow sectional grievances and their seductive rhetoric of a revitalized national community, a corporatist structure with a place once more for the Mittelstand, seemed to offer any relief for its frustration.[47] The 1924 elections, concludes Thomas Childers, represented an important first step on its migration to Hitler, and "although it would be an oversimplification to suggest that artisans, retailers and peasants had been irrevocably radicalized by the dislocations of the inflation and stabilization, their identification with the traditional representatives of bourgeois politics had been profoundly shaken."[48] It took another decade and the reality of the Third Reich to make it clear just how empty Nazi promises were to the Mittelstand.[49]

Some Theoretical Considerations

Curiously perhaps, our knowledge of the German inflation has until recently stemmed largely from the work of economists rather than historians.[50] And this fact reminds us that inflation has always been the subject of sharp controversy in economic theory, particularly in regard to its causes.

In the years after the First World War the debate over inflation's causes was essentially between the supporters of the quantity theory of money and those of the balance-of-payments school. Quantity theorists placed the main emphasis on increases in the supply of money and saw both price rises and currency depreciation as internally generated consequences of those increases.

47. For the middle-class social character of Nazi support after 1923, see Thomas Childers, *The Nazi Voter: The Social Foundations of Fascism in Germany, 1919–1933* (Chapel Hill, 1983), and his articles, "Inflation and Electoral Politics in Germany, 1919–1929," in Nathan Schmukler and Edward Marcus, eds., *Inflation through the Ages: Economic, Social, Psychological, and Historical Aspects* (New York, 1983), pp. 373–85 and "Inflation, Stabilization, and Political Realignment in Germany, 1924–1928," in Feldman et al., *Zwischenbilanz*, pp. 409–31. Also Larry E. Jones, "The Dying Middle: Weimar Germany and the Fragmentation of Bourgeois Politics," *Central European History* 5 (1972): 23–54.

48. Childers, *The Nazi Voter*, p. 79.

49. For the Nazis' "schizoid relationship" with the Mittelstand, see David Schoenbaum, *Hitler's Social Revolution: Class and Status in Nazi Germany, 1933–1939* (New York, 1967), pp. 136–43; also Heinrich A. Winkler, "Der entbehrliche Stand zur Mittelstandspolitik im Dritten Reich," *Archiv für Sozialgeschichte* 17 (1977): 1–40.

50. This point is made by Holtfrerich, *Die deutsche Inflation*, p. 1. The best examples of economists' work in the field are, besides Bresciani-Turroni's *The Economics*, Frank D. Graham, *Exchange, Prices, and Production in Hyperinflation: Germany, 1920–1923* (Princeton, 1931), and Karsten Laursen and Jorgen Pedersen, *The German Inflation of 1918–1923* (Amsterdam, 1964).

Adherents of the balance-of-payments school judged the external deficit to be the key; it depressed the exchange rate of the currency, thus raising import and domestic prices, which in turn enlarged the budget deficit and prompted an expansion of the note issue. Although the quantity theory was widely accepted abroad, most German economists subscribed to the balance-of-payments doctrine and followed Karl Helfferich in believing that it was the burden of reparations that was depressing the mark's exchange rate.[51] For a pronounced nationalist such as Helfferich, it was a more palatable explanation for Germany's misfortune in the years of recrimination following the onerous Versailles settlement that the Reich's former enemies were to blame.

While the causes of inflation are complex and may be hotly debated, its consequences are probably of more lasting interest to the historian. Inflation's most significant effect is its tendency to redistribute wealth and this redistribution applies with equal force whether the inflation is of the creeping variety, common to many present-day economies, or a hyperinflation such as the one with which Germany had to cope in 1923; the difference is only one of degree. Inflation transfers wealth from people whose income and assets do not change as the price level changes to people whose income and assets do change as the price level changes. In practice this means a relative impoverishment of those living on rent and interest payments – rentiers – and a relative enrichment of those who benefit from higher prices for their goods and services – entrepreneurs. A shifting of wealth on this scale can be disturbing for society, particularly if it takes place rapidly, but it may not always be seen as undesirable. Indeed it can be attractive to a government that is a large debtor because inflation always favors debtors over creditors.

In inflation, consumers generally lose in relation to producers and well-organized labor because companies with rising costs can

51. Ragnar Nurkse, *The Course and Control of Inflation: A Review of Monetary Experience in Europe after World War 1* (League of Nations, Washington, 1946), pp. 16–17. Chief proponents of the quantity theory in relation to Germany have been Bresciani-Turroni, *The Economics*, and more recently Philip Cagan, "The Monetary Dynamics of Hyperinflation," in Milton Friedman, ed., *Studies in the Quantity Theory of Money* (Chicago, 1956), pp. 25–117. Graham, by contrast, sided more strongly with the balance-of-payments school in *Exchange, Prices, and Production*. For an outline of the contemporary debate amongst German economists, see Karl Hardach, "Zur zeitgenössischen Debatte der Nationalökonomen über die Ursachen der deutschen Nachkriegsinflation," in Hans Mommsen, Dietmar Petzina, and Bernd Weisbrod, eds., *Industrielles System und politische Entwicklung in der Weimarer Republik* (Düsseldorf, 1974), pp. 368–75.

always pass on increases to their customers. In this way consumers become accustomed to rising prices and adjust their behavior accordingly, with trade unions bargaining on the basis of anticipated price rises and everyone abandoning saving in favor of the immediate purchase. In fact expectations play an important role in the mechanism of inflation, so that when it becomes rapid, the flight from cash into goods can, of itself, bid up prices. In the final analysis, inflation's impact depends upon the ability of individuals to predict its course and adapt in an appropriate manner. In theory, if everyone had the same competence in this respect, inflation would have no redistributive effects whatever and its social and economic consequences would be nil. Of course, such ability is not equally spread and it is this fact that leads to inflation's inequities.[52]

Amongst the working population, inflation has a tendency to harm people on fixed incomes and especially those with poor bargaining power. Worst hit are those who live off pensions and other forms of fixed income. The tragedy is that these are generally old people who do not know how to adapt to extreme inflationary conditions and are too proud to go to the authorities for help. Within wage and salary groups, inflation upsets earnings relativities by reducing differentials between skilled and unskilled workers, higher- and lower-paid workers, and men and women. In Germany, according to one source, average wage differentials sank from 30 percent to 9 percent between 1913 and 1923, a leveling process brought about largely by the granting of equal cost-of-living supplements.[53] There will be cause to return to this particular feature of the inflation at various points in the coming pages, but for the moment it is worth noting that one of the most important features of this narrowing of wage and salary differentials is the profound psychological effect it has upon the disadvantaged: as their relative earnings are eroded so is their feeling of worth in society.

The reaction of governments to inflation and its victims is usually determined by the location of its political constituency. If its support is drawn from the working class, then it is unlikely to tackle inflation at the cost of other economic desiderata, such as low unemployment and high social welfare, particularly since these

52. Martin Bronfenbrenner, "Inflation and Deflation," in *International Encyclopedia of the Social Sciences*, vol. 7 (New York, 1968), p. 298. The same idea is expressed in G.L. Bach, *Inflation: A Study in Economics, Ethics, and Politics* (Providence, 1958), p. 57.

53. Gerhard Bry, *Wages in Germany, 1871–1945* (Princeton, 1960), p. 8. See also Holtfrerich, *Die deutsche Inflation*, pp. 232–33.

command a higher degree of attention in society and are usually threatened by the traditional cures for inflation. Knut Borchardt puts the matter succinctly when he notes that

> precisely because the manifold distributive effects of inflation are so varied and unexplained, inflation can continue for so long a time without becoming an acute scandal. The effects do not suddenly become clear to everyone in a visible manner as in the case of unemployment, where no scientific investigation is necessary to determine who is unemployed. . . . because of this asymmetry in the social effects of unemployment and inflation one can probably see why full employment has until now indisputably been the higher aim of economic policy.[54]

Of course, not all governments are so solicitous towards the workers or so concerned to maintain full employment. Since 1980 some Western countries, most notably Britain under Margaret Thatcher, have accepted a level of unemployment unknown in the second half of the twentieth century in their battle to get inflation under control – and have done so with a remarkable degree of social acquiescence. And one should not forget that fifty years before the onset of Thatcherism, Germany was so stricken with inflation angst that the drastic anti-inflation policies of Heinrich Brüning's administration retained support through the domestic policy conflicts of 1931–32, despite a prevailing unemployment rate of over 40 percent.[55]

The German Inflation of 1914–1923

It is evident that the response of government to the economic problem of inflation is invariably governed by political factors, and Germany's inflation was no exception. However one approaches the subject, it seems incontestable that increases in the money supply over the decade 1914–23 bear the main long-term responsibility for the inflation and that these increases were essentially made to fund successive budget deficits.[56] But given the prevailing politi-

54. Knut Borchardt, *Strukturwirkungen des Inflationsprozesses*, Schriftenreihe des Ifo-Instituts für Wirtschaftsforschung, 50 (Berlin/Munich, 1972), pp. 15f.

55. Dietmar Petzina, *Die deutsche Wirtschaft in der Zwischenkriegszeit* (Wiesbaden, 1977), pp. 16–17. On the fear of inflation in the event of a devaluation of the German mark, both before and after the Nazi seizure of power in 1933, see Harold James, *The German Slump: Politics and Economics, 1924–1936* (Oxford, 1986), pp. 390, 396–97.

56. Nurkse, *Course and Control*, p. 17. For a modern view, see Andrea Sommariva and Giuseppe Tullio, *German Macroeconomic History, 1880–1979: A Study of the Effects of Economic Policy on Inflation, Currency Depreciation, and Growth* (New York, 1987), pp. 121–59.

cal circumstances, this deficit financing was practically impossible to avoid. Economists may point to mistakes made by the German government in handling the inflation, but its actions need to be set fully in context. Germany after 1918 was a weak-rooted democracy struggling to survive in an atmosphere of assassinations, uprisings, and internecine political strife; the early Weimar administrations had reasons enough to assume that a deflationary policy with accompanying unemployment, such as that pursued by Britain or the United States, would have catastrophic consequences.[57] As it was, the inflation called forth very high levels of employment and a growth rate from 1919 to 1922 (measured as net national product per capita) of around 12.5 percent per annum. Conversely, the first hint of a stabilization in the spring of 1920 threw people out of work.[58]

If there was something approaching an inflation consensus within the corporatist framework that emerged with the revolution in 1918, then the chief partners in that framework were industry, labor, and government.[59] For them inflation served three very compelling functions. First, it facilitated a measure of social pacification, bought with concessions to labor like the eight-hour day, public works, continuous pay increases, and controlled prices and rents. Indeed the *Zentralarbeitsgemeinschaft* (central work alliance) represented very clearly a strategy based on inflation, a strategy upon which the early Republic depended for its survival. Second, the inflation was a tool of economic recovery. It fueled an export boom with high export profits in 1919–21 and generally "enabled Germany to revive its economic life both in terms of domestic productivity and foreign trade at a pace faster than would have been possible had it pursued a deflationary policy."[60] It also facilitated a high level of industrial investment, although just how useful this

57. This is the view of Laursen and Pedersen, *German Inflation*, p. 88; Holtfrerich, *Die deutsche Inflation*, p. 297; also Peter Czada, "Große Inflation und Wirtschaftswachstum," in Mommsen et al., *Industrielles System*, esp. pp. 390–92.

58. Sommariva & Tullio, *Macroeconomic History*, p. 133; Holtfrerich, *Die deutsche Inflation*, pp. 198–99.

59. See Charles Maier's discussion of "inflation coalitions" in "The Politics of Inflation in the Twentieth Century," in Fred Hirsch and John Goldthorpe, *The Political Economy of Inflation* (London, 1978), pp. 37–72, esp. pp. 42–43. For an exhaustive analysis of the joint exploitation of the inflation – or at least its toleration – by industry and labor, see Heinrich A. Winkler's massive *Von der Revolution zur Stabilisierung: Arbeiter und Arbeiterbewegung in der Weimarer Republik, 1918 bis 1924* (Berlin/Bonn, 1984).

60. Gerald D. Feldman, "The Historian and the German Inflation," in Schmukler and Marcus, *Inflation through the Ages*, p. 388. See also Feldman's *Iron and Steel*.

investment turned out to be in the poststabilization period is doubtful.[61] Third, it forced the Entente to modify its demands for reparations. Since the predominant balance-of-payments theorists in Germany felt that the inflation's cause lay in the unjust level of reparations and the discrimination against Germany in export markets, they considered it necessary for the former enemy to moderate its demands before stable monetary conditions could be restored.[62] It hardly seemed to matter that industrialists and politicians were prepared to practically wreck their country's economy and that of other nations in an effort to prove the impossibility of fulfilling the terms of the Versailles *Diktat*. The bitterness that the unsatisfactory conclusion to the war had bred in Germany produced an unreal and certainly irresponsible reaction to questions concerning the nation's future. "A fatalistic attitude towards the inflation could thus be legitimized on the highest patriotic grounds."[63]

If the inflation was the least objectionable course for German industrial leaders to take after 1918, then it was probably the only one for the government. Having inherited from the Empire a debt of billions of marks owed to those patriotic Germans who had subscribed to the War Loan between 1914 and 1918, the Republic began life in serious debt. Seen from this perspective, the inflation was a convenient device for the Reichsbank to abdicate its responsibilities to the rentier. Franz Eulenburg, who wrote the first and for a long time the only treatment of the inflation's social consequences, reckoned that of the 150 to 160 billion marks' worth of German rentier capital in 1914, only a "small fraction" remained in 1924.[64]

It is in this atmosphere of irresponsibility, represented in some contemporary accounts even in terms of immorality, that the inflation's victims take on a sort of poignancy. The image of savings evaporating before the eyes of the elderly and the infirm has been a typical feature in portrayals of the inflation and one of the main reasons for its enduring disrepute.[65] There is the notion that

61. The view that inflation investment in industrial plants was wasted is presented in Bresciani-Turroni, *The Economics*, p. 197. A contrary position can be found in Holtfrerich, *Die deutsche Inflation*, pp. 201–2.

62. The French actually viewed the inflation as a German plot to evade reparations. See Holtfrerich, *Die deutsche Inflation*, p. 278.

63. Feldman, "The Historian and the German Inflation," p. 391.

64. Franz Eulenburg, "Die sozialen Wirkungen der Währungsverhältnisse," *Jahrbücher für Nationalökonomie und Statistik*, n.s. 3, 67 (1924): 755–57.

65. In addition to ibid., pp. 757–58, see Bresciani-Turroni, *The Economics*, pp. 315–29 and Laursen and Pedersen, *German Inflation*, pp, 118–20. See also the

people who saved and were careful with their money, who, in short, held to the puritan financial virtues, were somehow victimized by rapacious capitalists (entrepreneurs) who sold their souls to the devil inflation. The astute contemporary observer Moritz Bonn even talked of "a capitalist variant on the communist policy of dispossession. Instead of their class enemy, they plundered the broad mass of their co-capitalists [the rentier]."[66]

But rentier cannot be used interchangeably with Mittelstand; the latter may have exhibited an inclination for saving and the avoidance of debt, but it had no monopoly on these traits. One can speak of the dispossession of savers, but not, as Arthur Rosenberg does, of the Mittelstand. Attention might instead be focused on how victims from the Mittelstand were treated differently from those from the working class. There was a sense that whatever evils the inflation might inflict upon the German people, some sections of society deserved greater consideration, pity even, by virtue of their status. For example, it is interesting to note that welfare authorities actually received instructions to handle needy cases from the Mittelstand with more tact and consideration than was normally given to workers' families. A circular from Berlin in the spring of 1922 instructed municipalities to avoid humiliating veterans and pensioners from the Mittelstand who were compelled to seek aid from the state, even to the extent of conducting interviews with them in separate rooms where they would not be required to discuss their problems in public.[67] Such special treatment probably fed the myth of a "destruction (*Vernichtung*) of the Mittelstand," the evocation of which became the stock-in-trade of much reactionary political propaganda at the time. One must however be careful to avoid such generalizations. There was no such thing as the total destruction of a social class or estate in the inflation. Certain forms of wealth were eroded, some to a devastating degree, but class allegiance and social awareness survived. Savers were undoubtedly a primary casualty, but saving was not limited to the Mittelstand.

The real hardship in the inflation came at the end. With the hyperinflation in 1923, all the advantages of inflation were exhausted

---

anecdotal literature on the inflation such as Adam Fergusson, *When Money Dies* (London, 1975), or William Guttmann and Patricia Meehan, *The Great Inflation* (Farnborough, 1975).

66. Moritz J. Bonn, *So macht man Geschichte: Bilanz eines Lebens* (Munich, 1953), p. 272.

67. StA.H, *Kriegsbeschädigten- und Kriegshinterbliebenenfürsorge*, 351–59 D.IIa.21, Reichsarbeitsminister to Hauptfürsorgestellen, 23.3.1922.

because everyone started calculating in foreign currency and German domestic prices rose to world levels. The very industrialists who had benefited most from the inflation were now willing and eager to call a halt to it. The price for the stabilization was paid almost completely by the worker and the little man, in higher levels of unemployment, cuts in real earnings, a lengthening of the working day, and a pervasive credit drought. It was a depression, but one which received a broad measure of popular tolerance; after the economic hysteria of 1923, people were ready for an economic "cold shower" in 1924.

The stabilization had not only an economic price, but a political one too. The inadequate revaluation of debts that had been repaid during the inflation and the proliferation of special interest parties that followed the Reichstag elections of 1924 caused a fundamental destabilization of the Weimar party system. For many Germans who might otherwise have sustained the liberal center of Weimar politics, the party system took on all the negative connotations associated with interest politics and the shabby compromises of parliamentary government.[68] During the inflation successive governments had insisted that "a mark = a mark," despite determined petitioning by small savers to prevent the repayment of loans and mortgages in devalued currency. After the stabilization the response of the government was the same, for to revalue fully all debts from the inflation period would have been politically and economically impossible. It may have been depicted by champions of the dispossessed creditors and the enemies of the Republic as proof of Weimar's immorality and desertion of every traditional economic virtue, but really it was simple pragmatism.[69]

The failure of the early Weimar governments lay not in their inability to stop the inflation before 1923 or in the inadequate compensation for dispossessed savers that followed it, but rather in the lack of any institutions within the Republic which could channel and absorb the outrage of those dispossessed savers. Every crisis within a democracy will leave casualties in its wake; its success and

68. See Larry E. Jones, *German Liberalism and the dissolution of the Weimar Party System, 1918–1933* (Chapel Hill, 1988).
69. Thomas Childers, "Inflation and Electoral Politics," p. 376. For an interesting discussion of the legal aspects of the campaign to revalue debts which had been repaid during the inflation, see David B. Southern, "The Impact of the Inflation: Inflation, the Courts, and Revaluation," in Richard Bessel and E.J. Feuchtwanger, eds., *Social Change and Political Development in Weimar Germany* (London, 1981) pp. 55–76. Michael L. Hughes has dealt comprehensively with the legal and cultural aspects of compensation for creditors in *Paying for the German Inflation* (Chapel Hill, 1988).

survival however depends on providing an adequate safety net for those casualties. The problem for Germany after the First World War was not so much that it was asked to carry heavy burdens – reparations being only the most obvious – but that there was a total lack of agreement as to how those burdens should be carried.[70]

The French dealt swiftly with their obligations to the new German Empire after 1871 because, while they internalized their sense of grievance over the loss of Alsace-Lorraine, they never seriously challenged the validity of the Third Republic. For the Germans after 1918 there was no such unanimity of purpose. On the contrary, despite the parliamentary majority in favor of republican democracy, powerful sections of society were entrenched against it. The whole fabric of Weimar Germany was characterized by mutually antagonistic interests which were either unwilling to cooperate or did so only for a limited duration and in the pursuit of purely selfish goals. It was a structure with a corporatist design, but one built on shifting ground. Not surprisingly it did a poor job of shouldering the heavy burden of Versailles or, more important still, of carrying the costs of democratic government. Indeed, there are few better examples of Weimar's lack of consensus on basic issues than the attempts of the early administrations to raise the revenue necessary to meet its myriad commitments and to do so in as democratic a fashion as possible. It is therefore worth looking at the broad outline of republican taxation policy before proceeding further.

Republican Taxation Policies

Taxation is a vexed question in any country, but in Germany before 1918 it was particularly problematic. Under the federal system of the Bismarckian Reich, the central government had access only to the proceeds of indirect taxes and excise duties, with all the important taxes on personal income and property reserved for the states. Before any national goals requiring major expenditure could be accomplished, there had to be a broad measure of agreement between Berlin and the state governments, and this was rarely forthcoming.

At the end of the First World War Germany faced a vastly increased national debt and a current annual expenditure running at

70. An explanation for the inflation along these lines is given by Charles P. Kindleberger in "A Structural View of the German Inflation," in Feldman et al., *Die Erfahrung der Inflation*, esp. pp. 32–33.

several times the prewar level. And on the other side of the scale, the losses of territory, merchant fleet, and overseas assets had reduced the taxable wealth with which Germany could meet these expanded commitments. Clearly the government had to raise the level of revenue substantially, and in a series of reforms, usually named after their instigator Matthias Erzberger, a whole range of new taxes were introduced between August 1919 and March 1920 to enlarge the fiscal power of the Reich.

Erzberger's reforms represented not just a tax increase, but a bold overhaul of the entire revenue system facilitated by the change to republican government. Drawing on the provisions of the Weimar constitution, the new system shifted fiscal power from the states to the Reich. From now on Berlin was to collect taxes, including the income tax, and pass on revenue to the states according to their needs. The political rationale for this was not only the modernization of the tax system, but the transfer of power from states, with their generally oligarchic government, to the national level, where the new constitution served as a model of parliamentary democracy.[71] Erzberger's achievement was to establish Reich tax offices throughout the country and impose a single, unified tax code where previously there had been enormous variety between the rates and collection methods of the different states. The new taxes introduced included levies on profits and capital increases which had taken place during the war, an inheritance tax, and a one-time capital levy designed to hit large personal fortunes. There was also a capital gains tax on dividends and a special excess consumption tax for those wealthy people who chose to spend rather than save. But the main novelty was a new income tax, which was sharply progressive and amongst wage and salary earners was deducted at source, that is, pay-as-you-earn. It was universal and immediately replaced all the diverse state arrangements for income tax. The states themselves retained only the right to tax real estate.

The reforms were ambitious in scope and intention, but no one knew just how much the new taxes would contribute towards the budget deficit and reparations, particularly under conditions of

71. A good authority on German fiscal questions in this period is Peter-Christian Witt. See, for example, his "Finanzpolitik und sozialer Wandel in Krieg und Inflation, 1918–1924," in Mommsen et al., eds., *Industrielles System*, pp. 395–426; "Reichsfinanzminister und Reichsfinanzverwaltung, 1918–1924," *Vierteljahrshefte für Zeitgeschichte* 23 (1975): esp. 4–9. Also useful is Steven B. Webb, "Government Revenue and Spending in Germany, 1919–1923," in Feldman et al., *Die Anpassung*, pp. 46–82.

inflation. According to his biographer, "Erzberger's main aim was to establish, on paper at least, a balanced budget that would restore confidence in Germany's financial management at home and abroad."[72] In addition there was the difficulty of expeditiously implementing the reforms with an administrative structure that was only slowly adapting to the needs of a modern centralized system. However good the intentions of Erzberger and his successors may have been, they were dependent on the tax bureaucracy to carry out their plans and this showed itself to be less than ideal for the purpose, at least before 1923.[73]

Unfortunately the new taxes did not prove sufficient and never exceeded 50 percent of the sum which would have been necessary to cover expenditures in any year between 1920 and 1923. This was largely due to weaknesses in the system, which "exhibited little responsiveness to inflation."[74] The greatest miscalculation of the reforms was the assumption that the mark's value would remain stable. Over a year of price stability did follow their implementation in 1920, but lacking any kind of dollar indexing, the new taxes were bound to be affected when the mark's depreciation began anew in 1921. In the case of the income tax, the 1919 plan envisaged the twenty-five million taxpayers with low and medium earnings providing 30 percent of the total yield, while the five million taxpayers with top earnings contributed the remaining 70 percent. But things worked out very differently. Because the lower tax brackets were taxed at source, whereas the higher ones were subject to post-facto assessment, the former contributed a much higher level of real revenue; in other words, the higher earning categories had an opportunity to exploit the continuing devaluation of the currency in a way which was not available to wage and salary earners.[75]

The fate of other taxes was similar. The sales tax was assessed quarterly, so that after each quarter the taxpayer had to send in a record of his sales, then another month elapsed before his tax declaration was due, and then he had a further fourteen days in

72. Klaus Epstein, *Matthias Erzberger and the Dilemma of German Democracy* (Princeton, 1959), p. 345.

73. The bureaucracy had only shown initiative and high performance when there was a strong political leadership such as Erzberger's or, after October 1923, Luther's. Witt, "Reichsfinanzminister und Reichsfinanzverwaltung," p. 61.

74. Peter-Christian Witt, "Tax Policies, Tax Assessment, and Inflation: Towards a Sociology of Public Finances in the German Inflation, 1914–1923," in Schmukler and Marcus, *Inflation through the Ages*, pp. 457–58.

75. For the figures on taxation yields and the relative distribution of the tax burden, see Witt, "Tax Policies," pp. 461–67.

which to pay it. Even in a period of stable money values, this would have meant interest-free operating credit for the person owing the tax. In the inflation it meant that the treasury received only a portion of the outstanding amount in real terms, while the taxpayer retained the difference between the real value of the taxes when they were being created and when they were paid. The deleterious impact of the inflation on the whole process of tax collection was aggravated further by evasion and capital flight. Erzberger had made no secret of the fact that the new taxes were intended to squeeze the rich until the proverbial "pips squeaked" and that those who had made money from the war while others sacrificed their lives would pay with their pocketbooks. Not surprisingly the rich reacted with massive resistance: their capital fled the country, and their tax payments were delayed and evaded in every way possible. Indeed they even managed to portray tax evasion as almost patriotic, since a large proportion of the intended revenue appeared to be earmarked for reparations to the Entente.[76]

Tax assessment and collection during the inflation not only failed to meet the targets set by the German treasury, but also failed to effect a redistribution of the tax burden. Above all the inflation created a very strong incentive for both rich and poor taxpayers to delay at each step of the assessment process. Meanwhile the budget deficit at both state and Reich level grew as a consequence of the missing revenue, thereby heating the inflation further.[77] In the final analysis it was the consumer who bore the full extent of Erzberger's intended tax burden with the continuously rising prices he paid in the shops.

---

76. For the effect of capital flight and tax evasion, despite the government's attempts to stop it, see Witt, *Finanzpolitik und sozialer Wandel*, pp. 417–18.
77. Witt, "Tax Policies," p. 459.

2

Hamburg

> We have no nobles, no patricians, no
> slaves, even no subjects. All real
> Hamburgers have and recognise only
> a single estate, the estate of citizens.
> Citizens are we all, no more and no
> less.
> —J.K.D. Curio[1]

Hamburg offers some special advantages for the study of an urban
milieu in a time of crisis. Because it was both a city and a state
within the federation of the German Reich, it had a double administrative status. Not only was it spared the conflict between town
and country that affected other states, but unlike cities of equivalent
size such as Munich, Leipzig, or Cologne, it enjoyed a direct
relationship with the central government in Berlin. From the
methodological point of view, the choice of Hamburg benefits
from the city's excellent statistical records. From the broader
historical perspective, it is well placed for an analysis of the inflation's international repercussions, for as Germany's premier
trading port it was one of the areas of the country most sensitive to
fluctuations in the world economy.

This chapter is intended as an introduction to Hamburg's history
before 1914, and as such, a background to the events portrayed in
the chapters that follow. It is also an opportunity to look at the
city's demographic and social structure, the composition of its
working population, and the manner in which the various elements
of that population organized themselves.

---

1. Quoted in Percy E. Schramm, *Hamburg – ein Sonderfall in der Geschichte
Deutschlands* (Hamburg, 1964), p. 16.

Hamburg's Merchant Economy, 1866–1914

Hamburg, along with other Hanseatic cities like Bremen and Lübeck, was an example of a special development in German history, namely a republic amongst princely states. In contrast to the rest of the country it had always been governed by its own citizens and this was a source of intense pride, at least to those citizens who did the governing. For it must be said at the outset that while Hamburg was certainly distinguished from Prussia and the other German states by the total absence of an aristocracy, its government was nonetheless very largely in the hands of a wealthy minority.

Hamburg's rise as one of Europe's major ports began in the 1840s, encouraged by the decolonization of Latin America and the rise in German emigration to the New World. The liberation of the South American markets from Spanish and Portuguese monopoly brought new openings for the city's merchant houses, while the highly profitable transport of migrants enabled German ship owners to outbid their American competitors for carrying freight on the return journey across the Atlantic. The great advantage that Hamburg enjoyed lay in its geographical position as the most easterly of the major western European ports, with direct access both to the Atlantic shipping lanes and the extensive canal network that linked the river Elbe to the markets of central and southern Europe.[2]

The interests of trade and the merchant economy were paramount in the city; indeed they were the "hegemonic ideology of Hamburg society," as one knowledgeable commentator has put it.[3] Moreover the city's independent, laissez-faire tradition made it deeply suspicious of its powerful Prussian neighbor. Bismarck was regularly attacked in the local press, and within the German Confederation, Hamburg often sided with Prussia's chief rival, Austria. In the war of 1866, however, realpolitik overruled sentiment and the city reluctantly allied itself with Berlin. It is likely that Bismarck refrained from occupying Hamburg only because he realized that it would perform its valuable function as Germany's chief port more effectively as an independent state than as a Prussian province.[4]

2. Ludwig Wendemuth and Walter Boettcher, *The Port of Hamburg* (Hamburg, 1927), p. 8; Michael Grüttner, *Arbeitswelt an der Wasserkante: Sozialgeschichte der Hamburger Hafenarbeiter, 1886–1914* (Göttingen, 1984), pp. 19–21.
3. Richard J. Evans, *Death in Hamburg: Society and Politics in the Cholera Years, 1830–1910* (Oxford, 1987), p. 33.
4. Details of Hamburg's protracted struggle against Prussian hegemony in the

In 1871 Hamburg joined the new German Reich, but there remained strong resistance to entry into the German Customs Union (Deutscher Zollverein). For the merchants, the cause of commerce seemed infinitely more important than any political considerations at the time, and the protectionism of the Junker barons was rejected in favor of Anglo-Saxon free trade. After 1878, when Bismarck introduced import tariffs to protect landowners and industrialists from foreign competition, the case for Hamburg remaining outside the Customs Union seemed further strengthened. However a movement (known as the *Zollanschluß*) developed amongst the more forward-looking businessmen to join the union, on condition that the city be allowed to construct a special duty-free port area. In 1888, after years of negotiations, Hamburg entered the Customs Union with its free port, and in the following years, despite some remaining points of friction with Berlin, the dark prophesies of the die-hard Hamburg "particularists" proved unfounded.[5]

The *Zollanschluß* marked an important change in the character of the local economy. The customs privileges upon which Hamburg's trading strength had been built were sacrificed for a chance to participate in the growing industrial wealth of the German Reich. The wide network of overseas contacts built up during the past century by famous trading houses like Woermann and O'Swald was put to use channeling German factory products to the world. In the years remaining before the First World War Hamburg's strength and influence grew with the rapid expansion of international trade. The harbor had been in the process of development since the completion of the first modern quays and rail sidings at the Sandtor in the 1860s. Now the river Elbe was extensively dredged and new docks built to handle the much larger steamships which began to enter Hamburg's waters in the 1870s. While a high-tide shipping channel of 4.3 meters had sufficed in 1840, by the end of the century twice that depth of water was needed to handle the ocean liners of the HAPAG (Hamburg-Amerikanische Paketfahrt AG).[6] Already the largest shipping line in the world,

---

1870s and 1880s are given in Werner Jochmann and Hans-Dieter Loose, *Hamburg: Geschichte der Stadt und ihrer Bewohner*, vol. 1 (Hamburg, 1982), pp. 492–97. See also Evans, *Death*, esp. pp. 5–15.

5. Jochmann and Loose, *Hamburg*, pp. 505–27. Also still useful for a general history of the city at this time is Ernst Baasch, *Geschichte Hamburg, 1814–1918*, vol. 2 (Gotha, Stuttgart, 1925).

6. Eckart Klessmann, *Geschichte der Stadt Hamburg* (Hamburg, 1981), pp. 554–55.

this illustrious company had almost two hundred ships by 1914, amongst which were colossi like the 52,000 ton *Imperator*. Of more general significance was the decline in the predominance of British vessels using the harbor: in 1870 over 50 percent of ships berthing in Hamburg were British, but by 1912 the proportion had sunk to 30 percent and German ships now carried 60 percent of the total tonnage.[7]

With the rapid growth in trade came an expanded financial structure, so that Hamburg's banks grew hand in hand with its merchant houses and often exchanged directors. In 1913, for example, the Norddeutsche Bank had a Woermann and a Münchmeyer on its board, while the Hamburg Südamerikanische Dampfschiffgesellschaft had Herr Max Schinkel from the Norddeutsche Bank amongst its directors.[8]

Industry developed more slowly than trade, but Hamburg's entry into the Customs Union provided a catalyst for growth. The biggest industries were connected with the maritime economy, most obviously shipbuilding where the Blohm und Voss company was joined in 1909 by the Stettin-based Vulcan-Werft. By 1920 there were eight large shipyards on the Elbe employing about 25,000 workers directly, with a further 20,000 in machine working and ancillary industries.[9] In addition a major industrial branch developed in the free port area, where new concerns were established to process imported raw materials such as rubber, asbestos, phosphate, coffee, cocoa, and oil and then reexport them without being subject to the Reich's domestic duties. In 1880 there were about 600 firms with 18,000 workers – figures which had risen to 5,000 and 115,000 respectively by 1913.[10]

By the eve of the war Hamburg was the second most important entrepôt port on the European continent after Rotterdam. It was handling 20 percent of German exports – machines, chemicals, and textiles to the value of nearly 4 billion marks, some of it carried through the newly completed Kiel Canal (1895) to markets in the Baltic states. And on the import side, Hamburg's ships were bringing oil from Pennsylvania and coal from the collieries of northeast England for Germany's expanding industries.[11] The city

7. Grüttner, *Arbeitswelt*, pp. 23–24.

8. Dietrich Kersten, *Die Kriegsziele der Hamburger Kaufmannschaft im Ersten Weltkrieg* (Diss., Hamburg, 1963), p. 2.

9. Heinrich Hoebel, *Das organisierte Arbeitgebertum in Hamburg-Altona* (Diss., Hamburg, 1923), p. 11; Wendemuth and Boettcher, *The Port of Hamburg*, p. 154.

10. Jochmann and Loose, *Hamburg*, pp. 530–31; Grüttner, *Arbeitswelt*, pp. 26–27.

11. Klessmann, *Geschichte*, pp. 555–57; Heinrich Reincke, *Hamburg: Ein kurzer*

Table 1. Ships and Trade Tonnage (Imports and Exports) through Hamburg, 1866–1926

	Ships	Tonnage
1866	5,185	1,149,000[1]
1876	4,937	3,053,000
1886	6,384	5,245,000
1896	9,118	10,345,000
1906	12,982	18,944,000
1913	15,073	25,458,000
1919	2,234	2,343,000
1920	4,808	5,798,000
1921	8,401	11,011,000
1922	10,787	16,587,000
1923	13,192	20,932,000
1926	14,788	21,911,000

1. Imports only.
Source: Ludwig Wendemuth and Walter Boettcher, *The Port of Hamburg* (Hamburg, 1927), pp. 217, 219.

had witnessed a quarter century of unprecedented growth. Not only had trade tonnage risen almost fivefold since 1886 (Table 1), but the city had become rich; measured by per capita income, Hamburg and its sister Hanse town, Bremen, were at a level that was almost twice the German national average.[12] There was a relatively large number of taxpayers in the highest income bracket; workers' wages were amongst the best in the country; civil servants' salaries were without exception higher than in other cities; and, interestingly, the number of pensioners (*Rentner*) amongst taxpayers was lower (at 6 percent) than the average for the Reich.[13] The renowned city treasurer Leo Lippmann relates how in the postwar years he was obliged to make frequent official trips to Berlin and realized how other German states still saw Hamburg as a wealthy metropolis, not in need of federal funds. Although this

Abriß der Stadtgeschichte von den Anfängen bis zur Gegenwart (Bremen, 1925), pp. 269–71; Heinrich Meyer, *Hamburg als Güterumschlagsplatz vor und nach dem Krieg* (Hamburg, 1930), p. 16.
12. W.G. Hoffmann and J.H. Müller, *Das deutsche Volkseinkommen, 1851–1957* (Tübingen, 1959), p. 20.
13. Wiesbaden for example had 15 percent. Jürgen Brandt, *Hamburgs Finanzen von 1914 bis 1924* (Diss., Hamburg, 1924), p. 56.

was no longer true, it took "a lot of work [for Lippmann] to change this impression."[14]

Hamburg's Social and Political Structure

In its political structure Hamburg had a distinctiveness to match its economy. As a federal state it was to a large degree self-governing and independent from Berlin. Executive power rested with the Senate, which was composed of a number of senators who were responsible for the various government departments and who were presided over by a mayor (*Bürgermeister*) elected from their midst. The senate was Hamburg's government, and not as the name might suggest simply a parliamentary upper house. Besides its responsibility for the administration of the state, it was also the city municipality. Senators served for life and were invariably chosen from the ruling elite, a privileged circle of "senatorial families." These dynasties of rich merchants and lawyers – the latter taking the main load of actual administrative work – were, broadly speaking, of liberal economic views but with political sympathies that were conservative and particularist, disdaining alignment with national party organizations.[15]

The strength and influence of the ruling elite was nowhere more clearly illustrated than in the control it exerted through the Chamber of Commerce (Handelskammer). Indeed the fact that the building which housed this institution, the *Börse*, was physically adjacent to the city hall only served to reinforce the impression of a common purpose linking Hamburg's politicians and its leading businessmen.[16] As entry to the Chamber of Commerce was limited to independent owners of family firms, such families controlled both the city government and its links to Berlin. In 1914, for example, eighteen out of the twenty-four committee (*Vorstand*) members of the Chamber of Commerce came from traditional Hamburg merchant houses, another four from banks, and the remaining two were a shipowner and an industrialist.[17] Their idea of government was conditioned by their commercial interests; in other words they took the view that those with a financial stake in the city had the

14. Leo Lippmann, *Mein Leben und meine amtliche Tätigkeit* (Hamburg, 1964), p. 351.
15. James J. Sheehan, *German Liberalism in the Nineteenth Century* (Chicago, 1978), pp. 226, 229.
16. Ekkehard Böhm, *Anwalt der Handels- und Gewerbefreiheit: Beiträge zur Geschichte der Handelskammer Hamburg* (Hamburg, 1981), p. 193.
17. Kersten, *Kriegsziele*, p. 4.

right to govern it. The influential banker Max Warburg was typical amongst them in thinking that "politics" belonged in Berlin; in Hamburg it was the economy that mattered.[18]

Collaborating in the process of senatorial appointment and government was Hamburg's legislative body, the Citizens' Assembly (Bürgerschaft). This was elected under a highly restricted franchise, half by taxpaying male citizens who had to pay for the privilege of citizenship, and half by property owners and notables.[19] The atmosphere in the assembly was gentlemanly, with debates aimed at reaching a compromise between the interests of the participants, that is, big and small merchants, industrialists, bankers, property owners, and artisans. Like local urban politics elsewhere in Germany, the issues were generally unrelated to national questions.

It was a convivial atmosphere for the private businessman. The state's role in the conduct of the city's affairs was minimal and so was its expenditure. Taxes were low and esteem for the profit motive high. There may have been a degree of civic conscience amongst the senatorial families, but there was no civic money for "frivolities" like the arts or even a university.[20] The government agreed to spending money only in areas where the economy would benefit most, such as reinforcing the harbor defenses against the river Elbe. In matters of pressing social concern, the city's record was lamentable. The general level of health was poor because of inadequate funding for clean water provision, and until the turn of the century many of Hamburg's poorer citizens continued to live in appalling slums.

This political status quo was only challenged when industrialization brought a dramatic increase in the number of workers in the population. Already in 1869 and 1870 there were serious strikes and although Bismarck's 1878 anti-Socialist law was not applied at first with great vigor in Hamburg, concern grew amongst the ruling elite after 1883 when both the Reichstag districts within the city were represented by the Social Democratic party (SPD).[21] The SPD promised to end the neglect of the social infrastructure by

18. Ibid., p. 6.
19. For a history of the Citizens' Assembly, see Jürgen Bolland, *Die hamburgische Bürgerschaft in alter und neuer Zeit* (Hamburg, 1959). On the restrictive nature of Hamburg's suffrage laws in the late nineteenth century, see Jochmann and Loose, *Hamburg*, pp. 536–37.
20. Hamburg had to wait until 1919 until it acquired a university; see Fritz K. Ringer, *The Decline of the German Mandarins: The German Academic Community, 1890–1933* (Cambridge, Mass., 1969), pp. 75–76.
21. Jochmann and Loose, *Hamburg*, p. 535.

going straight to the national level, but to achieve any meaningful improvements for the workers, power in the Citizens' Assembly was required, and this was blocked by the discriminatory local franchise. Only the small minority who earned enough to pay local income tax had the citizenship rights that allowed them to vote in assembly elections. In 1875 a mere 8.7 percent of the city's population were citizens, and fifteen years later the percentage was even less. Moreover as property owners had two votes and notables three, the masses had virtually no representation at all.[22]

Roughly speaking, there were four socioeconomic groups spread out across the city's residential areas: the wealthy and influential in Harvesthude and Rothenbaum on the western side of the Alster Lake; the better-off white-collar workers of the new Mittelstand in Hohenfeld and Uhlenhorst on the eastern side of the Alster; the "respectable" working class in outer suburbs such as Barmbeck, Eppendorf, Eimsbüttel, and Hamm; and the dockworkers and casual laborers concentrated in a poverty-stricken area near the harbor known as the Alley Quarters (Gängeviertel).[23]

Hamburg's dockworkers had to live in this notorious district because the casual nature of their employment made it necessary for them to be close to the harbor and the agencies that organized dock labor. The neighborhood had altered little since the Middle Ages and over the years the houses had been extended in a jumble of annexes and attics that by the 1890s were so chronically overcrowded that the inhabitants spilled out into the narrow, unsanitary alleyways. The area was long seen as a source of criminal violence and political unrest, but it took the catastrophic cholera epidemic that hit Hamburg in 1892, claiming thousands of lives, to galvanize the government into action. Unfortunately, while many of the worst dwellings in the Alley Quarters were demolished in the following years, the chief beneficiaries were the owners, who were granted extravagant compensation by the state, and not the tenant workers who were forced either to relocate on the outskirts of the city or pay much higher rents for space in the remaining overcrowded premises. In the 1890s rents there were 50 percent higher than on the outskirts, although the latter accommodations were far superior. The result was that amongst the poorest families earning under 900 marks per year, that is, casual laborers, some small artisans, and widows with children, anything between a third and a half of their annual earnings was spent on rent for accommodations

22. Evans, *Death*, p. 48.
23. Ibid., pp. 56–58.

that typically consisted of two rooms plus a kitchen, measuring no more than twenty square meters – and with toilet facilities shared by four or five other families.[24]

A second consequence of the cholera epidemic and the major dock strike that followed it in 1896/97 was a change in the rules governing election to the Citizens' Assembly. But it was a change of little use to the Social Democrats, for citizenship and the right to vote in assembly elections now called for proof that a taxable annual income of 1,200 marks had been earned for five years in succession, a figure which was far beyond the means of the average working man. Only with the arrival of the new century, in 1901, did Otto Stolten – a machinist and editor of the *Hamburger Echo* – take his place as the first Social Democrat in the assembly. His success was an inspiration to the workers, many of whom now paid taxes on 100 marks per month, although actually earning less, for the sole purpose of gaining citizenship and the right to vote.[25]

By the end of 1904 the SPD had thirteen members in the Citizens' Assembly and the party's enemies on the Right were growing increasingly anxious that the dreaded workers would soon gain control of Hamburg's parliament. It was at this point that they acted in collusion with the Senate to change the franchise regulations even further in their favor. A blatantly unfair three-class suffrage was proposed, under which a third of the seats in the Citizens' Assembly (twenty-four) were reserved for voters with annual incomes over 6,000 marks and another third for those earning between 3,000 and 6,000 marks. This left only the remaining twenty-four seats for the workers and effectively prevented the SPD from gaining a majority. The new changes were hotly contested, not only by the Social Democrats, but also by many Left Liberals who saw the continued obstruction of working-class representation as a fraud and not worthy of a modern political institution. In protest they founded a new United Liberal party (Vereinigte Liberalen), but neither they nor a series of violent demonstrations in Hamburg's streets in January 1906 could prevent the new voting system from being implemented that year.[26]

---

24. Clemens Wischermann, *Wohnen in Hamburg vor dem Ersten Weltkrieg* (Münster, 1983), pp. 252–53; Grüttner, *Arbeitswelt*, pp. 102–23. To try to make ends meet, single rooms were often sublet to lodgers.

25. Klessmann, *Geschichte*, p. 532; Reincke, *Ein kurzer Abriß*, p. 280.

26. In the final version the three-class suffrage was reduced to two, with the upper (richer) class having twice the seats of the lower. For the details, see Klessmann, *Geschichte*, pp. 533–34. A biographical sketch of the United Liberal leader, Carl Petersen, is given in Erich Lüth and Hans-Dieter Loose, *Bürgermeister*

Although the SPD faction in the Citizens' Assembly continued to expand its numbers to twenty representatives by 1910, the party could do nothing to alter the fundamental concentration of political power held by the ruling elite other than attack it from its far-off platform in the Berlin Reichstag.[27] Unlike Social Democrats elsewhere in Germany, the Hamburg SPD was gradualist in its approach to political change and quickly disassociated itself from the radical behavior of the 1906 rioters. Richard Evans has suggested a number of reasons for the "undeviating" reformism of the local party, including its strong artisan tradition dating back to the 1840s and the city's robust particularist culture. Even when the SPD gained complete power in Hamburg after 1918, it shared control of the government with representatives from the old senatorial families and thereby lost many disillusioned working-class supporters to the German Communist Party (KPD). A further important reason for the local party's moderation was its desire to gain support amongst the fast-growing ranks of white-collar workers in the city. To do this, it had to turn its back on "the 'rougher' side of working-class life and project an image of solid and sensible reformism."[28]

Hamburg's Demographic and Occupational Profile

At the end of the First World War Hamburg was the second largest city in Germany and had already experienced phenomenal population growth since the beginning of the twentieth century. Between 1910 and 1925 the number of people registered in the city rose by over 13 percent, a rate of increase exceeded only by Cologne, Essen, and Düsseldorf (Table 2). The rise was in line with the general shift of population from the countryside to the city taking place throughout German society at this time. In addition cities such as Hamburg absorbed large numbers of returning soldiers at the time of the demobilization in 1918, as well as displaced persons from former colonies and ceded territories in the east.

Parallel to the trend to urbanization, there was also a tendency

---

Carl Petersen, 1868–1933 (Hamburg, 1971). For a good account of the popular protest to the new law, see Richard J. Evans, "'Red Wednesday' in Hamburg: Social Democrats, Police, and Lumpenproletariat in the Suffrage Disturbances of 17 January 1906," *Social History* 4 (1979): 1–31.

27. Evans, *Death*, pp. 81–84.
28. Ibid., p. 555.

Table 2. The Ten Largest Cities in Germany, 1910 and 1925

	1910	1925	Percentage of increase
Berlin	3,734,258	4,024,165	7.8
Hamburg	953,103	1,079,126	13.2
Cologne	600,291	700,222	16.6
Munich	607,592	680,704	12.0
Leipzig	644,644	679,159	5.3
Dresden	608,841	619,157	1.7
Breslau	514,979	557,139	8.2
Essen	410,214	470,524	14.8
Frankfurt	414,576	467,520	12.8
Düsseldorf	358,728	432,633	20.6

Source: Statistik des hamburgischen Staates, No. 32 (1925), Volkszählung, pp. 39–42.

for people to leave the city center for the new suburbs on the outskirts. It is clear that Hamburgers were becoming suburbanites from the fact that, while the overall city population was growing swiftly between 1910 and 1925, the number living in the inner-city neighborhoods actually decreased by about 10 percent.[29] It was those districts, like the Alley Quarters after 1897, that were under the greatest pressure to make room for business and administration buildings.

The city's occupational profile also shows significant changes during the period, and these can best be demonstrated by reference to the two Reich censuses of 1907 and 1925 that straddled the inflation period. Table 3 presents an analysis of Hamburg's working population according to its percentage of participation in the various economic sectors and occupational classifications laid down by the Reich statistical office. It reveals a number of developments during the eighteen-year period. Most striking is the increase in the number of white-collar workers and civil servants. This is largely explained by the overwhelming importance of trade and transport in the local economy. The proliferation of shipping lines, merchant houses, and banks provided a steady demand for clerks and book-keepers, so that by 1925 this sector was employing almost half the working male population.

In Table 4 the connection between white-collar labor and Ham-

29. Bericht über die medizinische Statistik des hamburgischen Staates bis zum Jahre 1927, in *Hygiene und soziale Hygiene in Hamburg* (Hamburg, 1928).

Table 3. Hamburg Working Population by Occupational Categories and Economic Sectors, 1907 and 1925 (In Percent)

	1907		1925	
	Men	Women	Men	Women
Occupational categories				
Independents	21.8	20.2	18.4	10.5
White-collar/civil service	**17.2**	**6.7**	**31.4**	**32.6**
Workers	60.2	32.6	49.8	26.8
Working family members	0.8	40.5	0.4	30.1
Total	100.0	100.0	100.0	100.0
Economic sectors				
Agriculture and fishery	2.9	2.5	2.4	2.7
Industry and artisans	41.6	27.1	38.3	25.8
Trade and transport	**45.1**	**24.9**	**48.6**	**38.3**
Administration and professions	6.5	4.2	6.9	5.1
Domestic service	1.7	38.1	0.7	22.5
Health care and welfare	2.2	3.2	3.1	5.6
Total	100.0	100.0	100.0	100.0

Source: Aus Hamburgs Verwaltung und Wirtschaft, Special Issue 1 (July 1927): 194–97. Hamburgische statistische Monatsberichte, Special Issue 1 (June 1926): 145–49.

Table 4. Distribution of White-Collar Workers in the Hamburg Economy, 1907 and 1925

	1907			1925		
	Men	Women	Total	Men	Women	Total
Agriculture	214	8	222	831	58	889
Industry	10,581	1,698	12,279	21,249	8,808	30,057
Trade and transport	**32,600**	**5,372**	**37,972**	**78,204**	**37,854**	**116,058**
Civil service	11,486	313	11,799	22,906	6,131	29,037
Health and welfare	579	60	639	4,401	5,329	9,730
Domestic service	5	—	5	186	403	589
Total	52,534	7,445	59,979	127,777	58,583	186,360

Source: Hamburgische statistische Monatsberichte, Special Issue 1 (June 1926): 145–49.

burg's trade and transport is demonstrated in absolute figures. It is interesting to note the rise in the proportion of female employees in the sector. Explanations for this are diverse, but in general it can be seen as evidence of the greater participation of women in the postwar German economy. Apart from the liberating effects of the war itself, the increasing mechanization of office procedures led to a higher level of female employment.[30]

By the turn of the century Hamburg already had a higher proportion of white-collar workers than most other German cities – Berlin, for example. The reason is clearly attributable to the prominence of the harbor and the trade and transport sector in the local economy. By comparison with this private white-collar sphere, the number in public service was below the Reich average.

By contrast, blue-collar workers, while the single largest group in 1925, were below the national average as a proportion of the work force. Furthermore when artisans are subtracted from the sector "Industry and Artisans," the figure falls from 38 to 33 percent (Table 3). While the shipyards employed skilled men, many workers were unskilled dockers and this is one of the features that distinguishes Hamburg, with its relatively slow-growing processing and chemical industries, from, for example, the Ruhr cities where steel mills and coal mines employed large numbers of the "labor aristocracy."[31]

The Reich company censuses, carried out at the same time as the 1907 and 1925 population surveys, provide information on the number of enterprises in Hamburg. In the industry and artisans sector, amongst those employing less than six persons, there was a decrease of about 13 percent during the period. This suggests that the process of industrial concentration was taking place more rapidly in the large urban centers, but one should not deduce from this statistic that the artisan economy in Hamburg was in decline. The list of trades shows that in building-related crafts, for example, there was plenty of growth. In trades with traditional guild skills, such as butchers and bakers, there was steady development, while in the new fields of electricity and photography, there was a very noticeable expansion between 1907 and 1925 (Table 5).

The overall impression is distinct: in comparison with the rest of Germany, Hamburg had a high proportion of white-collar and a

---

30. Günther Hartfiel, *Angestellte und Angestelltengewerkschaften in Deutschland* (Berlin, 1961), pp. 46–47. See also Ludwig Preller, *Sozialpolitik in der Weimarer Republik*, (Düsseldorf, 1949), pp. 115–29.
31. Ursula Büttner, *Hamburg in der Staats- und Wirtschaftskrise, 1928–31* (Hamburg, 1982), pp. 90–94.

Table 5. Registered Enterprises in Hamburg, 1907 and 1925

| | 1907 | | 1925 | |
	Total enterprises	Enterprises employing under six	Total enterprises	Enterprises employing under six
Agriculture, fisheries	1,380	1,210	288	252
Administration, entertainment, etc.	1,413	1,169	3,922	3,491
Trade and transport	44,786	37,460	54,226	46,911
Industry and artisans	**30,849**	**25,028**	**26,438**	**21,853**
Total	78,428	64,867	84,874	72,507

Fifteen selected trades in the industry and artisans category

Tailors	6,161	5,609	5,008	4,689
Shoemakers	2,892	2,747	2,366	2,331
Hairdressers	1,559	1,483	1,815	1,734
Painters	1,248	1,000	1,474	1,259
Plumbers	848	679	973	789
Bricklayers	490	270	182	118
Builders	381	148	672	425
Glaziers	367	335	419	404
Butchers	996	811	1,240	1,115
Bakers	561	257	658	347
Smiths	276	225	196	169
Electrical work	251	153	1,300	1,059
Watchmakers	247	213	391	381
Printers	426	233	394	213
Photographers	184	149	278	268

Source: Statistik des Deutschen Reiches, 215 (1907): 440, 442–51; 416 (1925): 6a, 54–55.

low number of blue-collar workers and a strong preponderance towards trade and away from industry. In short, it had an unmistakable demographic bias towards the new Mittelstand.

The Mittelstand

The major problem encountered in any analysis of the Mittelstand is the difficulty of defining and statistically measuring it. As we have already seen, more than anything else it was a common ideological identity that kept the concept alive into the twentieth century. For the purposes of this study a Mittelstand model is constructed, composed of selected occupations taken from Hamburg's working population. In line with the division between old and new, the target groups selected are artisans and retailers on the one hand and white-collar workers, including civil servants, on the other. An additional group – house owners – is also examined. This is a more nebulous category because it is not based on a single occupation, but there are good reasons for its inclusion here. Theodor Brauer suggested that their parasitic role as speculators in the property market disqualified them from Mittelstand membership.[32] But the majority of house owners were not speculators in the sense of those who engage in commercial operations that involve the risk of loss as well as profit. Rather, in Hamburg at least, they had an almost class-based conception of their role in society as landlords, and of particular importance, they shared that affection for small property and enterprise that was one of the few common attributes capable of binding together the Mittelstand's diverse strands.

Artisans and Retailers

Artisans and retailers occupied a similiar position in German society.[33] Both prized their economic independence as small businessmen and both were prepared to go to great lengths to maintain it. Many of them would probably have earned higher incomes in wage labor, but any sacrifice seemed justified to avoid losing their precious independence.[34] Perhaps the key characteristic of both groups was their satisfaction of local needs; indeed it was their orientation to the immediate neighborhood that goes a long way to explaining their survival into the twentieth century.

Artisan enterprises typically consisted of a master craftsman presiding as sole owner over a workshop in which, besides himself, a limited number of journeymen and apprentices might work. The whole business generally supported fewer than six people, including the master himself.[35] So far as capital was concerned, the artisan usually raised it himself through saving, although occasionally loans would have been taken out to purchase major pieces of

32. Brauer, "Mittelstandspolitik," p. 398.
33. The term artisan (*Handwerker*) here refers only to independent artisan masters, not to skilled workmen in the employment of others.
34. Crossick and Haupt, "Shopkeepers, Master of Artisans, and the Historian," in Crossick and Haupt, eds., *Shopkeepers*, pp. 8–9.
35. This does not mean that larger units did not exist, merely that the majority fit this description and that the distinction has the methodological benefit of coinciding with the categorization in the official Reich statistics.

equipment. Whatever the method used, there were certainly no joint-stock companies within the artisan economy. Where others might have placed their assets in a savings account or the stock market, the artisan invested every penny in his business, his future survival in an independent existence being more important to him than the maximum return on his capital.[36]

An indication of how many artisans were active in Germany during the inflation period can be gained from the company surveys carried out in 1907 and 1925. In the sector "Industry and Artisans," there was a slight fall from 1,618,781 to 1,616,080 in the number of enterprises employing fewer than six people – a smaller percentage fall than in Hamburg (see above). Of these 1.6 million small units (over 80 percent of the total number of German enterprises in 1925), informed estimates suggest that at least 1.3 million were craft-based workshops or artisans.[37]

Until the nineteenth century artisans had been strictly regulated by guilds, which not only controlled the terms of employment in a craft, but also determined the methods of manufacture and the price at which the goods were to be sold. It was a corporatist system in which "the advantages inherent in mechanical efficiency and competitive individualism were renounced for the sake of security and order."[38] But in the wake of the Napoleonic occupation of western Germany, this "pastoral economic world" was threatened by the movement towards *Gewerbefreiheit* (freedom of trade). Starting with a Prussian decree in 1810, the various German states pushed through legislation to reduce the power of the guilds, and in so doing, opened the way for large-scale factory production. In Hamburg industry not only came late, as we have seen, but it was actively discouraged, at least in the first half of the nineteenth century. While the ruling elite celebrated the virtue of market forces in commerce, its attitude to industrial development was more reminiscent of feudal times, and only in 1865 did the tra-

---

36. Carl Brenke, *Die Finanzierung des Handwerksbetriebes* (Stuttgart, 1936), p. 18.

37. Data from the two censuses are not entirely compatible because the methods of classification and presentation used in 1925 differed from those of 1907. For problems of measuring Mittelstand enterprises, see Hans Tobis, *Das Mittelstandsproblem der Nachkriegszeit und seine statistische Erfassung* (Diss., Grimmen, 1930), pp. 14–15. The 1907 figures were calculated according to Reich territory of 1925. *Wirtschaft und Statistik*, 8, Nr. 2 (1928), p. 48. See also Wilhelm Wernet, *Handwerkspolitik* (Göttingen, 1952), p. 77; Wolfram Fischer, *Wirtschaft und Gesellschaft im Zeitalter der Industrialisierung* (Göttingen, 1972), p. 353; *Enquete Bericht*, "Das deutsche Handwerk," 3. Unterausschuß, 8. Arbeitsgruppe (Berlin, 1930), vol. 2, pp. 18–19, 393.

38. Theodor S. Hamerow, *Restoration, Revolution, Reaction: Economics and Politics in Germany, 1815–1871* (Princeton, 1958), p. 21.

ditional privileges and rigid organization of the guilds give way to *Gewerbefreiheit*. "In sharp contrast to its views on the freedom of trade, the Senate maintained the rights and privileges of the 38 Hamburg guilds as a guarantee of economic stability and social order."[39]

By 1870 industrialization was well advanced, and in the half century between the beginning of the Great Depression in 1873 and the end of the inflation in 1923, two trends are clearly discernible in the German artisan economy. The first was the progressive disappearance of many uncompetitive enterprises and the growth of a few successful ones into large-scale capitalist firms. But this process was by no means complete by the outbreak of the First World War and the reason was to some extent the result of the second trend, namely, the renaissance of guild power.[40] For what the *Gewerbefreiheit* had called forth was not only the free forces of the market, but also an appeal for aid from the state.

Theodor Brauer observed that the most striking aspect of the artisan was his "hypnotized gaze upon help from above."[41] Such help would have been doubtful, had it not been for the fact that it coincided with the political movement towards Mittelstandspolitik that we have already noted. For their participation in this coalition of forces, the artisans were rewarded with new laws in the 1880s and 1890s reauthorizing and strengthening the power of the guilds, and extending authority to compulsory guilds, which were permitted to exercise monopoly rights within a given craft.[42] The new legislation served as an institutional life raft for artisans at exactly the moment when their demise, once predicted by Marx and Engels, seemed most threatening.[43] In fact in markets where quality remained at a premium, artisans remained superior to the factory assembly line, and in other areas they often succeeded in adapting themselves to the needs of mass production – usually in part work and repairs.[44]

39. Klessmann, *Geschichte*, p. 438. See also Jochmann and Loose, *Hamburg*, pp. 531–32.

40. Shulamit Angel-Volkov, "The Decline of the German Handicrafts – Another Reappraisal," *Vierteljahrschrift für Sozial- und Wirtschaftsgeschichte* 61 (1974): 170–71.

41. Brauer, "Mittelstandspolitik," p. 376.

42. The monopoly power did not extend to the right to fix prices. Under the terms of the 1897 law, free guilds could convert themselves to compulsory guilds when the majority of members agreed. Wernet, *Handwerkspolitik*, p. 52.

43. Karl Marx and Friedrich Engels, *The Communist Manifesto* (Penguin edition, 1967), p. 91.

44. Wherever special skills or quality production were required, artisans survived well. J. Dethloff, "Das Handwerk in der kapitalistischen Wirtschaft," in Bernard

While artisans remained guild conscious and proud that entry into their trade was restricted to those who had passed a rigorous examination, retailers had no such professional pride. Despite their overt anticapitalist outlook, they were nonetheless a modern phenomenon, having grown up as a direct consequence of mass production and the need to develop distribution between factory and consumer.[45] The typical German small retailer ran a grocery or hardware store, helped by family members and possibly a shop assistant. He struggled to survive on small capital reserves and narrow profit margins by working long hours and granting liberal credit to retain the custom of the immediate neighborhood.

With the rapid growth and urbanization of the German population in the years before the First World War, the number of entrants into retailing increased swiftly, so that by 1914 the trade was generally overcrowded. Many lacked the necessary capital and experience to survive, having opened a shop with the erroneous idea that easy profits were to be made.[46] In view of the difficulties, their rise in number between 1882 and 1925 is extraordinary. While the German population grew 36 percent in those forty-three years (from 45.7 million to 62.4 million), the ranks of small retailers (i.e., those employing fewer than six persons) increased 143 percent (from 434,785 to 1,056,603).[47] No exact figure is available for the number of Hamburg retailers at the outbreak of the war, but we do know they totaled just over 18,000 in 1925.[48]

Retailers could not claim an organizational structure reaching back into the Middle Ages. Indeed the shallowness of their traditions gave them something of an inferiority complex when compared to the artisans whose corporatist aspirations they gener-

---

Harms, ed., *Strukturwandlungen der deutschen Volkswirtschaft* vol. 2 (Berlin, 1928), p. 20. Artisans were also able to exist in a sort of symbiotic relationship with neighboring factories, carrying out repairs on their products, or accepting subcontract work. See, for example, Wilhelm Keil's "Erlebnisse eines Sozialdemokraten," in Wolfram Fischer, ed., *Quellen zur Geschichte des deutschen Handwerks*, (Göttingen, 1957), p. 171.

45. L.D. Pesl, "Mittelstandsfragen," in *Grundriß der Sozialökonomie*, chap. 4, sec. 9, pt. 1 (Tübingen, 1926) pp. 49–54.

46. Robert Gellately, *The Politics of Economic Despair: Shopkeepers and German Politics, 1890–1914* (London, 1974) p. 29; Pesl, "Mittelstandsfragen," pp. 104–5.

47. *Statistik des Deutschen Reichs, 1882–1907*, reproduced in Pesl, "Mittelstandsfragen," p. 104; *1925: Wirtschaft und Statistik*, 8. (1928), Heft 2, p. 46; 1925 figures based on reduced territory of postwar Reich.

48. *Statistik des Deutschen Reichs*, vol. 416 [1925] p. 54–55, 66–71. A comparable figure for 1907 is not available because in that census retailers and wholesalers were counted together. Between 1907 and 1925 this joint figure for Hamburg rose from 22,922 to 26,883.

ally shared. Their economic situation was in any case more precarious; not only did they represent the most poorly financed enterprises struggling to survive in an overcrowded market, but they also faced formidable competition from the 1890s onwards from large-scale undertakings such as department stores and consumer cooperatives.

The latter were feared not only because they used the advantages of bulk purchasing to offer the customer lower prices, but also on account of their strong Socialist influence.[49] Department stores by contrast were resented for being big business concerns – using financial muscle and "unfair" practices to drive their smaller rivals from the field. Both were seen as a pernicious threat to Mittelstand enterprise.[50] The defense associations formed to combat them were really the first form of retailer organization, but they lacked support even amongst the small shopkeepers they were intended to protect and served in no way to halt the inevitable progress towards large-scale retailing in Germany.[51] The growth of these new concerns serves to illustrate once again how fragile the Mittelstand coalition was; whatever solidarity existed between small retailers and artisans was severely strained by the frequency with which the latter patronized department stores like Tietz.[52]

As early as 1904 the Hamburg retailers achieved a long-standing goal when the Chamber of Retailers (Detaillistenkammer) was established.[53] It was intended to give institutional representation to the retail trade on a par with that enjoyed by the merchants and wholesalers in the Chamber of Commerce, but in reality it remained a poor relation in the city's influential business community and never offered any serious protection to the struggling shopkeeper. The Hamburg Senate, dominated as it was by representatives from the rich merchant families, ensured that the Chamber of Retailers did not become the fighting organ that the small retailers wanted through the expedient of restricting its voting procedure along the

49. For a good introduction to German consumer cooperatives, see Hans Crüger, "Konsumvereine," in *Handwörterbuch der Staatswissenschaft*, vol. 5 (Jena, 1923), pp. 875–78.

50. Gellately, *Despair*, pp. 37–40.

51. Ibid., pp. 86–89.

52. Wernicke, *Kapitalismus*, p. 562.

53. Elsewhere in Germany the retailers had not been so successful. A *Kleinhandelskammer* (retailers' chamber) was set up in Bremen in 1906, but in most centers the shopkeepers had to be content with a department within the local Chamber of Commerce. See Brauer, *Mittelstandspolitik*, pp. 393–94. For a detailed history of the Hamburg Detaillistenkammer's first quarter century, see H.T. Götz, *Die Detaillistenkammer Hamburg, 1904–1929* (Hamburg, 1929).

lines of the prewar Citizens' Assembly franchise. In practice only the more prosperous store owners could afford to take the time off from their businesses to attend the Chamber of Retailers' meetings or stand for its offices, with the result that the views of the little man were seldom heard.[54]

White-Collar Workers and Civil Servants

The white-collar worker is a modern figure, but unlike the small retailer, devoid of any attachment to the past. In an influential work published in 1912, Emil Lederer suggested that his defining characteristic was the engagement in intellectual activity (*geistige Tätigkeit*) instead of manual labor. He made it clear, however, that the qualification applied not to technical function, but to the "analogous social position" that all white-collar workers held and that gave them coherence as a group. This so-called intermediate position between capitalists and proletariat was fluid at the edges, so that the top was often indistinguishable from the independent entrepreneur and the bottom melted into the working class.[55] The emphasis that Lederer's definition placed upon brain work had the weakness that it could lead to awkward anomalies. Why, for example, should a highly skilled typesetter working on a foreign language publication be classified as *Arbeiter*, while an unskilled office girl was *Angestellte*?[56] Still, the importance of his contribution remains, namely, the ideological nature of the group identity. White-collar workers strove to avoid classification with the workers and imitated the life-style of the middle classes, even if this involved actually depriving themselves of necessities like food.[57]

In the nineteenth century white-collar workers enjoyed a close relationship with their employer; they supervised workers, administered the accounts, and represented the firm to customers. This proximity not only gave them a feeling of separateness from the workers, but also cultivated the notion that they too, after acquiring a suitable amount of training and experience, could become independent like their boss. This was particularly the case with shop assistants. Often living with their employer's family, they tended to look upon their position as a stepping-stone to the

---

54. Gellately, *Despair*, pp. 106–8.
55. Emil Lederer, *Die Privatangestellten in der modernen Wirtschaftsentwicklung* (Tübingen, 1912), p. 23.
56. Fritz Croner, *Soziologie der Angestellte* (Cologne, 1962), p. 81.
57. Lederer, *Privatangestellten*, pp. 100–11. Also Jürgen Kocka, "Zur Problematik der deutschen Angestellten, 1914–1933," in Mommsen et al., eds., *Industrielles System*, pp. 792–811, esp. 792.

establishment of their own shop. Despite low pay and a general lack of skills, they saw themselves as members of the Mittelstand.[58]

Marxists may take the view that white-collar workers were simply a novel addition to the proletariat, temporarily suffering from "false consciousness,"[59] but this is to ignore a crucial and enduring element in the white-collar worker's make up, namely, his attachment to the social prestige of his position.[60] His desire for a separate identity led him to adopt life-styles and political views that were probably at odds with his economic reality, particularly as the gap between him and the workers narrowed after the outbreak of the First World War, but then human behavior can never be explained entirely in terms of economic criteria. In fact the more his material superiority over the blue-collar worker diminished, the more he compensated by stressing his ideological distinctiveness.[61]

In Germany the number of white-collar workers began to rise in the second half of the nineteenth century as the growth of large-scale production caused a separation in the functions of management and ownership. At the same time the expanding role of the state led to an increasing number of civil servants who, with white-collar workers in the private sector, formed a new clerical class. Estimating its exact size in the Weimar Republic presents some difficulties,[62] but we know that the figure for white-collar workers and civil servants in the national statistics rose from 3.15 million in 1907 to 5.27 million in 1925 – an increase of 67 percent.[63] In Hamburg the corresponding figures were 59,979 and 186,360 – an increase of over 200 percent (Table 4).

Determining the number of civil servants alone depends on the definition of the term. Otto Hintze, for instance, noted that when one considered the German civil service, one thought naturally of government officials, but that teachers, army officers, priests, and

---

58. Hans Speier, *Die Angestellten vor dem Nationalsozialismus: Ein Beitrag zum Verständnis der deutschen Sozialstruktur, 1918–1933* (Göttingen, 1977), pp. 22–23.

59. Hartfiel, *Angestellte*, p. 98.

60. Speier, *Die Angestellten*, p. 85.

61. Jürgen Kocka, "The First World War and the *Mittelstand*: German Artisans and White-Collar Workers," *Journal of Contemporary History* 8 (1973): 103.

62. The procedures adopted in the censuses of 1907 and 1925 differed from each other in important respects. Besides the distortions caused by the reductions in Reich territory, there were changes in the classification of some occupations, for example, a salesman was classed as a blue-collar worker in 1907, but became a white-collar worker in 1925. Preller, *Sozialpolitik*, p. 117.

63. *Statistik des Deutschen Reichs*, vol. 408 (1925), pp. 116–17.

employees of the post office and railways should also be included.[64]
Civil servant numbers increased dramatically with the greater
organization of the economy during the war and the subsequent
demobilization in 1918–19, so much so in fact, that one authority
talks of "an inflation of officials to match the inflation of prices."[65]
By 1923 their strength had reached 2.156 million including post
office and railway employees, but the stabilization brought a severe
cutback to around 1.886 million.[66]

In Hamburg the career civil service had developed in a different
way than in other parts of Germany. In contrast to Prussia, for
example, where a full-time professional civil service had existed
since the end of the eighteenth century, Hamburg had no paid
higher civil servants until the 1890s and relied instead on a system
of deputations under the leadership of an unpaid senator. This
rather amateur form of government was in keeping with the
laissez-faire spirit of the merchant elite to whom the very idea of
professional bureaucrats would have been anathema.[67] Until the
Disziplinar- und Pensionsgesetz (disciplinary and pension law) of
1884 employees of the Hamburg state actually had terminable
positions, something unheard of in other parts of the Reich. But
with the 1892 cholera epidemic, a sharp jolt was delivered to
Hamburg's leisurely administrative apparatus. Within four years
long-overdue changes had been implemented and a Prussian style
higher civil service introduced. It was an important moment in
Hamburg's history for the power of the old merchants – the
government of elevated "citizens" – was diminished.[68]

The civil servant had a number of exclusive traits beyond the
sense of superiority shared with the white-collar worker in the
private sector. His relationship with his employer – the state – was
a much closer one than that of the typical white-collar worker, and
his salary was not just pay for service rendered in the manner of
normal wages, but contained an element of compensation for the
fact that he placed himself at the disposal of public administration

64. Otto Hintze, *Beamtentum und Bürokratie*, ed. Kersten Krüger (Göttingen, 1981), p. 17.
65. Emil Lederer and Jacob Marschak, "Der neue Mittelstand," in *Grundriß der Sozialökonomie*, chap. 5, sec. 9, pt. 1 (Tübingen, 1962), p. 126.
66. *Reichsarbeitsblatt*, Sonderheft 30 (Berlin, 1925), p. 25; Lederer and Marschak, "Der neue Mittelstand," pp. 129–30.
67. Evans, *Death*, p. 26.
68. Reichszentrale für Heimatdienst (Landesabteilung Hamburg Lübeck), *Die wirtschaftliche Lage Hamburgs unter besonderer Berücksichtigung der Einwirkungen des Krieges und des Vertrages von Versailles* (Hamburg, 1921), p. 12; Reincke, *Ein kurzer Abriß*, p. 278; Evans, *Death*, pp. 544–45.

for life.[69] The state demanded from its employees a degree of allegiance quite unlike that required of other workers, making, for example, indebtedness into a disciplinary offense. In return it offered the civil servant status, prestige, and an unsurpassed measure of economic security – in short, a job for life.

The relationship between the civil servant and the state was thus one of mutual dependence: the state relied on him to serve it at all times, while he trusted his employer to protect his livelihood whatever the prevailing conditions. It was a relationship really "outside the commercial realities of a capitalist society," as one writer has pointed out,[70] and it worked well enough until the state found itself in difficulties of the kind experienced during the Weimar Republic. While some civil servants may have seen the revolution and the fall of the monarchy as a calamity, many more saw it as an opportunity to demand better conditions. The lower ranks, in particular, formed trade unions to strengthen their position vis-à-vis the state and in doing so had to reconcile their action with their conception of themselves as reliable representatives of that state. In fact the seeming convergence of civil servant and worker interest that took place during the inflation did not last. As we shall see, with the stabilization in 1923, civil servants abandoned their brief affair with the class war and reverted to prewar elitism.

Although the two groups are understandably lumped together as new Mittelstand, research conducted by Sandra Coyner suggests that in the Weimar Republic civil servants had patterns of consumption different from those of white-collar workers in the private sector. For example, civil servant household budgets showed a strong inclination towards traditional family-oriented expenditure, such as books, education, and furniture, while white-collar workers favored more modern spending patterns with a significant share devoted to entertainment, cinema attendance, and listening to the radio.[71] There is also statistical evidence that white-collar workers had a higher degree of childless marriages than any other group, including civil servants, which suggests that they were avoiding the added expenditure involved in having a family in order to maintain

69. H. Koeppe, "Besoldung und Besoldungspolitik," in *Handwörterbuch der Staatswissenschaft*, vol. 2, 4th ed. (Jena, 1924) p. 603.

70. Jane Caplan, "The Imaginary Universality of Particular Interests: The "Tradition" of the Civil Service in German History," *Social History* 4 (1979): 312–13.

71. Sandra Coyner, "Class Consciousness and Consumption: The New Middle Class during the Weimar Republic," *Journal of Social History* 10 (1976/77): 314–16.

a particular life-style.[72] Spending patterns are of course a rather limited guide to ideological and political inclination, and for this reason Coyner's thesis that white-collar workers were more the "harbingers" of modern consumerism than Mittelstand members is somewhat overstated. Clerks and salesmen, while imitating the latest fashions, could still have held overtly reactionary views. However her work does illustrate the diverse nature of the Mittelstand and the difficulty of establishing any kind of common response to the pressures of the Weimar "system."

It is in organization that the differences between the old and new Mittelstand are probably clearest. While the artisans and retailers looked to the establishment of chambers or guilds for their salvation in a hostile market economy, the white-collar workers allowed their clublike associations of the late nineteenth century to evolve into full-fledged trade unions.

In Hamburg one of the earliest of the white-collar associations was the Verein der Handlungs-Commis von 1858, founded, as the name indicates, in 1858 and known universally as the 58er Verein. It was an organization more concerned with cultural activities than wage bargaining and held to the belief, typical of the time, that the white-collar worker's job was a mere staging post on the road to economic independence. Indeed a large proportion of the 58er Verein's members were not employees at all, but independent businessmen who would have sat at the other side of the table had there ever been any collective negotiations on pay or working conditions.

Partly in reaction to this cozy arrangement, but also out of distinct ideological motivation, the Deutschnationale Handlungsgehilfenverband (DHV) was established in Hamburg in 1893. This was a white-collar association, particularly well represented amongst shop assistants, with a strong nationalist flavor. Originally it was involved in anti-Semitic and pan-German politics, but later it devoted more time to the material interests of white-collar workers, while continuing to propagandize them as a respectable professional group.[73] The DHV was the clearest example of a bridge between the old and new Mittelstand in that they exhibited a distinct attraction to the corporatist formulas of the artisans and

72. See the figures assembled by Merith Niehuss in "Lebensweise und Familie in der Inflationszeit," in *Anpassung*, ed. Feldman et al., p. 240.

73. For a history of the DHV, see Iris Hamel, *Völkischer Verband und nationale Gewerkschaft: Der Deutschnationale Handlungsgehilfen-Verband, 1893–1933* (Frankfurt a.M., 1967).

retailers; clerks and salesmen should belong to an honorable and secure estate like craftsmen and farmers.

By the eve of the First World War the nationwide membership of the white-collar associations had reached about half a million for commercial employees and in excess of 100,000 for technical staff. The latter were concentrated in industry rather than trade, and because they had closer contact with industrial workers, their associations were run more along trade union lines.[74] Few of the individual organizations had impressive support; however, the largest in the country was the Hamburg-based DHV with 107,688 members in 1907.[75]

House Owners

Housing was a private affair in Germany before the First World War, hardly touched by controlling regulations. The vast majority of lower paid workers lived in overcrowded tenement houses, paying high rents for unhealthy and demoralizing accommodations.[76] It was a market where demand far outstripped supply, and the idea that he had any obligation other than that of maximizing his profit would have struck the average landlord as utterly foreign. Naturally he opposed any legislation intended to improve the lot of his tenants if it involved a reduction in his income.[77]

In Hamburg there were 20,483 house owners in 1913, comprising about 2 percent of the city's population.[78] They may have lacked numerical strength, but they made up for it in economic and political power. This was partly because their Grundeigentümer-Verein was one of the most influential political bodies in

74. Emil Lederer, "Privatbeamtenbewegung," *Archiv für Sozialwissenschaft und Sozialpolitik* 31 (1919): 215 ff.; Lederer and Marschak, "Der neue Mittelstand," p. 132.

75. Hartfiel, *Angestellte*, p. 132.

76. See, for example, Albert Gut, "Die Entwicklung des Wohnungswesens in Deutschland nach dem Weltkrieg," in Albert Gut, ed., *Der Wohnungsbau in Deutschland nach dem Weltkrieg* (Munich, 1928), p. 22.

77. Peter-Christian Witt, "Inflation, Wohnungszwangswirtschaft und Hauszinssteuer. Zur Regelung von Wohnungsbau und Wohnungsmarkt in der Weimarer Republik," in Lutz Niethammer, ed., *Wohnen im Wandel* (Wuppertal, 1979), pp. 387–88.

78. *Statistik des hamburgischen Staates* 29 (1913): 3. The term *Grundeigentümer*, strictly translated, means landowner, but this has strong rural connotations that are inappropriate to describe a purely urban environment like Hamburg. Property owner is also unsatisfactory because its use is ambiguous in the context of the inflation when possession of any kind of material assets was the key to survival. In this study therefore house owner and landlord are used interchangeably to render the meaning of *Grundeigentümer*.

the city, partly because their representation in the Citizens' Assembly was disproportionately high[79] and partly because they made a substantial contribution to the city's tax revenue.[80]

The Grundeigentümer-Verein (GVH) was one of the earliest associations for house and property owners in Germany, being founded in 1832.[81] Basically it represented the interests of landlords or those who received all or part of their earnings from rents. It helped them, for example, in disputes with tenants by compiling a blacklist of those who had left premises with rent owing or who had committed some other transgression. In 1879 there were only 600 members out of the approximately 11,000 house owners in Hamburg and its suburbs, but by 1906 the number had risen tenfold, with a particular spurt in membership after the 1892 cholera epidemic and the new legal restrictions on urban property that followed it. Membership was predominantly of the old Mittelstand with many artisans and small traders amongst the leadership.[82] Their hostility to the ruling elite, which they held responsible for tax burdens on property, was only exceeded by their fear and loathing of the workers and their champion, the Social Democratic party. Indeed the GVH saw opposition to the SPD as an article of faith – social democracy being a threat to the welfare of Hamburg in its eyes – and it was one of the chief instigators of the 1906 franchise changes.[83]

For its part the Hamburg SPD clashed bitterly with the GVH over state intervention in the housing sector and actually found itself supporting the senate in its plans to clear the slums in the Alley Quarters. But the dominant position of the house owners in the Citizens' Assembly made housing improvements for the workers a slow process. They blocked every initiative aimed at improving housing conditions in the Citizens' Assembly on the grounds that it was an unreasonable burden on the house owners or an "interference in landlords' rights."[84] Even after the cholera epidemic,

79. Because of the restricted franchise for the prewar Citizens' Assembly, the house owners held no fewer than 40 of the 160 seats. Reincke, *Ein kurzer Abriß*, p. 280.
80. The land tax, to which all Hamburg house owners were liable, yielded 26 percent of total revenue in the fiscal year 1913/14. *Einzelschriften zur Statistik des Deutschen Reichs* 10 (1930), 670. Also Brandt, *Hamburgs Finanzen*, p. 65.
81. For a history of the association, see Renate Hauschild-Thiessen, *150 Jahre Grundeigentümer-Verein in Hamburg von 1832 e.V.: Ein Beitrag zur Geschichte der Freien und Hansestadt Hamburg* (Hamburg, 1982).
82. Evans, *Death*, pp. 42–43.
83. Wischermann, *Wohnen*, pp. 220–21.
84. Evans, *Death*, pp. 518–19; Grüttner, *Arbeitswelt*, pp. 105–6.

they "delayed and diluted" legislation so that only in 1898 did minimum requirements for space and ventilation in lodgings become law. After the state had paid exorbitant compensation for demolished premises in the Alley Quarters, private developers and market forces, firmly defended by the GVH, determined the expansion of the city's housing stock up to the outbreak of the First World War.[85] Cooperative building societies, which many saw as the solution to the need for cheap housing, were likewise opposed by the GVH as "lowering house values."[86]

One of the effects of the suffrage reform debate in the years from 1893 to 1896 was an increase in friction between the house owners and the ruling elite, with the latter blaming the landlords for holding up housing legislation that might have mitigated the effects of or even prevented the cholera epidemic.[87] In similar fashion the slum clearance plans drawn up in 1897 produced a conflict of interest between the house owners and the big employers in the Hamburg docks. The employers wanted to build new low-cost dwellings within close proximity of the harbor in order to avoid paying higher wages for their workers to come in from the outskirts, but the house owners were interested in profitable exploitation of their expensive inner-city real estate, not cheap homes for the poor.[88]

It was a steady development which shows that not only was this propertied Mittelstand faced with bitter hostility from poor working tenants, but it was also making enemies in the years after 1892 amongst the ruling elite that felt its grip on the city's government increasingly threatened. And the 1905 franchise revisions did nothing to calm its fears, for it was the house owners and the GVH, rather than the Senate, who gained the most in the Citizens' Assembly as a result of the new electoral arrangements. The confrontation between these three blocs – workers/tenants, house owners, and the ruling elite – was to smoulder on in Hamburg's local politics until it finally burst into flame with the 1918 revolution. In the events which followed that event, it was the house owners, symbol of the propertied Mittelstand, who were to be the chief losers.

85. Wischermann, *Wohnen*, p. 129.
86. Evans, *Death*, p. 520.
87. Ibid., pp. 541–42.
88. Grüttner, *Arbeitswelt*, p. 116.

3

War, 1914–1918

> It is as though we are living in a mad
> house when one reflects that the
> Great Powers of Europe are involved
> in converting Europe into a heap of
> ruins, all to the advantage of America
> and Japan.
> —Albert Ballin, 1915[1]

The inflation had its origins in the First World War.[2] The pattern in
which the German war effort would be financed was set at the very
outset in 1914 when the Reichsbank abandoned its obligation to
redeem banknotes in gold. Shortly afterwards new laws were
enacted which not only permitted the discounting of treasury bills
against bank notes, but also rendered meaningless the statutory
requirement that 30 percent of the note circulation be backed by
gold. New credit banks were allowed to circulate their own currency alongside regular notes; in a matter of days the German
government had secured itself a "license to print money" and it was
determined to use it.[3]

Under the financial leadership of Treasury Secretary Karl Helfferich, Germany covered the massive expenditure needed to prosecute the war with borrowing. Some attempt was made after 1916
to increase taxation, but the ensuing gains in revenue did little more
than keep pace with the rise in the nonmilitary budget.[4] The belief

---

1. Quoted in Lamar Cecil, *Albert Ballin: Business and Politics in Imperial Germany,
1888–1918* (Princeton, 1967), p. 296.
2. Holtfrerich, *Die deutsche Inflation*, p. 4.
3. The legislation remained in force until the stabilization in 1923. Rudolf
Stucken, *Deutsche Geld- und Kreditpolitik, 1914 bis 1953* (Tübingen, 1953), pp. 17–18.
Statistics on the issue of credit bank notes are given in K. Roesler, *Die Finanzpolitik
des Deutschen Reichs im Ersten Weltkrieg* (Berlin, 1967).
4. Roesler, *Die Finanzpolitik*, pp. 196–97. For the role of the states in the war's

that Germany's dependence on borrowing to finance the war was itself inflationary and that she might have avoided the problem had she followed the path of Britain, where a higher percentage of expenditure was covered by tax revenue, has recently been challenged. Balderston has argued that inflationary pressure was greater in Germany than Britain, not because of differing fiscal policies, but because, lacking an equivalent to the London money market, the Germans could not take up state debt or place it abroad so easily as the British.[5] In any case Helfferich believed that taxation in time of war would have a demoralizing effect on the German people, and he expected his country to win and be in a position at the end of the conflict to present the enemy with the bill.[6] This was not simply patriotism, but a recognition that any effective tax would have to include a levy on the rich, and in particular on war profits. For Helfferich, this would have meant not only squeezing his own political allies, but would also have required the expropriation by the central government of the states' right to impose income tax, and it seems he had no stomach for the hard fight in the Federal Council (Bundesrat) which this would have involved.[7] There is a certain irony in the fact that, having lost the war, Germany was practically compelled to adopt a centralized taxation system, introduced under the auspices of Helfferich's archenemy Matthias Erzberger.

Of course the war produced a great deal more than simply a bankrupt treasury.[8] It heralded the arrival of far-reaching state intervention in the German economy, both in terms of the supervision of industrial output for the war effort itself and in the rationing and price control of goods for domestic consumption. The latter aspect of this *Zwangswirtschaft* was pursued by the authorities with seemingly relentless energy, much to the disgust of artisans, retailers, house owners, and, to a certain extent, the consumers themselves. But during the war at least, it was easily

---

financing, see Witt, "Finanzpolitik und sozialer Wandel," in Mommsen et al., eds., *Industrielles System*, pp. 406–10.

5. T. Balderston, "War Finance and Inflation in Britain and Germany, 1914–1918," *Economic History Review* (May 1989): 222–44.

6. J.G. Williamson, *Karl Helfferich, 1872–1924: Economist Financier, Politician* (Princeton, 1971), p. 125.

7. For a full, if rather sympathetic, treatment of Helfferich's war financing, including his arguments over taxing war profits, see ibid., esp. chap. 4.

8. The war cost Germany approximately 164 trillion marks, most of which was held either in the war loan by individual subscribers, or in short-term credit extended by institutions outside the Reichsbank in exchange for government treasury bills.

justified on the grounds that it was necessary to deter those traders who might otherwise be tempted to exploit customers' fears over shortages by charging excessive prices.[9]

As the Reichsbank dutifully followed Helfferich's lead and increased the quantity of money, so the external value of the mark fell. This had only a marginal effect on the internal purchasing power of the currency because the German economy during the war was to a large degree isolated from the outside world. However, with its rationing and the burgeoning black market, the war economy itself forced prices up, so that while the foreign exchange index moved only from 1.00 in July 1914 to 1.77 in November 1918, the retail food price index moved in the same period from 1.00 to 2.44.[10]

In Hamburg the war meant a severe shock to the city's prosperous existence. The source of its former strength, its overseas connections, became an immediate liability as international trade collapsed. Within months its extensive port facilities were taken over by the navy and many of the dock sheds were commandeered for storing munitions.[11] By the end of 1914 shipping was at a standstill and the only trade still being plied was with Scandinavia through the Kiel Canal. The proud motto of HAPAG chief Albert Ballin, "My field is the world," had suddenly become a meaningless echo. His death in November 1918 spared him the sight of the HAPAG's dismemberment by the Entente.

For the next five years Hamburg's maritime lifeline with the outside world was cut by the British blockade and an acute shortage of bunker coal.[12] In addition the export of weapons, vehicles, optical equipment, chemicals, foodstuffs, and oil was banned and for most other items, export permits were required. No other state in Germany suffered to the same extent from the war's effects, for only Hamburg had so large a proportion of its population dependent on overseas relationships. The scale of the disaster in terms of imports and exports can be seen in Table 1.

While trade languished and dockers were made redundant, Hamburg's industry expanded in areas where orders could be taken

9. Holtfrerich, *Die deutsche Inflation*, p. 77.
10. "Zahlen zur Geldentwertung in Deutschland, 1914 bis 1923," in *Wirtschaft und Statistik*, Special Issue 1 (Berlin, 1925), pp. 6, 16 (hereafter cited as *Zahlen*). In July 1914 the U.S. dollar was worth 4.20 marks. For a discussion on exchange rates and domestic prices during the inflation period, see Holtfrerich, *Die deutsche Inflation*, pp. 13–23.
11. Wendemuth and Boettcher, *The Port of Hamburg*, p. 157.
12. Meyer, *Güterumschlagsplatz*, p. 14.

from the military. The great shipyards of Blohm und Voss and Vulcan-Werft made good profits building submarines for the navy and by 1917 the total shipyard work force had grown to 27,000 (compared with 18,000 in 1914).[13] However, living standards for workers fell. According to calculations made by Jürgen Kocka, the average real annual wage of a male worker at the national level fell by 23 percent between 1914 and 1918 in war industries and by 44 percent in the civilian sector.[14] The figures for Hamburg metal-workers show a similar picture: wages rose between 80 percent and 87 percent, while the cost of living increased by over 100 percent. Moreover working hours were much extended, with fifteen hours per day and weekend working becoming the norm in the shipyards.[15]

Parallel to the mass conscription into the army, workers in peacetime jobs were mobilized for war production, and labor shortages soon brought women and girls into the explosives factories on Hamburg's outskirts. Women were especially hard hit. Besides worrying about their conscripted husbands at the front, they had to work long hours in these munitions plants and then queue up with their ration cards in front of butchers and bakers in the hope of getting something with which to feed their families. These shopping lines gave them the opportunity to vent their spleen against the authorities and the war in general; meanwhile their children roamed the streets uncontrolled.[16]

The chronic deficiencies of the food distribution system and the spreading black market led to great bitterness amongst the workers, particularly as the rich middle class seemed to be avoiding the shortages. In August 1916 and again in February 1917 there were hunger riots and shop plundering, involving mainly women and youths. The 1916 disturbances, which inevitably led to clashes with the police, were restricted to the working-class districts of Barmbek and Hammerbrook, but the 1917 riot spread to the rest of the city, indicating that even the Mittelstand was now affected by the food shortage.[17]

13. Volker Ullrich, *Kriegsalltag: Hamburg im Ersten Weltkrieg* (Cologne, 1982), p. 78.

14. Jürgen Kocka, *Facing Total War: German Society, 1914–1918* (Cambridge, Mass., 1984), p. 23.

15. Volker Ullrich, "Massenbewegungen in der Hamburger Arbeiterschaft im Ersten Weltkrieg," in *Arbeiter in Hamburg*, ed. Arno Herzig et al. (Hamburg, 1983), p. 407.

16. Ibid., p. 411. See also Volker Ullrich, "Everyday Life and the German Working Class," in Roger Fletcher, ed., *Bernstein to Brandt: A Short History of German Social Democracy* (London, 1987).

17. Ullrich, *Massenbewegungen*, p. 413.

Trade union activity suffered from a lack of skilled functionaries and the rapid influx of workers without previous industrial experience. In addition many temporary shipyard workers feared that union membership could lead to their dismissal and a subsequent call to the trenches. Nonetheless spontaneous action by rank-and-file workers grew as union authority faded. Young workers were particularly rebellious because they could not be threatened with the draft. There was a series of stoppages for cost-of-living supplements from 1916 onwards at Blohm und Voss and Vulcan-Werft, but the shipyards also provided the stimulus for the two major mass actions in Hamburg during the war: the August 1917 peace demonstration and the January 1918 strike. It was the shape of things to come and a testing ground for how far the majority Social Democratic party (SPD) in Hamburg could control the growing wave of workers' protest. The majority SPD was torn between cooperation with the authorities in the spirit of the *Burgfrieden* (truce) and reclaiming the grievances of the masses from the left-wing Independent Social Democratic party (USPD). In the January 1918 strike it took the latter course and, in anticipation of its action ten months later in the November revolution, worked on the strike movement to deradicalize it.[18]

As the war drew to a close Hamburg's businessmen looked to a speedy dismantlement of the *Zwangswirtschaft* and the restoration of Germany's position as a trading nation.[19] Alfred O'Swald, head of the famous merchant family, confidently expected the Entente to allow Germany back into the world's network of commercial relations, while in its 1918 annual report, the chamber of commerce talked optimistically of the postwar economy being reconstructed with speed. It recommended a "just peace" in which Germany would lose neither its merchant fleet nor its colonies. Above all there should be a minimum of restrictions; the free, responsible merchant would revive economic life in Germany without the need of state interference.[20]

18. Ibid., pp. 409–12, 416.

19. Guenther Jantzen, *Hamburgs Ausfuhrhandel im 20. Jahrhundert* (Hamburg, 1953), p. 55.

20. See Alfred O'Swald, "Der Handel," in *Hamburg in seiner politischen, wirtschaftlichen und kulturellen Bedeutung*, ed. Deutsche Auslandsarbeitergemeinschaft (Hamburg, 1921), p. 87; *Jahresbericht der Handelskammer Hamburg über das Jahr 1918*, pp. 28–29.

The Artisans

While guild membership was rising between 1911 and 1913, the artisan economy in Hamburg was not in particularly good shape on the eve of the First World War, and according to the last annual report of the Chamber of Artisans (Handwerkskammer), all branches were reporting diminishing sales. The bakers were threatened by larger concerns and many lacked the necessary capital to modernize. Despite a rising demand for the most basic of foodstuffs, the number of members in the bakers' guild fell during 1913. The printers had an equally depressed year and those producing advertising material were hit by the general downturn in the economy. Amongst the tailors the news was little better, and there were frequent complaints about a flood of imported garments from England and "the completely dishonest" advertisements that London tailors were placing in German newspapers. An interesting feature of the 1913 report was the considerable difference between crafts in journeymen's wage rates. Sculptors earned 9.50 marks for an eight-and-a-half-hour day, while smithies were paid only 5.50 marks for nine hours of work. The variation was attributable not only to the different skills required, but more significantly to the fact that the sculptors had negotiated a wage agreement with their guild that was binding on their masters, whereas the smithies had not. In general, journeymen with such collectively agreed contracts were better paid than those without; for the masters and journeymen alike it was an indication of how things would develop in the future.[21]

With the outbreak of the war the first reactions of some artisans bordered on panic and the Chamber of Industry (Gewerbekammer) found it necessary to ask the Hamburg government building department to speed up orders to maintain confidence in the future.[22] In fact the early months of the war were less disastrous than expected. Some artisans were conscripted into the army, but guild membership did not fall significantly and most of those called up

21. *Jahresbericht der hamburgischen Handwerkskammer für 1913*, pp. 99, 105, 119. Regrettably the 1913 report was to be the last until after the inflation period. The *Handwerkskammer* was in fact one half of the Hamburg *Gewerbekammer*, which was founded in 1873 as a self-governing administrative organ for both the artisan and industrial economies within the city. In 1908 it was divided into two relatively independent sections responsible for industry and trade respectively. The two terms *Gewerbekammer* and *Handwerkskammer* are used here interchangeably to describe the artisans' chamber.

22. StA.H *Gewerbekammer*, A.13, Bd. 1, Protokolle, Handwerkerabteilung, 23 October 1914.

were apprentices.[23] Many of those apprentices who did not go to the front found their way instead into the munition factories that sprang up on Hamburg's periphery. The artisan masters, unable to match the high wages paid in these factories, had great difficulty trying to lure them back.[24]

When the master himself was conscripted, however, the resulting burden was often too much for those who were left in charge. Unlike the retailers, who could march off to war in the knowledge that their wives could mind the shop as competently as themselves, the artisan had no replacement for his skilled labor, and even the presence of an apprentice or two was often not enough to support the business at a profitable level. Moreover the war brought with it new problems which would have taxed a fully manned artisan enterprise. Consumer demand fell as people tightened their belts and difficulties in procuring raw materials had to be faced in common with the rest of the city's business community. Profits were typically low, but some branches were hit worse than others. Those that could acquire military orders often did good trade – tailors were kept busy making uniforms, while cartwrights turned out gun carriages. On the other hand, bakers suffered from a shortage of flour and, even more severely, of coal to fire their ovens. Likewise the difficulty in procuring leather against the prior claims of military contractors forced many shoemakers into liquidation by 1916.[25]

Another serious difficulty was the almost total drying up of credit. As the retailer depended on credit from his wholesaler (and gave it in considerable measure to his customers), so the artisan relied on credit for raw material purchases. With the outbreak of war, new credit banks were set up throughout Germany, but in Hamburg an additional state enterprise called the Relief Fund for Retailers and Traders (Hilfskasse für Detaillisten und Gewerbetreibende) was established with a mixed capital of six million marks coming from private and public sources. It made loans to both artisans and retailers, usually against the collateral of stock or

23. This was borne out by the fact that there was a sizable drop in craft examinations taken in 1914. StA.H *Aufsichtsbehörde für die Innungen*, A.3, Bd. 2, Jahresbericht, 1914.

24. The resulting apprentice shortage was not serious. According to the Hamburg vocational guidance office, a government department, in early 1918 there was still 88 percent of prewar apprentice strength available for work. StA.H *Gewerbekammer*, A.13, Bd. 1. Protokolle, Handwerkerabteilung, 7 March 1918.

25. StA.H *Gewerbekammer*, A.12, Bd. 4, Protokolle, Plenarsitzung, 7 March 1918. These were generalized problems experienced by all artisans in the war. See Winkler, *Mittelstand*, pp. 27–28.

property, with the largest payment being made in 1914 (1.56 million marks) when the need was greatest.[26] As the war progressed loans from the relief fund diminished, until by October 1918 nearly 60 percent of the total funds loaned had been repaid with interest.[27] However, while it performed a useful role in relieving the financial situation of some artisans, the total sum loaned by the relief fund was not especially large, and in fact most of it went to the retailers.

With the structural changes in the economy which accompanied the implementation of the Hindenburg Plan in the autumn of 1916, the Chamber of Industry called for greater participation in the fulfillment of army contracts to replace the "dried-up business in the private sector." It also recommended greater cooperation between artisans in the national interest.[28] In fact mergers between struggling workshops did become more common in the remaining years of the war, particularly in branches such as tailoring where military orders assumed crucial significance. At the outbreak of the war the tailors' guild had placed itself at the disposal of the local army uniform office; by the end of the conflict the combined output of the guild's members amounted to 50,993 pairs of trousers, 34,221 battle dresses and shirts, and 10,958 greatcoats.[29]

The effect of the war years on the socioeconomic outlook of the artisans is hard to describe. While the demands of the war economy forced a desirable measure of rationalization into their production methods, it cannot be said that it favored the growth of either the artisan economy as a whole or its institutional structure. What is more certain is that the guilds were strengthened by their repeated dealings with the military purchasing authorities, and this may have enhanced their influence in the postwar inflation years. Undoubtedly there were artisans who returned as demobilized soldiers in 1918 to find their workshops gone and their families facing destitution. The fact that a new Loan Relief Fund for Traders (Darlehnshilfskasse für Gewerbetreibende) was founded in the spring of 1918 "to help those enterprises which had suffered

26. StA.H *Deputation für Handel, Schiffahrt und Gewerbe*, II Spezialakten, XXXIV. 59, 28 August 1914.
27. StA.H *Deputation für Handel, Schiffahrt und Gewerbe*, II Spezialakten, XIX A.3.31. Geschäftsbericht der Hilfskasse für Gewerbetreibende in Hamburg, 1917–1918.
28. StA.H *Gewerbekammer*, A.12, Bd. 4, Protokolle, Plenarsitzung, 20 November 1916.
29. StA.H *Schneider-Innung*, 612–1/49b 4., Bericht über die Festsitzung am 19. April 1922 anläßlich des 50-jährigen Bestehens der Schneider-Innung zu Hamburg, p. 14.

Table 6. Artisan Guilds in Hamburg, 1911–1926

	Compulsory guilds			Free guilds		
	No.	Members	Percentage of organized artisans	No.	Members	Percentage of organized artisans
1911	19	8,875	87	14	1,372	13
1913	19	9,739	88	14	1,369	12
1914	19	9,561	87	14	1,377	13
1919	19	9,247	85	15	1,694	15
1926	37	17,267	95	9	967	5

Source: StA.H, *Aufsichtsbehörde für die Innungen*, A3, 2.

because of the War" supports this view.[30]

Table 6 shows an essentially stable trend in Hamburg artisan guild membership. In 1914 there were thirty-three guilds with 10,938 members. In 1919 there were thirty-four guilds with 10,941 members – an increase of exactly three. While these figures certainly do not contradict the claim put forward by Feldman and Czada that the Mittelstand underwent a process of proletarianization towards the end of the war,[31] they do confirm that the artisan organizational structure was durable enough to withstand the rigorous social pressures of the First World War.

The Retailers

If the years before 1914 had been bad, then the war made everything worse for the retailers. Their prewar difficulties were compounded by shortages and rationing, while new forms of wartime control gave them an endless list of things to grumble about.

Their first reaction to the announcement of hostilities had been to join in with the patriotic fervor that swept the nation and in a gesture of solidarity, they offered to continue paying the salaries of employees who had volunteered for the front.[32] But such sentiment

30. StA.H *Gewerbekammer*, A.12, Bd. 4, Protokolle, Plenarsitzung, 13 March 1918.
31. Gerald D. Feldman, *Army, Industry, and Labor in Germany, 1914–1918* (Princeton, 1966), pp. 464–65; Peter Czada, "Ursachen und Folgen der großen Inflation," in Harald Winkel, ed., *Finanz- und Wirtschaftspolitische Fragen der Zwischenkriegszeit* (Berlin, 1973), p. 33.
32. HKH 102.1.A.6.11. Detaillistenkammer, Vollversammlung, 8 August 1914.

did not last long. Prices started to rise immediately in the autumn of 1914 and the retailers, never especially popular before the war, now became the target for the concentrated wrath of the consuming public.

Government controls quickly started to intrude into the free market. Faced with the threat of a growing black market, the city authorities started to take over the business of food procurement and distribution. That they made little attempt to employ the expertise of the retailers in the management of the supply operation was irritating enough; far worse was their response to rising prices: at the very outset of the war the local military government imposed maximum price limits on vital foodstuffs and fuel.[33] It was to be the first step in a long process of price regulation which lasted until 1923.

Early price control measures gave local authorities the power to fix maximum retail prices and prosecute those who either overcharged or who withheld goods from sale with the object of driving up the price. The law was not comprehensive and lacked any provision for controlling the wholesalers – a further source of retailer grievance.[34] Because it was rigid and formalistic in its approach to profiteering, it had the unfortunate effect of making all prices challengeable, so that even legitimate differences in the price of the same good became suspect.[35]

As the war continued new legislation appeared at intervals to extend and refine the price control system. In July 1915 a law was passed to combat excessive price increases.[36] In theory it offered more justice than its predecessor because it aimed at profits rather than prices, but it was also infinitely more complicated to enforce and soon needed a new bureaucratic watchdog to determine what actually constituted excessive profits.[37] These were called price control offices or *PPS*. They were independent, yet conversant with local conditions, and monitored retailers' prices through a supervisory structure. Where charges of profiteering were brought, they arranged for experts to give evidence for the prosecution at the ensuing trials.[38] In Hamburg the Chamber of Retailers provided five

33. 4 August 1914, *RGBl.* 1914, p. 339.
34. HKH 102.1.A.6.11, Detaillistenkammer, Vollversammlung, 2 September 1914.
35. Hans Geithe, *Wirkungen der Lebensmittelzwangswirtschaft der Kriegs- und Nachkriegszeit auf den Lebensmitteleinzelhandel* (Berlin, 1926) pp. 18–19.
36. Verordnung gegen übermäßige Preissteigerung, *RGBl.* 1915, p. 467.
37. Geithe, *Lebensmittelzwangswirtschaft*, p. 20.
38. The *PPS* also had an information service that gave material on pricing to the

members of the *PPS* as retailer representatives, but this did not prevent the greatest antagonism developing between them and the new body. Apart from the fact that only fixed profit margins, based on prewar averages, were allowed, the retailers were angry that the "real profiteers" appeared to escape attention, "while reputable shopkeepers are hounded by courts and public alike."[39]

In 1916 controls were further tightened by an order against "chain trading." This was defined as the "insertion of an intermediate stage in the distribution process, unnecessarily lengthening the time taken for goods to reach the consumer and thus making those goods more expensive." This particular swindle had increased in occurrence as a direct result of the 1915 laws setting guidelines for acceptable profit levels.[40]

Another wartime development concerned one of the retailer's archenemies, the consumer cooperatives. Consumer societies were cooperatives whose members joined together to buy consumer goods in quantity with the object of distributing these goods, mainly to members. Because of the close ties between them and the official food distribution points, large cooperative outlets like Hamburg's Produktion were assigned the right to distribute meat and fats imported by the Reich as food rationing was intensified after 1915.[41] According to its enemies, Produktion may also have received vital credit before it was offered to other retailers and certainly in 1923, at the height of the hyperinflation, the co-op received financial aid from the Hamburg state in equal proportion to the Chamber of Retailers, which was responsible for all the small retailers.[42]

What is certain is that, despite great losses during the inflation like those experienced by all retail organizations, Produktion nonetheless enjoyed a steady increase in support throughout the period. Taking the twenty-year period from 1903 to 1923, mem-

---

public, traders, and the press. In this way it was hoped that price movements could be influenced in the right direction. StA.H *Deputation für Handel, Schiffahrt und Gewerbe,* Jahresbericht der Preisprüfungsstelle, 1925, Anlage 4. p. 1.

39. HKH 80.A.2. Bd. 1, Deutscher Industrie- und Handelstag, Kommission betr. Kleinhandel, Bericht, 28 August 1916.

40. Verordnung zur Bekämpfung des Kettenhandels, *RGBl.* 1916, p. 581.

41. Max Mendel and Josef Rieger, *Die "Produktion" in Hamburg, 1899–1924: Geschichte einer genossenschaftlichen Verbrauchervereinigung von der Gründung bis zum 25. Geschäftsschluß* (Hamburg, 1924), p. 90.

42. See the pamphlet of the DNVP Citizens' Assembly representative J. Henningsen, *Steuer- und Wirtschaftsfragen in der Hamburger Bürgerschaft nach dem Umsturz* (Hamburg, 1924), p. 31.

bership of this successful co-op rose steadily, including during the war years, from 16,240 to 136,954 in 1922, falling slightly in 1923 to 131,176. At the same time the number of outlets belonging to Produktion increased from 27 to 143.[43] Although this impressive growth may not have represented a significant loss of custom to the small private retailers, it was a source of continual concern to them. The co-op's presence seemed to be felt on every street corner, and now with the war, it appeared to be receiving preferential treatment from the authorities.

In general, the legislative control of German retailing that was developed during the First World War tended to confuse and demoralize the shopkeepers, without quite achieving its purpose. On the one hand, business confidence sank amid rumors that everyone but the retailers was ignoring the regulations; on the other hand, the popularly held notion that they were exploiting the war economy to enrich themselves was constantly revived by much-publicized cases of genuine profiteering. In addition there was the problem of the black market. As in most wars, it grew rapidly with the imposition of rationing and the contraction of supply of food and other necessities. Unfortunately no reliable information on its extent in Hamburg during the war years exists, although according to one assessment of the national picture, by 1918 the black market was responsible for between one-eighth and one-half of all flour, potatoes, milk, butter, cheese, eggs, meat, and vegetables sold – and at prices up to ten times the prewar level.[44]

One important consequence of the price controls, and indeed of the whole organization of the economy that had taken place as a result of the war, was the subordination of market instincts to the rule of the statute book. In the case of the retailers, it had the paradoxical effect of tending to push them towards a greater appreciation of market dynamics and an abandonment of some of those traditional anticapitalist views with which they are often associated in this period.[45] At a more practical level, it forced the retailers to become more sophisticated in their methods of accounting and costing. In the past they had added 20 percent to every purchase price or simply followed the costing practice of their fathers. Now, with prices rising and the state playing a greater

43. Mendel and Rieger, Die "Produktion," pp. 98–99.
44. Adolf Günther, "Die gesunkene Kaufkraft des Lohnes und ihre Wiederherstellung," quoted in Holtfrerich, Die deutsche Inflation, p. 84.
45. The idea that as German capitalism became more organized during the First World War, small traders began to lose their anticapitalist outlook is introduced in Kocka, "First World War and the Mittelstand," p. 119.

role in their business, they were compelled to consider their prices more carefully and take into account those costs which had previously been ignored, for example, the labor of family members. Before long the retailer was "calculating wages, running costs and the interest on his capital with every pound of sugar he sold."[46] Inevitably he sometimes got his sums wrong and wound up either bankrupt or in the profiteering court.

The White-Collar Workers

White-collar workers tended to be paid more than their manual colleagues and, in addition, received the privilege of monthly payment, but what was their real living standard? Information on prewar earnings is patchy, but a survey conducted by the DHV in 1908 gives some clues. Its conclusions are presented with the proviso that it was biased, in so far as the purpose of the study was to demonstrate that the needs of DHV members were not being met by employers.

The survey investigated the economic circumstances of 33,611 people, or about 30 per cent of the DHV membership, and was weighted towards younger members and those living in the north of Germany. The highest rates of income were found in the northwest, as were the highest rents paid.[47] Those in wholesaling and industry earned considerably more (up to 2,700 marks per year) than those in retailing (up to 2,000 marks per year). Indeed the majority of shop assistants were under twenty-five years of age and earned only in the region of 1,200 marks per year.[48] The sample was small, but nonetheless there is a clear indication that northwestern Germany, with Hamburg at its center, was both a high-cost and a high-earnings area for white-collar workers.

If white-collar workers had any grounds for complacency before 1914, then the war sent a shock wave through their ranks. Not only was the previous slow increase in their real earnings reversed, but the circumstances of the war started to undermine their sense of status and superiority to the blue-collar worker. It was the industrial workers, for whose manual skills the war economy now had an insatiable demand, who were best able to keep up with the rising

---

46. Götz, *Detaillistenkammer*, p. 61. See also Adolf Lampe, *Der Einzelhandel in der Volkswirtschaft* (Berlin, 1930), p. 7.
47. *Die wirtschaftliche Lage der deutschen Handlungsgehilfen im Jahre 1908* (DHV, Hamburg, 1908), pp. 28, 38–39, 47, 49.
48. *DHV Survey*, pp. 50, 55, 101, 116.

cost of living. Moreover the white-collar workers felt forgotten in the *Burgfrieden* between labor and industry, since this celebrated cease-fire was between the opposing sides of a class war from which they had conspicuously excluded themselves. In some cases they were faced with salary cuts and even unemployment, but it was their self-esteem upon which the new conditions "weighed especially heavily."[49]

It was not long before white-collar organizations started to reflect these changes. Previously their associations had taken a conciliatory approach towards employers and eschewed any kind of industrial action or strike.[50] Generally speaking, there had been too many of them with too many different objectives to make any important contribution to the white-collar worker's welfare.[51] But wartime conditions brought an end to petty rivalries and within a short time two main streams emerged in their midst. The *mittelständisch* groups continued to hope for harmonious relations with employers, while recognizing that the new conditions demanded collective action to maintain living standards. The socialist groups moved rapidly towards the formation of full-blooded trade unions and closer ties with the blue-collar workers.[52]

By the autumn of 1917 the socialist groups had formed themselves into the Allgemeine freie Angestellten-Bund (AfA-Bund), which propagated a united white- and blue-collar labor front against the employers. However its early support had less to do with its political stance than with its uncompromising fight for wage increases; falling real earnings brought in the members.[53] The war ended before the middle-class associations had coalesced into two other major groupings: the liberally inclined Gewerkschaftsbund der Angestellten (GdA) and the Christian-oriented Gesamtverband Deutscher Angestelltengewerkschaften (GEDAG), dominated by the nationalist DHV.[54] The emergence of all three of these umbrella organizations was facilitated by the deterioration in earn-

49. Kocka, "First World War and Mittelstand," pp. 108–9.

50. Kocka, "Zur Problematik der deutschen Angestellten, 1914–1933," in Mommsen et al., eds., *Industrielles System*, p. 792.

51. Hartfiel, *Angestellte*, p. 131.

52. Ibid., pp. 142–43.

53. Otto Suhr, "Die Angestellten in der deutschen Wirtschaft," in *Angestellte und Arbeiter* (an AfA-Bund publication, Berlin, 1928).

54. The principal associations in the GdA were the 58er Verein and the Leipzig-based Verband Deutscher Handlungsgehilfen. For the history of the GdA, see Hans-Jürgen Priamus, *Angestellte und Demokratie: Die nationalliberale Angestelltenbewegung in der Weimarer Republik* (Stuttgart, 1979). Also William L. Patch, *Christian Trade Unions in the Weimar Republic* (New Haven, 1985), pp. 45–48.

ings between 1917 and 1919, as thousands of hitherto unorganized white-collar workers and public sector employees sought for the first time some mechanism to protect their livelihoods.

An idea of white-collar pay rates during the war can be obtained from the salary scales of the Hamburgische Electricitäts-Werke (HEW). This was the local power-generating plant, employing a considerable number of blue- and white-collar workers. In Table 7 the salaries of forty-eight of the latter are given for the years 1914 to 1919. The majority were clerks, cashiers, and typists, although a manager was hired in 1898 and a statistician in 1918.

Clear patterns are difficult to establish, but average earnings increased in the order of 40 percent during the war. Typical in these figures is the diminution of pay differentials; in line with the trend in most white-collar earnings, the higher the starting salary, the lower the proportional increase taking place between July 1914 and the end of 1919. The strong rise in incomes in 1919 was a direct result of the first serious bout of inflation that hit Germany in that year and the response of employers like the HEW in granting supplements and bonuses to help their workers keep up with the cost of living. When their earnings are compared with the rudimentary cost-of-living data then available, HEW employees certainly lost ground in real terms during the war. There was also a clear erosion of wage differentials and a general closing of the gap between white- and blue-collar workers in the manner described by Jürgen Kocka.[55] Obviously white-collar workers at the HEW suffered from the lower demand for their labor and their relative lack of organizational strength. But the Kocka thesis that the convergence of white- and blue-collar positions caused a "proletarization" of the former is more difficult to substantiate. It is hard to see how an increase in the conflict between a converging bloc of wage and salary earners on the one hand, and private and state employers on the other hand, can be reconciled with a war economy characterized by *Burgfrieden* and *Arbeitsgemeinschaft*. On the contrary, it would seem that a reduction in class conflict was taking place – admittedly on a temporary basis only – at the cost of the white-collar workers who had the least to offer and the least to gain by any rapprochement between labor and capital.

One interesting wartime development was the replacement of white-collar positions with female labor. Of course the war caused a dramatic influx of women into the labor force in general, but the jobs of male white-collar workers were particularly at risk since

55. Kocka, *Facing Total War*, pp. 84–87.

Table 7. Staff Salaries at the HEW, 1914–1919 (Marks per Month)[1]

	Joining year	Starting pay	1914–15	1916	1917	1918	1919 1	1919 2	1919 3	Bonus
1.	1898	125	290	315	340	390				
2.	1898[2]	125	340	400	475	700				
3.	1898	175	260	275	290	315				
4.	1902	100	240	260	285	310				
5.	1902	100	260	260	260	300				
6.	1904	112	210	KIA[3]						
7.	1905	100	225	225	225	250				
8.	1906	200	360	360	360	435				
9.	1907	90	175	175	175	240				
10.	1907	90	190	KIA						
11.	1907	150	250	KIA						
12–13.	1908	100	175	175	175	240				
14–16.	1909	100	175	175	175	240				
17–18.	1909	100	175	175	175	240	300	500	680	1225
19.	1909	140	235	KIA						
20.	1910	100	150	KIA						
21.	1910	100	170	170	170	240				
22.	1911	110	150	175	200	220				
23.	1911	100	170	KIA						
24.	1912	105	125	135	135	185				
25–27.	1913	105	120	120	120	180				
28–36.	1914	105	105	125	125	185	200	350	500	900
37–38.	1915	125	125	125	125	185	200	350	475	975
39.	1915	110	110	110	125	135	195	340	475	945
40.	1915[4]	105	105	105	125	135	170	320	450	945
41.	1915[5]	100	100	100	125	125	155	280	430	885
42–46.	1915	90	100	90	100	115	155	275	390	825
47.	1916[6]	80	90	80	90	100	160	290	440	
48.	1918[6]	220				220	240	400	475	1200

1. Wartime salaries of forty-eight clerks, cashiers, and typists.
2. Managr.
3. Killed in action.
4. Unmarried females.
5. Ibid.
6. Statistician.

Source: Uncatalogued HEW records.

they required no particular physical strength or dexterity. Indeed for many of the simple office procedures of the day, women were probably better suited than men. The reaction of the male colleagues was predictably hostile; they felt that the entry of women into their working environment lowered their much-vaunted status, quite apart from endangering their livelihoods. The DHV, for example, exhibited a robust antifeminism to add to its previous prejudices, including anti-Semitism, and campaigned actively to exclude women from the workplace.[56]

The Civil Servants

For the civil servants, as well as for the white-collar workers, the First World War was a "catalyst for social mobilization and organizational concentration."[57] In the nineteenth century they had been a cohesive group only insofar as they had a special legal status (pension rights, etc.) and a common employer – the government of the day. Considering themselves as a loyal pillar of the state and reasonably content in the security and comparative privilege of their position within the workforce, they had little need of a strong national organization to represent their interests. Only in the last decade before the war did the loose federation of regional local civil servant associations begin to move towards more unified structures. As trade union activity by civil servants was strictly opposed by the imperial government, this was a slow and difficult process, but the rising cost of living in the last few years before 1914 was an increasing incentive to strengthen their organization – particularly for lower grade civil servants.[58]

In Hamburg the unwillingness to tolerate civil servant unionization, which was evident in Berlin, was married to a strong hostility on the part of the city fathers to bureaucracy in general. As the representatives of untrammeled free enterprise liberalism, there was nothing they disliked more than interfering officialdom; civil servants were a necessary evil and the less spent on them the better. It was small wonder therefore that they preferred to ignore the falling living standards of Hamburg civil servants on the eve of the war. In February 1914 the journal of middle and lower ranking

56. The DHV's Hamburg headquarters, a lavish building constructed in the 1920s, was actually designed without any women's washrooms.
57. Andreas Kunz, *Civil Servants and the Politics of Inflation in Germany, 1914–1924* (Berlin and New York, 1986), p. 93.
58. For details, see ibid., pp. 94–101.

clerical staff, *Der Bureaubeamte*, was giving a fair depiction of the situation when it referred to the rising cost of living, from which "civil servants have been suffering for years," and demanded cost-of-living supplements for those with large families.[59]

With the outbreak of the war, the civil servants joined in the general euphoria, promising that "henceforth our interest turns to the honor and defense of the fatherland,"[60] but after 1915 the spirit of self-sacrifice had once again given way to one of self-interest. Throughout Germany civil servants suffered a severe loss of purchasing power – the higher grades relatively more than the middle and lower ones – and their loyalty to both Reich and state government was subject to greater strain than at any time since the foundation of the Empire.[61]

In Hamburg civil servants were receiving special war supplements long before white-collar workers in the private sector were paid bonuses to cover rises in the cost of living. In March 1916 the Senate raised the salary qualification for the supplement from 166 marks per month to 208 and laid down that it would be determined in the future by the number of children in a family, that is, for two children an extra five marks per month was paid, for four children an extra ten, and so on.[62]

In the remaining years of the war, the supplement system was developed continuously, with the Hamburg authorities generally following Prussian practice. As Table 8 shows, Hamburg bonuses lagged behind those of Prussia, and since that state included the neighboring city of Altona, it was a source of particular annoyance for the Hamburg civil servants. They complained not only about their treatment in relation to colleagues elsewhere, but also in comparison with white-collar workers in the private sector. Already one of the most critical features of the inflation was making itself felt: the ability to upset the fine gradations of earnings and status that existed between different categories of workers.

As early as 1916 long lines had become a familiar sight outside Hamburg food shops. Workers' wives stood side by side with the

---

59. "Kollegen, Beschäftigt Euch mit Volkswirtschaftlichen Fragen!" *DB*, 14 February 1914; "Familienzulagen," *DB*, 21 February 1914. In the latter stages of the inflation, such supplements were a regular feature of white-collar pay; it is interesting to note that they were being discussed amongst civil servants even at this early stage.

60. "Bureaubeamte!" *DB*, 8 August 1914.

61. For the trends in income for Reich civil servants from 1913 to 1923, see *Zahlen*, p. 43.

62. In all cases the children had to be under 15 years of age; "Die Neuregelung der Kriegsbeihilfe," *DB*, 15 April 1916.

Table 8. Cost-of-Living Supplements for Married Civil Servants in Hamburg and Prussia, 1917–1918 (Marks per Month)

	Upper salary limit	Supplement					
		Hamburg			Prussia		
		Basic	Children		Basic	Children	
			2	4		2	4
September 1917	192	49	76	111	60	94	132
	400	57	89	125	72	107	146
	500	57	89	125	60	93	130
	650	60	93	130	75	111	151
	833	75	90	105	75	90	105
April 1918	250	75	112	153	90	137	189
	417				102	152	206
	500	82	119	160			
	583				100	151	206
	750	80	117	158			
	1,223				108	141	206
	1,250	90	108	126			

Source: Compiled from the *Hamburgische Beamtenzeitung (HBZ)*, 27 October 1917, "Beamtenfürsorge hier und anderswo"; 30 March 1918, "Die Erhöhung der Teuerungszulagen"; 25 May 1918, "Die Unzulänglichkeit der Teuerungszulagen."

wives of civil servants; they were competitors for food, yet fellow sufferers in a world of rations and shortages.[63] It was an experience which tended to lower the antipathy between the two groups, but then war produces a great deal of temporary social solidarity, the durability of which should not be exaggerated. Indeed there were other manifestations of the war that merely strengthened the mutual fear and disregard which existed between white-collar workers and civil servants on the one hand and the workers on the other. When the high earnings of young men in the munitions factories were contrasted with the salaries of experienced officials of the Hamburg government, there was indignation amongst civil servants. "Eighteen-year-olds in industry today," lamented *Der Bureaubeamte* in 1916, "earn more than an office assistant [*Bureauassistent*] in the health department, and electrical fitters more than a

63. Ullrich, *Kriegsalltag*, p. 85.

senior clerk [*Oberassistent*] . . . yet the rights and duties of the two groups are not comparable.''[64]

The fact that making shells and ammunition was extremely dangerous and accidents were practically daily occurrences in the powder factories was apparently ignored by the civil servants. Their traditional sense of superiority to people who worked with their hands remained acute, and the nature of the market forces that dictated that a munitions worker in time of war would earn more than a junior clerk in government administration was viewed as something almost perverse. Yet grudgingly the conviction was growing amongst them that only the organizational methods of the workers could help them regain their accustomed position in society. By 1917 the work of national activists like Albert Falkenberg and Ernst Remmers had born fruit in the creation of the Interest Community for Reich civil servants, which had a membership of over half a million by the end of the war.[65] Then with the revolution in 1918, trade unions became respectable and lost their previous odium of hostility to order (*Odium der Ordnungsfeindlichkeit*) as the state itself – their employer – took on a new appearance. The momentum towards organizational unity amongst the civil servants was now irresistible. Within weeks in early December a new one million strong umbrella organization known as the Deutscher Beamtenbund (DBB) was created, embracing civil servants and their separate organizations from the railways, the postal service, the teaching profession, the police force, as well as the combined ranks of Reich, state, and municipal officialdom.[66]

The House Owners

When the war broke out in 1914, it brought the comfortable existence of Hamburg's house owners to an abrupt halt. As tenants were recruited into the army, demand for accommodations in Hamburg slackened.[67] In fact the market had been moving against

---

64. "Die wirtschaftliche Lage der Beamten," *DB*, 15 June 1916.

65. See Kunz, *Civil Servants*, pp. 106–10.

66. Ibid., pp. 132–45; see also Lederer and Marschak, "Der neue Mittelstand," p. 137.

67. The number of empty dwellings in Hamburg during the war was above the average for large German cities. This may be accounted for by the fact that the war had a greater effect on the local economy, that is, the standstill in shipping caused a large exodus of families to the countryside. See Gustav Lorenz, *Die Wohnungsproduktion und ihre Regelung in dem letzten Jahrzehnt, 1914–1924* (Diss., Würzburg, 1927), p. 27.

landlords even before 1914. According to the official statistics, the number of dwellings in the city between 1910 and 1917 rose by 31,859 to 275,053, of which the proportion that were empty held steady at around 6.4 percent; in other words there was an overall rise in the supply of available living space. In the same period the number of households increased by 27,906 to 262,522.[68] Under normal circumstances, or rather in the absence of the war, the Hamburg landlords might have responded to this unfavorable shift in market conditions by turning over empty dwellings to commercial usage or even by combining two smaller units to make one larger, and therefore more expensive, apartment. However conditions were not normal. The war brought radical changes to the relationship between landlord and tenant and the first moves towards the protection of the latter's rights.

As early as August 1914 emergency legislation prohibited rent increases and obliged landlords to grant rent reductions to soldiers' families.[69] In December all the German states were authorized to establish rent arbitration offices (*Mieteeinigungsämter* or *MEA*), which would be responsible for reconciling disputes between landlords and tenants, as well as between mortgagees and mortgagers.[70] In 1917 the authority of the *MEA* was extended to cover the administration of rent control and the adjudication of eviction cases.[71] The following year, in 1918, further legislation gave the *MEA* the right to extend tenancies in contested cases.[72]

Like the retailers and other members of the urban Mittelstand, the landlords professed a willingness to make their contribution to the war effort and ease the housing conditions of soldiers' families. But they were also alarmed at the implications of the new legislation and the prospect of losing their long-held advantage within the housing market. With the rent reductions and freezes, they soon started to notice a fall in income and turned to their Grundeigentümer-Verein (GVH) for assistance. In a speech to the Citizens' Assembly in February 1915 the GVH leader Friedrich Eddelbüttel appealed for a reduction in the amount of land tax that house owners were expected to pay to be commensurate with the shortfall in rents. Apparently a survey amongst GVH members had revealed a loss of 3.4 million marks in the first five months of the

68. *Hamburger statistische Monatsberichte* (December, 1925): 293–94.
69. The legislation was the *Kriegsnotgesetz*. For rent reductions see "Die Mieteverhältnisse Hamburgs, 1918/1919," *Hamburger Fremdenblatt*, 14 August 1919.
70. *RGBl.* (1914), p. 511.
71. *RGBl.* (1917), p. 659.
72. *RGBl.* (1918), p. 1140.

war. Nevertheless the Hamburg Senate was unimpressed by the landlords' request and was not inclined to weaken its fiscal armory by making concessions to a small and relatively unpopular minority. In wartime, it pointed out, everybody was expected to make sacrifices.[73] It was a sign that the tide was turning against German house owners. Even before the arrival of Social Democratic administrations dedicated to improving the welfare of the workers, the requirements of the war were changing the face of urban housing relations.

By 1918 falling revenue and rising repair costs had led to the deterioration of many city buildings, particularly those "housing the low-priced dwellings of combatant families."[74] The costs of running city properties had risen significantly – coal prices were up by 300 percent, gas by 43 percent, and water by 37 percent – and none of these increases could be passed onto tenants because of wartime restrictions. Brass and copper fittings had all been requisitioned by the military, and building supplies were generally impossible to obtain for house maintenance.[75] Total losses suffered by the house owners during the war were in the region of eighty million marks, of which over fifty million were attributed to the years 1916–1918.[76] As the newspaper closest to the landlords' interests described their situation four months before the armistice,

The War legislation has caused great sacrifices on the part of the house owners in the interests of the combatant families. . . . Many have suffered such a high loss of rental income that they now enjoy no return on their investments, indeed they have no longer the means to maintain them properly.[77]

But worse was to come. With the demobilization a chronic housing shortage arose as thousands of soldiers returned home and found themselves competing for accommodations with the refugees from former German colonies and exiles from the ceded territories in the east. It was a nationwide problem, but Hamburg was struck particularly hard.[78] Under free market conditions such a

---

73. StA.H *Steuerverwaltung*, IIA 1a IA, Finanzdeputation 29 February 1915.

74. "Die Lage des Grundeigentums," *HGZ*, August 1918.

75. Hauschild-Thiessen, *150 Jahre Grundeigentümer-Verein*, p. 251; "Gas und Wasser," *HGZ*, 29 December 1916.

76. These were figures from Hamburg's statistical office. "Die Kriegsverluste des Hamburger Grundeigentums," *HGZ*, 29 August 1919.

77. "Hergabe staatliche Mittel für Grundeigentümer," *Hamburger Nachrichten*, 30 June 1918.

78. Gut, "Die Entwicklung des Wohnungswesens in Deutschland nach dem

shortage would have been to their advantage as they exploited the laws of supply and demand. But no return to normality was in sight. A new German state was emerging that had assumed the social responsibility for housing people, while ignoring market forces and the interests of the landlords. Indeed if there was a single development at the birth of the Weimar Republic which encapsulated Mittelstand concern about the future, it would be hard to find a more obvious one than the changes which took place in housing.

Weltkrieg," in Gut, ed., *Der Wohnungsbau*, p. 24. For an analysis of the similar crisis that developed in Munich, see Martin H. Geyer, "Wohnungsnot und Wohnungs-zwangswirtschaft in München, 1917 bis 1924," in Feldman et al., eds., *Die Anpassung*, pp. 127–62.

4

Revolution and Inflation, 1918–1921

> The situation needs to be clearly en-
> visaged. 100,000 sailors had mutin-
> ied. All the guns were in their hands.
> The lives of their officers were at
> their mercy. The German Empire
> was breaking up under their action.
> And these same revolutionaries were
> concerned with the question as to
> whether they should say "you" in-
> stead of "Sir" to their officers! The
> political naivete and inexperience of
> the Germans finds adequate express-
> ion here. At the beginning of
> November 1918 the sailors thought
> neither of a Republic nor of over-
> throwing the Government, nor even
> of the introduction of Socialism.
> —*Arthur Rosenberg*[1]

This was a period of revolution and counterrevolution, inflation and temporary stabilization. It opened with the Kaiser's abdication in November 1918, continued with the doomed rising of the Spartacists, the reluctant signing by Germany of the Versailles treaty, and the abortive Kapp *Putsch*, and ended with the Allied ultimatum on reparations in May 1921. It was the period in which the immediate consequences of defeat fell upon the German econ-omy, first in the loss of material, territory, and population and then in reparations.[2] And these new burdens were further increased by the erection of protective tariffs in export markets and the

---

1. Arthur Rosenberg, *Imperial Germany: The Birth of the German Republic, 1871–1918* (Boston, 1964), p. 267.
2. For a discussion of the influence of reparations on the course of the inflation, see Holtfrerich, *Die deutsche Inflation*, pp. 135–54.

continuation of the wartime blockade, causing an inevitable deterioration in Germany's balance-of-payments situation and a fall in industrial output during 1919. Transport difficulties brought on by the confiscation of the German merchant fleet and railway rolling stock and by revolutionary activity further crippled production.[3]

In 1919 the Germans experienced the worst inflation since the beginning of the war. The depreciation of the currency was largely induced by domestic factors including the determination of the government to carry out its pledge to introduce the eight-hour day and comprehensive support for the unemployed. It must also be remembered that the signing of the Versailles treaty in the second half of 1919 provoked "a psychological crisis in certain German circles." There was a lack of confidence in Germany's future, manifested in a "flight from the Mark" and a demand for foreign currency.[4] After March 1920 there was a period of relative stability when calm returned to the domestic scene in the wake of the Kapp *Putsch*. The exchange rate for the mark steadied against the U.S. dollar, import prices fell, and there was some decrease also in wholesale prices (Table 10). Although domestic debt rose, the circulation of money did not expand greatly and in comparison with 1919 exports were strong, benefiting from the earlier fall in the mark's overseas value.[5] Contributing factors to this temporary stabilization were the rise in capital imports from abroad – largely American speculation on an appreciation in the mark's value – and the agreement of the Allies to close the so-called hole in the west that had existed since the occupation of the Rhineland.[6] This was regarded by German leaders as an important factor in the mark's depreciation and its cessation was a psychological boost.

The rise in exports improved the balance-of-payments situation, but whether the government was able and willing to bring about a permanent stabilization is doubtful. There was no serious attempt to limit the note issue or curb public expenditure, which would have endangered the generous social policies that prevented

3. Ibid., pp. 179–82.

4. Bresciani-Turroni, *The Economics*, p. 54.

5. Gerald D. Feldman, "The Political Economy of Germany's Relative Stabilization during the 1920/1921 World Depression," in Feldman et al., eds., *Zwischenbilanz*, p. 188.

6. The "hole in the west" was the open trade frontier with France through which large quantities of underpriced raw materials left Germany and uncontrolled French exports poured into the country for precious foreign exchange. For the influx of American capital until 1922, see Carl-Ludwig Holtfrerich, "Amerikanischer Kapitalexport und Wiederaufbau der deutschen Wirtschaft, 1919–1923," *Vierteljahrschrift für Sozial- und Wirtschaftsgeschichte* 64 (1977): 497–529.

domestic unrest. In addition there was an incentive to delay a full stabilization until the reparations bill was fixed at a more acceptable level.[7]

Erzberger's tax program had been adopted in March 1920, but the man himself had resigned. He had probably made his vital task as finance minister more difficult by provoking the Right in the summer of 1919. "His drastic tax program was bound to be resisted by the upper classes in any case; it was unfortunate that he had further stirred their anger by taking the lead in blackening their wartime record."[8] The tax reforms did not succeed in changing the general course of deficit financing. The growth in expenditure outpaced the growth in revenue, which because of the inflation lost real value steadily from the time of assessment to the time of payment.

In Hamburg the new tax regime was one of the most intrusive changes to have accompanied the revolution. As a rich city before the war, it had experienced little trouble raising the revenue necessary to cover its multifarious expenditures. But within five years all this had changed. The manifold costs connected with the war, plus the sudden increase in expenditure after the revolution, stretched the city-state's fiscal system beyond its limit.[9] Moreover Versailles had eroded the city's favorable tax base to such a degree that the loss in assets liable to the wealth tax was greater than almost anywhere else in Germany.[10] It would have been necessary, therefore, even without the sweeping changes brought about by Erzberger's program, to rebuild Hamburg's fiscal structure. But the reforms added to the difficulty by stripping the Hamburg treasury of half its revenue sources.[11]

Designed to strengthen the Reich's financial power at the cost of the states, the reforms met with sustained protest throughout Germany, and Hamburg was no exception. Taxes are naturally

7. Feldman, "Relative Stabilization," p. 206.
8. Epstein, *Erzberger*, p. 331.
9. In 1913 there had been an insignificant budget deficit of 183,583 marks; in 1919 it had risen to 370 million marks, which even allowing for the depreciation of the mark in the intervening years was a staggering increase. For this and other details of Hamburg's increased expenditure in the early postwar years, see Brandt, *Hamburgs Finanzen*, pp. 15, 25, 32–42.
10. The loss of such assets between the end of 1913 and the end of 1923 amounted to 68 percent. In comparison Prussia lost 48 percent and Saxony 59 percent. Lippmann, *Mein Leben*, p. 383.
11. Of greatest importance, the Reich expropriated the right to impose income tax. Brandt, *Hamburgs Finanzen*, p. 25.

unpopular, but in this case the ever hostile Hamburg particularists thought they saw the centralizing tendencies of Prussia as the chief motive for the reforms.[12] Moreover attacking tax proposals, however desperate the need for additional revenue, was a sure vote winner amongst the small business community, and nationalist DNVP Citizens' Assembly members responded to every new tax with the objection that it would "bring about the final ruin of the Hamburg economy."[13]

For the Chamber of Commerce, new taxes, either local or Reich, were of less concern than the kind of postwar order that Hamburg's merchants would have to face abroad. The expectation that the trading strength and goodwill which the city had enjoyed before the war would be rapidly restored with the return of peace was misfounded. Hamburg's maritime ties proved to be a disadvantage as the terms of the Versailles treaty became known. Germany's colonies, the overseas possessions of her merchants, and the bulk of her merchant fleet were all confiscated. In addition British and French colonies were practically closed to German traders, and mutual suspicions made the reestablishment of trading links extremely difficult.[14] It seemed a catastrophe for many Hamburg citizens; the historian Percy Schramm, himself from one of the city's great families, spoke of the work of generations being lost and the necessity for Hamburg merchants to start again, virtually where they had begun a century before.[15]

In fact such stern predictions were as inaccurate as the Chamber of Commerce's hopes for a "just peace." Hamburg's fleet was actually rebuilt quite quickly with subsidies from the Reich, and many of her fishing trawlers had in any case been excluded from the confiscation process. The inevitable shortage of capital was alleviated by Reich funds, and the shipyards, which had happily built warships until 1918, now rejoiced in massive orders for cargo and passenger vessels. Before the end of 1920 the first postwar ocean-going liner (the *Hamburg*) had been launched for the Deutsch-Australische Dampfschiffgesellschaft. By 1924 nearly half the prewar merchant fleet tonnage had been replaced, some ships being bought abroad.[16]

12. "Die Finanzhoheit der Einzelstaaten," *Neue Hamburger Zeitung*, 9 August 1919.

13. Henningsen was the scourge of new taxes among the Hamburg nationalists. Lippmann, *Mein Leben*, p. 307.

14. Erwin Wiskemann, *Hamburg und die Welthandelspolitik von Anfängen bis Gegenwart* (Hamburg, 1929), p. 330.

15. Percy E. Schramm, *Hamburg, Deutschland und die Welt* (Munich, 1943), p. 653.

16. Reincke, *Ein kurzer Abriß*, pp. 275–76.

Trade also recovered, as Table 1 makes clear, with exports reviving rather more slowly than imports. This was partly because of protection in foreign markets against German goods and partly because of government restrictions (*Ausfuhrkontrollen*). The latter were particularly resented by Hamburg exporters, who would otherwise have been able to exploit the falling international value of the mark in 1919. In December the local exporters association joined with the Chamber of Commerce in sending a telegram to Berlin protesting the continuation of this aspect of the hated *Zwangswirtschaft*.[17] When Reich Economics Minister Scholz, who belonged to the People's party (DVP) and was therefore assumed to be closer to business interests than his SPD predecessor, visited Hamburg in December 1920, he was lectured for two days by the assembled luminaries of the city's business community on the need to abolish the government's restrictions on Hamburg's vital trade.[18]

The inflation had conflicting repercussions on exports. While the depreciating mark made German goods competitive abroad, the continually rising domestic costs made it practically impossible to price the goods correctly. Hamburg exporters often raised their prices after a figure had been agreed upon with the customer or left them simply subject to alteration. This was extremely irksome to foreign buyers and soured relations particularly with those neutral countries that had remained good trading partners during the war. Complaints poured into the Chamber of Commerce from the Netherlands, Norway, and Sweden, reporting all manner of un-scrupulous practices, and the German consul in Rotterdam warned that Dutch businessmen were compiling a black list of offending Hamburg suppliers.[19]

In view of their long hegemony over the city government before the war, Hamburg's ruling elite adapted without great difficulty to postwar political conditions. In early November 1918 the red flag flew over the city hall and all power seemed to have passed to the Workers' and Soldiers' Council (Arbeiter- und Soldatenrat) under the

17. HKH, 77.D.1.19. Bd. 1, 18 December 1919.
18. "Aussprache mit dem Reichswirtschaftsminister," *Hamburgischer Correspondent*, 19 December 1920. For a less charitable account of the proceedings, "Reichswirtschaft und Hanseatengeist," *Hamburger Echo*, 20 December 1920. The *Correspondent* was the oldest newspaper in the city and represented most closely the interests of Hamburg's leading trade and shipping circles. As the mouthpiece of the merchant class, it supported the National Liberals before the war and moved naturally towards Stresemann's People's party in Weimar. The *Echo* was the local organ of the SPD.
19. HKH, 77.D.1.53. Bd. 2, Heft 2, May 1920.

chairmanship of the USPD leader Heinrich Laufenberg. This revolutionary body announced that the Senate and Citizens' Assembly no longer existed, but that law and order would be maintained and, interestingly, that private property would be protected.[20] Max Warburg, the very incarnation of finance capital in Hamburg, relates how together with some associates he met Laufenberg, ensconced in the city hall with a company of sailors, and managed to get him to recognize the authority of the Finance Deputation to control the expenditure of the city government. The bankers did not know at this stage whether the Senate and Citizens' Assembly would ever be restored, but they were satisfied that the most important jewel in Hamburg's crown – its finances – had been rescued from the Bolsheviks.[21]

The council's claim to power rapidly became little more than a facade behind which Hamburg's old political practitioners reestablished themselves. The revolution could muster neither the skills nor the experience necessary to administer the city government, and the job soon fell to the old bureaucracy by default. Apart from the hostility of the new Reich government to the council idea, the Hamburg revolutionaries were doomed to failure by their general lack of any concept or plan. They never seriously addressed the prevailing property relationships of this quintessentially capitalist trading community and left the traditional power elites essentially undisturbed. In fact the degree to which the council was forced to collaborate with the previous government quickly revealed its weak foundations. Only the USPD was interested in the continuation of the council system, since the majority SPD welcomed free elections and trusted the people to vote for them. The SPD's participation in the council – in which it held a minority position – was really a tactical maneuver to ensure continued workers' support until a democratic parliamentary government could be established.[22]

In March 1919 a new Citizens' Assembly was elected and the council handed over its power to the legislature. The council had

20. Laufenberg's popularity with the workers rested on his resistance to the war at a time when the majority Socialists (SPD) were collaborating in the *Burgfrieden*. See Jutta Stehling, "Der Hamburger Arbeiter- und Soldatenrat in der Revolution 1918/19," in Herzig et al., eds., *Arbeiter in Hamburg*, pp. 419–27. For Laufenberg's own account of the revolution in Hamburg, see Heinrich Laufenberg, *Die Hamburger Revolution* (Hamburg, 1919). Also informative is Richard Comfort, *Revolutionary Hamburg: Labor Politics in the Early Weimar Republic* (Stanford, 1966).

21. Max Warburg, *Aus meinen Aufzeichnungen* (New York, 1952), p. 68.

22. Stehling, *Arbeiter- und Soldatenrat*, in Herzig et al., eds., *Arbeiter in Hamburg*, pp. 421–22.

held seventy-six meetings by this point and passed 135 laws, many of which were subsequently confirmed by the Citizens' Assembly.[23] The elections, which were the first to be conducted under universal suffrage, resulted in an absolute majority for the SPD, and in the Senate the nine existing members were joined by an additional nine SPD senators.[24] Although they had a majority in the Citizens' Assembly, the Hamburg Social Democrats never sought absolute power, ruling after 1921 in coalition with the Democrats (DDP) and later even with the DVP. The local SPD was of a pragmatic stamp, in keeping with the character of the Hamburg people.[25] In the Senate half of the seats remained occupied by Democrats or nonparty figures from the past, thus ensuring a strong element of continuity between the Wilhelmine Empire and the Weimar Republic. Even the position of first mayor was reserved for a traditional figure from the past. Werner von Melle was given the senior position in the government on the grounds that "at the head of the Hamburg state belongs a man from one of the old families," as the Social Democrat Otto Stolten (himself appointed second mayor) put it.[26]

In another illustration of continuity, the close relationship between the Senate and the powerful Chamber of Commerce was quickly reestablished after the revolution. Social Democratic regard for this temple of business expertise was surprisingly strong and attempts to democratize its election process encountered opposition even from an SPD Senator.[27] The Chamber of Commerce, unlike other professional bodies, was not simply a representative of a special interest, but stood between private business and the authority of the state, ready if necessary to take over certain state obligations towards the local economy. It spoke out for laissez-faire and against all forms of economic planning and particularly export controls. Chamber of Commerce president F.H. Witthöfft was not just attacking the *Zwangswirtschaft*, but was uttering the essence of Hamburg's long-standing mercantile philosophy when he told colleagues in the stock exchange in January 1919, "It is time that the gentle breeze of the free, Hanseatic trading spirit [*freien hanseatischen Kauf-*

---

23. Ibid., p. 420.
24. Reincke, *Ein kurzer Abriß*, pp. 281–83.
25. A good outline of political developments in Hamburg after 1918 is found in Ursula Büttner, *Hamburg in der Staats- und Wirtschaftskrise, 1928–1931* (Hamburg, 1982), pp. 24–49.
26. Klessmann, *Geschichte*, p. 537.
27. The senator was Paul Hoffmann. Büttner, *Hamburg*, p. 47.

mannsgeistes] swept away the stuffy air of the Berlin bureaucracy."[28] The support which the Senate gave to the Chamber of Commerce, particularly in its fight against the *Zwangswirtschaft* – an innovation closely identified with Socialist policy – demonstrates that, when it came to matters affecting the Hamburg economy, SPD senators were Hamburgers first and Social Democrats second.[29]

The Artisans

As producers rather than mere distributers of goods, the initial concern of Hamburg's artisans had been with the course of the revolution rather than the inflation. Was their traditional place in the German economy to be recognized by whatever new government emerged from the chaos of November 1918, or were they to disappear in a tidal wave of collectivization? The minutes of the Chamber of Industry's meeting on 9 November 1918 reveal the fear and confusion among Hamburg artisans at the prospect of what lay ahead. The first acts of the Workers' and Soldiers' Council had not been encouraging. In arbitrary fashion, fitters' and metalworkers' shops had been closed (they were still fulfilling military orders), while printers and brewers were left undisturbed, presumably because their products were of importance to the revolutionary process. Local builders actually received specific instructions to keep working, but the tailors' guild was at a loss as to what to do with a completed order for army uniforms that had to be delivered to a barracks now occupied by "revolutionary sailors."[30]

As the first chaotic days of peace passed, it became clear that, while the artisans might survive any future demands for nationalization of the economy, labor relations would undergo a fundamental change. The revolution had brought equality between the trade unions and the employers and it seemed that centuries of "patriarchal discipline dissolved" almost overnight.[31]

A new era of collective action had dawned in the German economy, and the artisans, long accustomed to individual agreements with their workers, were not sure how to react. In Hamburg

28. HKH, 77.D.1.3.H.1, Witthöfft to stock exchange, 16 January 1919. See also Peter Niehusen, *Die Hamburger Kaufmannschaft und ihre Haltung zur Exportförderung in der Wiederaufbauphase des deutschen Außenhandels von 1918–1929* (Diss., Hamburg, 1980), pp. 46–50.

29. Böhm, *Handelskammer*, pp. 192–93.

30. StA.H *Gewerbekammer*, A.12, Bd. 4, Protokolle, Plenarsitzung, 9 November 1918.

31. Herbert Sinz, *Das Handwerk: Geschichte, Bedeutung und Zukunft* (Düsseldorf, 1977), p. 221.

some thought that they should ally themselves with the industrial employers' organizations, while others viewed this as tantamount to joining the devil himself and hoped for an alternative way to protect themselves from the new power of organized labor.[32] An ambivalence of attitude on the part of the artisans towards capitalist industry was typical of this period: on the one hand they maintained a belief in the superiority of Mittelstand enterprise; on the other hand they recognized the need for a combined front by employers against the advancing forces of the working class.[33]

The earliest sign of a united purpose in Hamburg came in April 1919 with the launching of a new journal for businessmen, the *Allgemeine Industrie- und Gewerbezeitung (AIGZ)*. It was produced under the auspices of the Chamber of Industry and proclaimed in its opening message to readers that it would "build a visible bond of unity" between the industrial and artisan economies.[34]

There is some evidence that local artisan organizations were strengthened in Hamburg, including higher guild membership and increased support for cooperatives. Indeed the greater use of the cooperative paralleled the rising white-collar worker support for trade unions at this time. For example, during 1919 forty out of the one hundred members of the Hamburg Bookbinders' Guild formed a purchasing cooperative and a similar structure was set up by the Hamburg smithies. Small wonder that when the Chamber of Industry syndic Hampke proposed a cooperative to provide financial support for struggling artisans, the idea was greeted with wide applause.[35] In October 1919 a more visible expression of artisan solidarity came into being at the national level with the foundation of the Reichsverband des Deutschen Handwerks. The new association united over one hundred artisan chambers and organizations, including cooperatives, and had as its stated purpose the forwarding of the political interests and objectives of the German artisan. "At last," declared the president of Berlin Chamber of Artisans, "German artisans have grasped that they can no longer afford the luxury of internal disunity."[36]

32. StA.H *Gewerbekammer*, A.13, Bd. 1, Protokolle, Handwerkerabteilung, 27 November 1918.
33. Winkler, *Mittelstand*, p. 80.
34. "Zum Geleit," *AIGZ*, 1 April 1919.
35. StA.H *Gewerbekammer*, A.13, Bd. 1, Protokolle, Handwerkerabteilung, 16 January 1920. See also "Die Beschaffung von Handwerkerkredit," *AIGZ*, 7 and 14 June 1919. By the end of 1919 nearly all of the 190 members of the smithies' guild were in the purchasing cooperative. StA.H *Gewerbekammer* A.18 Bericht, 1914–1920.
36. "Die Gründung des Reichsverbandes des Deutschen Handwerks," *AIGZ*, 25 October 1919; Sinz, *Handwerk*, p. 222.

But it would take more than newspapers and associations to reconcile the artisans to the unwelcome novelties of the Weimar Republic. Already in 1919 new legislation had raised their taxes and lowered the working hours of their journeymen. Above all the burdensome *Zwangswirtschaft* was not only still in place a year after the end of the war, but actually seemed to be extending its grip over the whole economic life of the country. Unlike the retailers whose hostility was concentrated on the issue of price control, the artisans' protest centered on the question of supply, particularly of fuel and raw materials.[37]

In the summer of 1920, as the relaxation of controls on agricultural produce was causing price rises and the plundering of neighborhood shops, the Chamber of Industry was pressing the Hamburg government to remove controls on the supply of building materials, particularly bricks. The brick shortage was really a result of the difficulty in obtaining coal, but the artisans were convinced that the *Zwangswirtschaft* served only "to keep an army of bureaucrats busy making unnecessary regulations" and that a "return to free market operations" would revive the critical building sector.[38]

Beyond the central issue of economic controls, there was much hostile rhetoric delivered by the artisans at the new tax structure being developed in 1919–20. The sales tax and, in particular, the luxury tax were deeply disliked as an unnecessary extra cost levied on the craftsman's livelihood. Hamburg hatmakers complained of the classification of their wares as luxuries and therefore subject to the extra tax, while local horticulturalists grumbled that "naturally the cultivator is prepared to carry his share of the burden of reconstructing our destroyed fatherland, but why should simple flowers be classed as luxuries?"[39] Why indeed? A case can always be made for excluding some item or other from the tax net, but for the German artisans after 1918 there was a deeper grievance: their identification with the new republican regime was at best lukewarm. Their guild-bound production ethos left them with little sympathy for the aspirations of the organized workers or for the plight of those workers when they were unemployed, so the thought that their tax revenues might be going to support them was hard to bear. But after an early attempt to secure a lower rate of

37. "Geschäftsbericht der hamburgischen Gewerbekammer für 1919," *AIGZ*, 10 January 1920.
38. *AIGZ*, 17 July 1920.
39. StA.H *Gewerbekammer*, Nr. 29, Gartenbau-Verein für Hamburg, Altona und Umgegend, 4 May 1920.

taxation for artisans had failed, it was regretfully acknowledged in Hamburg that the artisans' influence in Berlin was very limited and few concessions in their direction could be expected in the future.[40]

After 1919 there was a greater degree of reconciliation to the new democratic system, yet an appreciation of the need for political representation in the Weimar Republic came as an almost painful awakening process for many artisans. That they still viewed the parliamentary apparatus in Berlin with the greatest distrust is clear from a despairing article by the general secretary of the Nordwest-deutschen Handwerkerbund in March 1920. In it he called upon artisans to join a political party, "any party, as long as it is not the Social Democrats! The main thing is that we are politically organized and realize that nothing can be accomplished in public life without participation in politics."[41]

Artisans were not only hostile to the Social Democrats, but apathetic to the whole party system, especially so in comparison with the workers. In the campaign preceding the June 1920 Reichstag election, it was still thought necessary to warn artisans against voting for the SPD. At a large meeting in May of the Bund der Innungen und fachgewerblichen Vereine, artisan candidates from the DNVP and the DVP addressed the gathering, the latter speaking of the "violation of the middle-class convictions by the Social Democratic government." The trend could only be reversed, claimed the speakers, by a vote for the parties of the Right.[42] Presumably there was satisfaction with the Hamburg results of the June election, since the DNVP and the DVP made considerable local gains.[43]

If the artisan masters were a potential constituency for the political Right, then their journeymen became targets for the Left. Trade union membership amongst their ranks rose steeply after the revolution, but even more unpalatable for their artisan employers was the introduction of the universal eight-hour day. It was this path-breaking symbol of workers' power, rather than the inflation

40. The approach to the government had been made by the Deutsche Handwerks- und Gewerbetag in 1919. StA.H *Gewerbekammer* A.13, Bd. 2, Protokolle, Handwerkerabteilung, 27 August 1923.
41. "Der Handwerker und die neue Zeit," *AIGZ*, 6 March 1920.
42. "Aus dem Vereins- und Innungsleben," *AIGZ*, 5 June 1920.
43. The task of the Bund der Innungen was to educate Hamburg artisans to the workings of the Weimar party system and to encourage them to participate in it. The object was not so much to gain support for the wider process of parliamentary democracy with its objective of national government, but to gain specific goals for the artisan estate. For an insight into its workings, see Karl Manecke, *Denkschrift zur 10-jährigen Gründungsfeier des Bundes der Innungen und fachwerblichen Vereine e.V.* (Hamburg, 1929).

Table 9. Daily Journeyman's Wage in Selected Crafts in Hamburg, 1913 and 1920

	1913 Marks per day	Hours per day	1920 Marks per day[1]	1913 to 1920 Wage increase (factor of)[2]
Bakers	5.20	11.0	40.00	10.6
Dyers	5.00	10.0	40.00	10.0
Cartwrights	6.00	9.5	44.00	8.7
Bookbinders	5.00	9.0	39.00	8.8
Carpenters	6.46	8.5	48.00	7.8
Coppersmiths	6.50	9.0	44.80	7.8
Fitters	6.50	9.0	41.60	7.5
Printers	6.50	9.0	41.66	7.3
Decorators	6.25	7.5	47.20	7.1
Builders	7.38	8.2	49.60	6.9
Plumbers	7.20	8.2	48.00	6.8
Glaziers	7.20	8.5	44.00	6.6

1. Universal eight-hour day.
2. Hours adjusted.

Source: Compiled from *Jahresbericht der hamburgischen Handwerkskammer für 1913* and *AIGZ*, 31 July 1920, "Übersicht über die derzeit in Hamburg gültigen Lohnsätze (zusammengestellt vom Arbeitgeberverband Hamburg-Altona)." The rise between 1913 and 1920 is approximated from an adjustment of the 1913 to a national eight-hour day. Where the payment was weekly (bakers, bookbinders, and printers), the figures have been adapted to a six-day workweek.

and higher wages, that caused the greatest resentment amongst artisans. In fact the figures suggest strongly that journeymen's wages were in any case hardly keeping pace with the cost-of-living index, which had multiplied during the period 10.6 times.[44] As Table 9 shows, this would have outstripped the wage rises of all but the bakers and dyers, and they, with the bookbinders, were the most poorly paid.

Artisans resisted the wage demands of their journeymen, not only because they held to the traditional belief that journeymen should sacrifice higher pay for the opportunity to become independent themselves – a variant on the concept of delayed gratification perhaps – but also because they were coming to adopt the tactics, if

44. *Zahlen*, p. 33.

not the philosophy, of industrial employers. For example, since the cost-of-living index during the inflation was generally rising, workers came to rely upon its figures as the basis for their next pay claim, and conversely, in the rare episodes when the index was steady or falling, employers used it to oppose claims. In the price plateau that set in after the first quarter of 1920, the latter case prevailed. In the second week of June, for instance, when a strike by cartwright journeymen had already been in progress for two months, artisan employers heard the argument from their leaders that "there could be no talk" of agreeing to journeymen's demands because the cost-of-living index had actually been falling since the strike began in April.[45]

Bearing in mind that this was the period when Hamburg's retailers were battling with complex price fluctuations, the artisans had more latitude than the retailers in their response to the currency depreciation. Unlike the retailers, they were not locked into a dependent relationship with a wholesaler, and as long as they could obtain raw materials, they could rely on the added value of their own skilled labor in any goods they sold. Neither pricing nor wage costs represented the greatest problem facing the artisans during the inflation; rather it was those changes in the legislative and institutional landscape that had arisen out of the wartime economy and continued on after the revolution. The best example of this was the raw material shortage that hit the artisans much harder than rising prices. Even the bakers, who should have been relieved of flour rationing after the relaxation of agricultural controls in 1920, still found themselves in difficulties the following year. The fact that 200,000 casks of Chinese flour, which had already been stored in England for three years, was imported into Hamburg in the spring of 1921 suggests that the bakers were fairly desperate to get supplies.[46]

The relief attempts of Hamburg's government proved as irksome to the artisans as the *Zwangswirtschaft*. The shoemakers were badly hit by the provision of cobbling services in public offices, and the threat of state-run shoe repair facilities hung over the entire Hamburg shoe trade. A questionnaire answered by 2,000 cobblers in January 1921 revealed that business in the previous three months had been exceptionally bad, with 1,291 reporting sales under 6,000 marks. If one takes into account the high cost of shoe leather at this

45. "Aus dem Vereins- und Innungsleben," *AIGZ*, 12 June 1920. The employers' association was the Bund der am Wagen- und Automobilbau beteiligten Arbeitgeber Groß-Hamburg e.V.
46. British Consular Report, Hamburg, *PRO FO.371/5940*.

time, then the claim that "many were not even making the minimum wage" seems probable.[47]

In the building trade, another new legislative feature was depressing the market. Rent control was reducing the return on capital and the amount of new investment in housing.[48] But whereas rent control affected only parts of the artisan economy, the eight-hour day touched all. It was a special source of indignation that journeymen now had the time to do extra work for their own profit after completion of their regular day's labor. The extent to which this black economy grew during the inflation is clear from the number of advertisements carried by local newspapers for the services of painters, carpenters, and plumbers to be performed after 4 P.M. at a price below the usual rate.[49]

The Retailers

So long as the war lasted, Hamburg's retailers had been careful to mute the tone of their attacks upon the antiprofiteering legislation that they so detested and concentrated their efforts instead on establishing the need to restore free trading with the peace. Moreover until the summer of 1918 most of them anticipated this would be a victorious peace, accompanied by a rapid dismantling of all controls.[50] The armistice and the revolution dashed their hopes. Far from vanishing, the controls were strengthened with more legislation introduced to deal with black market operations and to establish special profiteering courts.[51] These courts dispensed rapid justice and were particularly disliked by the retailers. Starting their proceedings at the beginning of 1920, the courts had dealt with over 27,000 cases in Germany by the end of the year – 513 in Hamburg alone.[52]

---

47. Meeting of the Kartell der selbständigen Schuhmacher von Hamburg und Umgegend, 4 January 1921, *AIGZ*, 15 January 1921.

48. *AIGZ*, 7 January 1922, Annual Report; 22 January 1922, Baugewerbs-Innung "Bauhütte zu Hamburg," Quarterly Meeting.

49. It was typical that the guild-conscious artisan masters found such moonlighting an affront. They also claimed, with doubtful logic, that it was robbing the German economy of work that would otherwise have employed thousands of journeymen in regular hours at normal prices. "Bekämpfung der Pfuscharbeit, ein Stück praktischen Wiederaufbaues," *AIGZ*, 29 January 1921.

50. HKH 102.2.C.3.2. Detaillistenkammer, Kriegsbericht 2 February 1919.

51. Verordnung gegen Schleichhandel, 7 March 1918, *RGBl.* 1918, p. 112; Verordnung über Sondergerichte gegen Schleichhandel und Preistreiberei, 27 November 1919, *RGBl.* 1919, p. 1909.

52. *Reichsarbeitsblatt*, 31 January 1922, Nonofficial section, pt. 2, pp. 56–57. In

Like the artisans, the small retailers neither liked nor understood the reality of postwar Germany. The revolution and the establishment of the Weimar Republic brought all manner of unwelcome developments. First there was the specter of socialization threatening the German economy. Retailers were concerned that their old enemy, the consumer cooperatives, would be strengthened and granted special privileges by a government dominated by Social Democrats, and the rhetoric at the cooperative conference in Hamburg in June 1919 would hardly have reassured them. "The cooperative movement looks to the democratization of the German economy," said co-op leader August Kasch, "the elimination of personal profit through collective work; . . . the cooperative idea will lead the future economic idea."[53] In fact plans for socializing German retailing never materialized, and although there was a strong rise in membership of the consumer cooperatives during the inflation, they suffered as much from price control and capital depletion as the privately owned retail shops.

A second and more serious problem for those retailers with employees was the new militancy of the *Angestelltenbewegung* (white-collar movement) and the limits on the working day. As with the artisans, the eight-hour day provoked the most vehement opposition.[54] "A pernicious and irrelevant concept" was how the syndic of the Chamber of Retailers described it at a meeting in May 1919. The prevailing attitude was that, while acceptable for factory workers, the eight-hour day was intolerable when applied to shop assistants because they were never required to work all the hours they were actually on duty.[55]

Like the journeyman in the artisan's workshop, shop employees had tolerated long hours and low pay because they still cherished the illusion – assiduously cultivated by their employers – that one day they would be able to establish themselves in an independent

---

fact the legality of the special courts was widely disputed because there was no means of appeal against their verdicts. See J. Wernicke, *Kapitalismus*, pp. 393–95.

53. 16th Meeting of the Zentralverbandes deutscher Konsumvereine (ZdK), 23–24 June 1919, quoted in Heinrich Kaufmann, *Kurzer Abriß der Geschichte des Zentralverbandes deutscher Konsumvereine* (Hamburg, 1928), pp. 200–201. The headquarters of the ZdK was in Hamburg; its leaders leaned towards the right-wing of the SPD.

54. The statutory eight-hour day – one of the central achievements of the Stinnes-Legien Agreement – was a particular grievance of most employers, whether corner shop owners or big industrialists. Ursula Büttner, *Politische Gerechtigkeit und sozialer Geist* (Hamburg, 1985), p. 164.

55. The meeting was at the Deutscher Industrie- und Handelstag in Berlin. HKH.80.A.2o.1. Bd. 2.

existence. Even before the war, this fantasy was disappearing as the growth of department stores with large numbers of employees helped narrow the gap in self-perception between white- and blue-collar workers. Indeed it was partly because department stores diminished the prospects of shop assistants and disabused them of any illusions they might have about future independence that small retailers opposed them.[56]

As their employees began to organize themselves into trade unions, the retailers tentatively began to close ranks. Faced with the necessity of negotiating collective agreements with people whom they had known for years and had always paid according to some private arrangement, they needed a new organization. In April 1919 the Retail Employers' Association (Arbeitgeberverband des Einzelhandels) was founded with the task of establishing "a sound working relationship between employers and employees and preventing improper stoppages. . . ." In fact many Hamburg retailers remained skeptical of the need for the new organization and membership remained low.[57] As with the Chamber of Retailers, the divisions and petty jealousies within the ranks of the shopkeepers left the new body without much authority.

1919 was the year in which the depreciation of the mark first assumed dramatic proportions, with, as Table 10 shows, its exchange rate value against the U.S. dollar falling from approximately one-half to less than one-tenth. For the retailers the critical factor was the manner in which the movement of both retail and wholesale prices lagged behind the falling exchange rate for the mark. The consequence of this price lag became apparent in March 1920 when the sharp decline in the mark's exchange value came to a halt and a stabilization of the currency seemed in sight. Retail prices at this juncture were about 16 percent behind wholesale prices and still rising; indeed they continued to rise for the rest of the year, while the dollar rate and wholesale index leveled off. Until this point the inflation had encouraged consumers to buy, and in Hamburg retailers had reported booming sales. Suddenly the customer's patience seemed exhausted and a consumer strike set in. The possibility that a stabilization might be at hand caused everyone to hope for imminent price falls, and purchases were delayed for the future.[58]

The vulnerability of the small retail enterprise is demonstrated as

56. Brauer, "Mittelstandspolitik," pp. 389–91.
57. Heinrich Hoebel, *Das organisierte Arbeitgebertum in Hamburg-Altona* (Diss., Hamburg, 1923), p. 100.
58. *Jahresbericht der Detaillistenkammer zu Hamburg*, 1920.

Table 10. Index of Exchange Rates and Domestic Food Prices in
Germany, 1914–1923

	Dollar rate (1914 = 1.00)	Wholesale price (1913 = 1.00)	Retail price (1914 = 1.00)
July 1914	1.00	1.04	1.00
December	1.07	1.30	1.34
July 1915	1.17	1.63	1.60
December	1.23	1.58	1.53
July 1916	1.31	1.76	1.63
December	1.36	1.59	1.65
July 1917	1.70	1.79	1.80
December	1.35	2.17	1.94
July 1918	1.38	2.22	2.20
December	1.97	2.34	2.44
January 1919	1.95	2.40	
April	3.00	2.54	2.82
July	3.59	2.95	3.00
October	6.39	4.57	3.45
December	11.14	5.89	4.15
January 1920	15.43	10.14	
March	19.97	12.85	11.01
April	14.20	11.27	12.29
July	9.40	11.43	12.52
December	17.38	12.50	14.27
January 1921	15.46	12.77	14.23
April	15.13	11.23	13.34
July	18.26	12.45	14.91
October	35.75	24.17	17.57
December	45.72	32.29	23.57
January 1922	45.69	35.09	24.62
April	69.32	60.86	43.56
July	117.49	94.42	68.36
October	757.73	564.20	266.23
December	1807.83	1161.00	807.02
January 1923	4281.00	2390.00	1366.00
February	6650.00	4308.00	3183.00
March	5048.00	3336.00	3315.00
April	5826.00	3952.00	3500.00
May	11355.00	6335.00	4620.00
June	26202.00	14840.00	9347.00
July	84186.00	64856.00	46510.00
August	1100632.00	658401.00	670485.00
September	23549000.00	16413891.00	17300000.00
October	6017000000.00	5435300000.00	4301000000.00
November	522286000000.00	678800000000.00	862000000000.00
December	1000000000000.00	111220000000000.00	1512000000000.00

Source: Zahlen zur Geldentwertung, pp. 6, 16–17, and Friedrich Hesse, *Die deutsche Wirtschaftslage von 1914–1923* (Jena, 1938), pp. 443–45.

clearly in the spring of 1920 as at any other time during the inflation. To break the consumer strike, the shopkeepers were obliged to reduce prices, often to a level below that at which they had purchased the goods. Then after July, as the mark began to show new signs of deterioration, the strike evaporated as consumers bought in anticipation of higher prices to come.

In the next twelve months the retailers had little success in anticipating future price trends. Having misjudged the spring stabilization and suffered damaging losses through price reductions, they now faced wholesale prices that were outstripping the permitted increase at retail level. Forced to sell their wares underpriced, their takings fell to the point where they were insufficient to cover the cost of stock replacement. A further problem was the gradual removal of controls in agricultural production that took place in 1920. While the change from an administered to a free market in produce from the countryside increased supplies and brought about a welcome collapse in the black market, it also pushed up retail prices. In Hamburg angry consumers reacted by plundering shops.[59]

With the removal of the *Zwangswirtschaft* from the agricultural sector, antiprofiteering legislation was strengthened in the retail sphere. To the syndic of the Hamburg Chamber of Retailers, it appeared like victimization and he called upon retailers to take action at the national level, including standing in the forthcoming Reichstag election.[60] To make matters worse, the small retailers' old enemy, the consumer cooperatives, appeared to be getting preferential treatment in those areas where supply rationing was still in force. In April 1920 the war provision office was accused of favoring the cooperatives with supplies of fresh meat, while other retailers had to be content with frozen stock.[61] In fact the cooperatives experienced the same difficulties as private retailers during the inflation, and they were certainly as enthusiastic about the removal of controls.[62] Clearly their closer political proximity to the

59. See "Die Plünderung in Hamburg," *Der Einzelhandel*, 15 July 1920. For an account of the dismantlement of agricultural controls, see Robert Moeller, "Winners as Losers in the German Inflation: Peasant Protest over the Controlled Economy, 1920–1923," in *Zwischenbilanz*, ed. Feldman et al., pp. 255–88.

60. "Einzelhandel und Reichstagswahlen," *Der Einzelhandel*, 1 June 1920.

61. There were other alleged instances of the office favoring the cooperatives, both in the field of rationed supplies and the waiving of import regulations. *Detaillistenkammer Vollversammlung*, 9 June 1920, 6 October 1920, HKH 102.1.A.6.17.

62. Heinrich Kaufmann, *Kurzer Abriß der Geschichte des Zentralverbandes deutscher Konsumvereine* (Hamburg, 1928), p. 198; also Mendel and Rieger, *Die "Produktion,"* p. 91.

ruling Social Democratic administration was what really made them suspicious in the eyes of resentful small shopkeepers.

More than the distribution of the burden of controls, it was the utter confusion accompanying their implementation at the local level that caused the greatest problems. What was needed from Berlin was not so much greater retailer representation in the Reichstag as clarification of the prevailing regulations, which had become so complicated as to be virtually incapable of objective interpretation. And if there was bewilderment in the streets as to what constituted the law on pricing, then this only reflected uncertainty at the top.

Two days after Kapp's soldiers marched into Berlin in March 1920, the *Reichsgericht* in Leipzig – the highest court in the land – handed down an important judgment in a profiteering case. The defendant, a small retailer, claimed that she had sold goods purchased in 1914 for higher prices in 1918 because to have done otherwise would have meant that she would have been unable to buy further stock. The court ruled that because the inflation had made a greater expenditure of capital necessary to keep the business operating, the higher prices she had charged were justified and did not amount to profiteering. In reaching this judgment the *Reichsgericht* overturned the verdict of a lower court and allowed small businesses to take currency depreciation into account when calculating their prices.[63]

The 1920 Leipzig decision, which covered pricing in the calculation of both the entrepreneur's profit and his own labor, was circulated around Germany to all the *PPS* for the information of their expert committees. It might have been considered something of a landmark decision, but being reached at a time when the inflation, after raging for a year, was showing signs of dying out, it was quickly overtaken by other decisions. Fifteen months later in July 1921, in judging another profiteering case, the *Reichsgericht* appeared to set a new precedent when it called for "the burden of currency depreciation" to be shared equally between retailer and customer.[64] Now it seemed that the inflation could not be taken into account in pricing, at least not fully. In any event the price that guaranteed the retailer's survival – the replacement cost – was not allowed under the 1921 verdict. Without a clear ruling from the national level, the onus of pricing control fell upon local bodies, in

63. *Juristisches Wochenblatt*, 15 October 1920, p. 839. Also "Zur Frage des angemessenen Gewinns," *Der Einzelhandel*, 15 September 1920.
64. Geithe, *Lebensmittelzwangswirtschaft*, p. 131.

particular the *PPS*, and here the profusion of opinions and sharply competing interests simply stoked the fires of resentment among retailers.

The White-Collar Workers

Although the agreement between industry and labor reached in the first days after the 1918 armistice did not last beyond the stabilization, it seemed initially that the trade unions had made substantial material gains. Naturally the newly organized white-collar workers wanted to share in this achievement and participation in the *Zentralarbeitsgemeinschaft* quickly came to be seen as a triumph of the "trade union idea in their movement."[65]

The example of the Hamburg 58er Verein (58er) is interesting. Before the war it had been a typical association for harmony (*Harmonieverband*), enjoying the trust of local businessmen, and even as late as March 1919 one of its leaders had demanded a "return to the old freedoms of trade upon which the dazzling glory of the Reich has been built" and an end to the "throttling of entrepreneurial initiative, the source of the white-collar worker's daily bread."[66] Within three months the 58er leadership had changed its tune and in a circular to members was calling for the creation of a proper trade union.[67] When shortly afterwards this was accomplished and the 58er merged with two other associations to form the 350,000 strong GdA, there were loud protests from the Hamburg business community, enraged over what they saw as an attempt to incite their employees.[68]

It was the relentless pressure of the inflation in 1919, rather than the leftward political momentum of the revolution, that had finally driven the seventy-year-old 58er to embrace trade unionism. For the majority of white-collar workers, the old concept of a transitional stage rapidly lost its validity in postwar Germany. Few of them now entertained any illusions that they would ever be independent, and to keep up with the workers, it was clearly necessary to adopt the workers' methods. Henceforth the cap-in-hand approach of the individual would give way to the collective action of the group.[69]

65. Hartfiel, *Angestellte*, p. 146; Eberhard Fehrmann and Ulrike Metzner, *Angestellte und Gewerkschaften: Ein historischer Abriß* (Cologne, 1981), p. 71.
66. *Der Handelsstand* (GdA Journal), April 1919.
67. HKH 80.A.7c.1, GdA, June 1919.
68. HKH 80.A.7c.1 Witthöfft to *Reichsverwertungsamt*, 12 January 1920.
69. The number of wage agreements amongst white-collar workers increased

For the nationalist DHV, which joined the loose gathering of Christian trade unions at this time, this meant accepting the wisdom of the trade union approach, although it played down the class struggle in favor of an emphasis on the national perspective in labor relations.[70] This did not mean acquiescence with the employers, "of whose costs the employee's salary forms but a tiny part," but that both sides should act in accordance with the national interest.[71] The DHV encouraged its members to have a sense of dignity in their position, something, it claimed, which was not satisfactorily encompassed by their archrival, the left-wing ZdA.[72] By 1920 there were over 1.4 million members in the three main white-collar umbrella organizations, with close to half of them in the Socialist-led AfA-Bund. The early dominance of the Left dissipated however after 1923, and following the stabilization, an enduring reaction set in amongst white-collar workers, which was ultimately to the detriment of the entire nation. In 1929, of the 1.6 million organized, only 450,000 were in the AfA-Bund and in the following year white-collar workers formed the largest contingent amongst the Nazi deputies in the Reichstag.[73]

The reaction of the employers to the growing militancy of the white-collar workers was hostile, for they were unwilling to lose the benefits of the harmonious prewar labor relations. But the attempts to organize, particularly amongst retailers, were not particularly successful. The Retail Employers' Association, founded in response to the *Angestelltenbewegung* with enthusiastic retailer support in the spring of 1919, was already suffering from "a noticeable lack of interest in concerted action" by October. Small retailers found it hard to alter the habits of a lifetime and preferred to continue managing their few employees on an individual basis, while the larger department stores felt strong enough to ignore the new trade unions altogether.[74] The fact that large and small retailers had traditional animosities of their own made it more difficult for them to combine their actions in the face of a new solidarity amongst their employees.

---

from zero before 1918 to 703 by the end of 1919. "Die Tarifverträge im Deutschen Reich am Ende des Jahres 1919," *Reichsarbeitsblatt*, Sonderheft 23, p. 30.

70. Hartfiel, *Angestellte*, p. 156.

71. *DHW*, Organ of the DHV, 15 September 1920.

72. Paul Broeker, *Die Arbeitnehmerbewegung* (DHV, Hamburg, 1919), p. 9.

73. *Jahrbuch der Berufsverbände im Deutschen Reich*, Sonderheft 52 zum Reichsarbeitsblatt (1930), p. 27; Kocka, *Zur Problematik*, p. 799; Fehrmann and Metzner, *Angestellte*, pp. 67, 78.

74. "Angestelltenbewegung," *Der Einzelhandel*, 1 October 1919.

The high-handed attitude of the large retail employers is typified by a case of crass exploitation in 1921 at Karstadt, the largest department store in Hamburg. It operated an illegal form of probationary contract for newly hired sales staff, who were obliged to pay a penalty fee if, at the end of their probation period, they decided not to stay with the company. Its illegality lay in the fact that Karstadt themselves reserved the right to fire the employee without either explanation or compensation if for any reason they found him or her unsuitable. The trade unions strongly condemned such practices, but had great difficulty prevailing against them.[75]

Unlike industrial employers who had grown accustomed to labor acting in concert and now had a range of collective agreements with the trade unions, retailers found it difficult to adapt to the new conditions. They were angry about their employees' organizations and not above breaking salary contracts if they thought the state of business warranted it. Such an occasion presented itself in early 1921 when the temporary stabilization of the mark caused a fall in wholesale prices in response to which employers in both the wholesale and retail chemical branches announced unilaterally that they would cut white-collar workers pay by 20 percent.[76]

Because retailing was commonly represented by a small-scale business in which the owner liked to feel he was the boss, any erosion of his authority was felt even more acutely than financial losses. Trade unions and new restrictions on his trading practices made him feel under siege. The eight-hour day and limits to shop opening hours were typical of the legislation arising out of the revolution and demobilization, which seemed to be "making employees lords of the firm."[77]

The reaction of all employers to white-collar strikes was predictably harsh. One of the earliest strikes was not over pay or working conditions, but in response to the 1920 Kapp *Putsch*. Many white-collar workers, particularly amongst the membership of the left-wing AfA-Bund, took part and subsequently found themselves

---

75. The unsuitability could derive from a confidential medical report. *GDA*, Journal of the GdA, 16 October 1921; *DHW*, 23 November 1921.

76. *DHW*, 13 April 1921.

77. "Die Angestelltenbewegung im Hamburger Einzelhandel," *Der Einzelhandel*, 15 June 1919. From March 1919 the working hours of Hamburg white-collar workers were limited to eight. On twenty days of the year they were allowed to work overtime, up to ten hours per day and not later than 10 P.M. "Regelung der Arbeitszeit der Angestellten während der Zeit der wirtschaftlichen Demobilmachung," 18 March 1919, *RGBl.* 1919, p. 315.

dismissed on the grounds that a political strike was in breach of their contract.[78] Although the nationalist DHV avoided the action against Kapp, it was not shy of industrial action. In June 1920 it proclaimed a great victory in the Hamburg docks where white-collar workers had struck for nine days in pursuit of a pay claim against shipyard owners. The strike was important to the DHV because it demonstrated that their members could bring big concerns to a standstill just as effectively as the blue-collar unions. It was proud to show the skilled shipyard workers that the pen pushers were equally important to the economy.[79]

Despite the pronounced concentration of white-collar workers in Hamburg's trading establishments, it was in industrial settings like the shipyards that the greatest incidence of disputes involving white-collar labor took place. Perhaps the closer contact with blue-collar workers made the white-collar worker more militant; perhaps they felt a greater need to prove the strength of their organizations before their proletarian colleagues. In 1922 and 1923 there were continual battles between the shipyard owners and the left-wing ZdA. Initially salary rates were fixed by arbitration with the support of the Reich Ministry of Labor, but the employers consistently refused to recognize that white-collar employees had the same rights as the workers. They rejected arbitrated solutions and took the matter to a succession of courts, the last of which – the Hamburger Oberlandesgericht – encouraged them to arrange a vote amongst their white-collar labor force to see how many wanted their salaries determined by collective bargaining. At stake was the right of employees to organize in trade unions, and a counterpoll was carried out revealing that employees were in favor of collective agreements by a margin of twenty to one.[80] The dockland disputes were eventually resolved more or less in favor of the employees. For the ZdA it was a victory to boast before the DHV.

The Civil Servants

By 1918 most civil servants belonged to organizations affiliated with the politically nonaligned Deutsche Beamtenbund (DBB), whose leaders were committed both to the Republic and to the

78. "Kündigungen und Entlassungen von Angestellten wegen Beteiligung am Generalstreik gesetzlich unzulässig," *Hamburger Echo*, 27 March 1920.
79. "Der Streik der Angestellten der Hamburger Seeschiffswerften," *DHW*, 15 June 1920.
80. ZdA, *Geschäftsbericht*, 1923, pp. 30–31.

protection of members' economic interests.[81] The DBB boasted a million members in 1919, but lost ground both to the Left and to the Right in the next four years of the inflation. In 1923 it had about 860,000 members, of which 200,000 were rail and postal workers and over 300,000 teachers and municipal employees. The Allgemeine Deutsche Beamtenbund, which had been set up in 1922 after the Socialist ADGB had failed to bring the DBB under its wing with the white-collar AfA-Bund, had a strength of about 350,000 – mainly rail workers who had left the DBB. Finally, the nationalist Gesamtverband Deutscher Beamtengewerkschaften had close to 400,000 members, who were closely associated with the white-collar DHV.[82]

In Hamburg civil servants struggled to regain the lost ground of the war years in an atmosphere of increasing organization. In 1914 the senate had rejected a proposal to establish a freely elected civil servants' committee to deal with salary and promotion claims on the grounds that the civil service was an integral part of the state and therefore could not establish a separate body with which to negotiate with the state.[83] But by the end of 1918 radical changes of view had taken place in the city. As power passed momentarily to the Workers' and Soldiers' Council, the civil servants found themselves caught up in the council movement, and their own Civil Service Council (Beamtenrat) was soon recognized.[84]

The Civil Service Council consisted of thirty-two elected representatives from the different government departments, from which an executive of five was chosen. In tune with the sentiments of the majority of civil servants, it was not a revolutionary body. Rather it was constituted to safeguard their interests in the chaos that erupted in Hamburg on 13 November.[85] Certainly there were radical elements who were encouraged by the revolutionary climate to make more far-reaching demands, such as the democ-

81. See p. 71.
82. Theodor Geiger, "Panik im Mittelstand," *Die Arbeit* 7 (1930): 641.
83. "Der Senat lehnt den Beamtenausschuß ab!" *Der Bureaubeamte (DB)*, 27 June 1914.
84. *Hamburger Amtsblatt* (1919), pp. 1, 930. The movement towards councils in German economic and political life grew out of the revolution and was actually anchored in Article 165 of the Weimar constitution. However, it never took hold beyond the shop floor level and by 1923 was essentially a dead letter. The Civil Servants' Council continued to exist until the Nazis took over the government in Hamburg in 1933.
85. Kocka, taking evidence from Bavaria, speaks of lower and middle civil servants "being at least, tolerant of the Revolution," in *Facing Total War*, p. 101. Similar sentiments apply to the Hamburg civil servants.

ratization of government departments, but such talk did not impress the real revolutionaries and only served to antagonize the patriarchs of the Hamburg business community.[86] At a meeting between the deputy chairman of the Workers' and Soldiers' Council and the Civil Service Council executive, it was the former who had to remind the gathering that the German people had to be liberated before any *Verwaltungsrevolution* (administrative revolution) could take place.[87]

As the early revolutionary zeal dissipated, the Civil Service Council evolved into a negotiating channel between government and employees. Committees were established in every department with the task of coordinating the demands of the personnel in order that a common front could be presented in negotiations with the Hamburg Senate. However, because of its middleman position, the Civil Service Council was incapable of exerting organized pressure on the employer. This was clearly the task of a trade union. In 1919 the Gewerkschaft der Bürobeamten des Hamburgischen Staates (GBHS) was launched, with many of its leading members drawn from the Civil Service Council executive.[88] Unfortunately its insistence on civil servant exclusivity and its refusal to accept members from amongst white-collar workers in the private sector weakened the union from the start. Both the DHV and the left-wing ZdA made it clear that the GBHS was not worthy of admission to the Hamburg trade union cartel. It was an irresolute approach to labor relations and reflected the civil servants' continuing ambivalence about their position in society.

In the first postwar year the Senate was compelled to raise the married civil servants' war supplement, at first in March to 200 marks per month across the board with an extra 40 marks for every child and then, a few weeks later, to 280 marks with the child allowance increased to 50 marks.[89] As a condition to granting the latter increment, the Senate reserved the right to reduce the rates as soon as prices started to fall. Its parsimonious attitude was sharply criticized by the civil servants, and indeed the city's reluctance to

86. "Demokratie und Beamtenhierarchie: Eine Warnung vor unbedachten Forderungen," *Hamburgischer Correspondent*, 16 November 1918. For the radicals' demands – which included equal rights for women – see "Aus der Tätigkeit des Beamtenrätes," *Hamburger Fremdenblatt*, 27 January 1919.
87. StA.H *Beamtenrat*, 18, 19 November 1918.
88. "An alle Berufsgenossen!" *DB*, 15 September 1919.
89. "Zur Neuregelung der Teuerungszulage," *Hamburgische Beamtenzeitung*, 15 February 1919. "Die Neuordnung der laufenden Kriegsteuerungszulagen," *Hamburgische Beamtenzeitung*, 14 March 1919. "Bürgerschafts-Angelegenheiten," *Hamburgischer Correspondent*, 9 May 1919.

provide the necessary relief for its own employees might seem odd in view of the fact that Hamburg's government was now in the hands of Social Democrats.[90] A more telling fact was the continued presence of many senior administrators, appointed in prewar days when the orderly conduct of municipal finances was considered a sacred part of Hamburg's mercantile constitution. For these men the inflation in 1919 was hardly more than a temporary consequence of Germany's defeat that should not give rise to changes in the salary system that might be difficult to revoke once things returned to normal.

That such views should have been held in the upper reaches of the Hamburg bureaucracy was scarcely astonishing; what is surprising is that the notion seems also to have been shared lower down. In September 1919 the Civil Service Council committee at the Deputation for Trade, Shipping, and Industry set up a commission to investigate civil servants' salaries. Its report revealed disagreement on the extent to which family situations should be taken into account in determining salaries. At stake were basic principles.

The opponents of the social wage, that is, the whole array of cost-of-living supplements awarded according to family size, argued that renumeration must be according to performance criteria only otherwise great resentment would develop amongst unmarried staff and possibly amongst the general public as well. Moreover they questioned whether the state had any responsibility towards the families of its employees. Against them, the supporters of the social wage contended that the state did indeed have a vital interest in the upbringing of civil servants' children because only through the next generation could the tradition of reliability and the spirit of public service be carried on among the German people. It was a position of some arrogance, tantamount to believing that civil servants were in some way guardians of a higher morality without which the state would not survive. Indeed it was made clear that the social wage should be restricted to civil servants because the liberality of the workers disqualified them from child benefits; also if they received assistance based on family size, then the treasury would be swamped and the vital role of the civil service threatened.[91]

Eventually the commission compromised. Childless employees

90. "Vom Abbau der Teuerungszulagen," *HBZ*, 21 June 1919.
91. StA.H *Beamtenrat*, 76. Bd. 1, Bericht der Kommission des Beamtenausschusses der Deputation für Handel, Schiffahrt und Gewerbe zur Beratung der Gehaltsreform entsprechend dem Antrag des Beamtenrates, 17 September 1919, p. 2.

should be paid according to the principle "equal work, equal pay," while those with families would receive the child benefit with the proviso that it would not count as pensionable income. On the question of pay levels, the commission recommended adoption of a twelve-tier system, with the lowest grade receiving a minimum wage "that would be just when conditions have returned to normal." This represented an extraordinary concession, tantamount to condemning the lower ranks to an impoverished limbo until normal conditions were restored. The constrained nature of the recommendation is clear when compared with average earnings in the Hamburg economy at this time. In the autumn of 1919 an unskilled worker earned approximately 6,300 marks per year, a sum which, according to the commission, would fall in real value to 4,800 marks with the return of monetary stability. Yet 4,800 marks was the proposed minimum salary for civil servants, including child benefits, for 1919.[92] The only explanation is that the commission expected a return to stabilized conditions in the very near future, although even then the marked negative differential between the unskilled worker and the lower grade civil servants would have remained.

As the civil servants entered the difficult winter of 1919/20, they were beset with doubts about their future. "How could it be," asked *Der Bürobeamte*, "that with our trusted colleagues in the Civil Service Council and department committees, we could have made so little progress?" The answer seems to be an overwillingness to compromise; the revolutionaries of 1918 had become the government lackeys of 1920. And parallel to a lack of determination at the top was a lack of power at the bottom; in particular the departmental committees – the visible evidence of *Betriebsdemokratie* (industrial democracy) – were ineffective without the immediate support of trade unions.[93]

The Civil Service Council, conceived as a channel between the government and its employees, had quickly become an obstacle. While in the private sector trade unions dealt directly with employers, the civil servants relied on this hybrid creation to present their demands. It was both unwieldy and impotent, yet proposals for a closer working relationship with the trade unions were rejected by the civil servants themselves, who seemed to share the Civil Service Council's position that "trade union affairs are not its

92. Ibid., p. 12.
93. See "Gibt es denn kein Halten?" *DB*, 1 December 1919; "Berechtigte Unzufriedenheit: Die Beamtenausschüsse und wir," *DB*, 1 February 1920.

101

business."[94] Its anomalous position was further revealed at the time of the Kapp *Putsch*. Although Hamburg remained loyal to the Republic and the majority of civil servants answered the *DBB* call for a strike, some nonunion staff continued to work. This lack of unanimity made the civil servants suspect in the eyes of the city's organizing union cartel, and the Civil Service Council was excluded from the decision-making process during the action against Kapp.[95]

Without the council – or for that matter the DBB – having much influence on developments, the fortunes of the civil servants in 1920 went from bad to good and back to bad again. In April a major change in the pay structure of Reich civil servants brought considerable rises in income, as well as a reorganization of the grading system. The previous 180 different pay groups throughout the country were reduced to just 13 in the "A" scale (9 in the "B" scale), and there was a substantial narrowing of the pay scales, thereby reducing differentials between higher, middle, and lower grades.[96] Hamburg adopted the Reich plan, and with cost-of-living supplements now fixed at 50 percent of basic salary, real incomes showed a significant index improvement (Table 13).[97] The city's conservative press complained predictably enough that Berlin's expensive plan would now have to be borne by the Hamburg taxpayer.[98]

In November however prices recommenced their precipitous climb, and by the end of the year earnings amongst civil servants had fallen again. The problem was that the DBB was not sufficiently united to push through civil servants' demands at the Reich level, and their case was not presented convincingly enough to the general public; they liked to see themselves as upholders of the state, but the generally hostile press portrayed them as a parasitical bureaucracy living off the backs of the people.[99] In many

94. "Die Beamten und die Gewerkschaften," *DB*, 1 February 1920.

95. StA.H *Beamtenrat*, 59, Verhandlungsniederschrift über die 140. Vollsitzung des Beamtenrates am 16 March 1920. See also "An die Beamten und Angestellten im Reichs-, Staats-, und Gemeindedienst von Gross-Hamburg!" *Hamburger Echo*, 14 May 1920.

96. For details of the April 1920 salary reform, including the political machinations in Berlin, see Kunz, *Civil Servants*, pp. 196–205. Kunz's argument that the extra expenditure incurred by the reforms reduced the chances for a permanent stabilization that year seems exaggerated when set in the wider economic and political context of Weimar in its second year.

97. "Die neue Besoldungsordnung," *DB*, 15 February 1920.

98. "Neuregelung der Beamtenbesoldung," *Hamburgischer Correspondent*, 6 June 1920.

99. "Unsere Niederlage," *DB*, 15 December 1920; "Beamtengehalts-Statistik," *Hamburger Nachrichten*, 25 January 1921.

Table 11. Households and Dwellings in Hamburg, 1919–1925[1]

	Households[2]	Dwellings		Homeless
		Total	No. empty	
				2,612[3]
1919	277,394	274,694	1,794	6,099[4]
1920	282,446	276,586	468	14,777
1922	292,935	280,906	389	32,056
1923	302,603	285,121	324	36,837
1925	310,257	288,100	361	38,077

1. Figures for 1921 are not available.
2. Includes those on ships in the harbor (Schiffsbevölkerung).
3. October 1919.
4. December 1919.

Source: Compiled from *Hamburger statistische Monatsberichte*, December 1925, pp. 293–94; Oberbaurat Peters, *Die Wohnungsnot in der Stadt Hamburg auf Grund der amtlichen Zählung der Wohnungssuchenden im Juli 1925*, p. 5.

ways their whole position was a result of the new uncertainties that civil servants faced after the political upheaval of 1918/19. For two generations they had been accustomed to serving on an imperial ship of state; now they were being asked to guide the vessel through the murky waters of parliamentary democracy. They were unsure of their way and anxious for their survival but, on the other hand, still retained a mentality attuned to the problems of government – in other words the difficulty the Hamburg treasury might face in paying their salaries. Unfortunately their rather sanctimonious attitude was out of step with the times. Since the war their economic circumstances strongly suggested that their interests would be better served by the recognition that they were a part – even if a rather exclusive one – of the German wage-earning classes. And in the new republican arena, they had to organize and fight like other wage earners if they wanted to survive the inflation.

The House Owners

Leo Lippmann noted that the two greatest problems facing the city at the end of the war were the inflation and the housing shortage (Table 11).[100] The new Reich government, having enshrined in Article 155 of the Weimar constitution the right of every German

100. Lippmann, *Mein Leben*, p. 312.

to a suitable place to live, was naturally concerned to solve the housing crisis expeditiously.

New construction was encouraged as far as possible,[101] but because of the shortage of building materials and labor, the response tended to concentrate on legislation to control and intensify the usage of existing housing stock.[102] With the housing shortage law of September 1918, local housing offices (*Wohnungsämter*) were established and empowered to procure unused living space for the accommodation of the homeless.[103] Later, in May 1920, compulsory billeting (*Zwangseinquartierung*) was introduced, which permitted the requisitioning of oversize dwellings and their reallocation to homeless families.[104]

These procedures were resented by both landlords and tenants alike, and the ethics of the compulsory billeting was particularly odious to the Mittelstand, whose large apartments were often chosen. It seemed a violation of their most cherished values of privacy and family life, and one contemporary account actually describes the billeting as hostile to culture (*kulturfeindlich*).[105] Moreover enforcing the system, which was a thankless task at the best of times, was made worse by abuse of the regulations, such as the purchase of exemptions. "As long as Germany lives by the law," complained one landlord to the Hamburg Housing Office, "it should be impossible for the rich to buy exemptions from the law that the greater part of the decent Mittelstand class has to bear."[106]

If arrangements to help the homeless offended the landlord's sense of propriety, then the regulation of his tenants' rents hit him in the pocket. As we have seen, rent control had been part of the Hamburg housing scene since 1914, although at that time it was

101. The new construction program is well documented. In addition to Gut, see for example, Hans-Günther Pergande and Jürgen Pergande, "Die Gesetzgebung auf dem Gebiet des Wohnungswesens und Städtebaus," in *Deutsche Bau- und Bodenbank AG, 1923–1973* (Bonn and Bad Godesberg, 1973), esp. pp. 54–99; or Dan P. Silverman, "A Pledge Unredeemed: The Housing Crisis in Weimar Germany," *Central European History* 3 (1970): 112–39. Also useful is Fritz Schmidthuysen, *Die Deckung der Wohnungsbauabgabe in Deutschland bis zur Stabilisierung* (Würzburg, 1928).

102. Hermann Hipp, "Wohnungen für Arbeiter? Zum Wohnungsbau und zur Wohnungsbaupolitik in Hamburg in der 1920er Jahren," in *Arbeiter in Hamburg*, ed. Arno Herzig et al., pp. 471–72.

103. *RGBl.* (1918), p. 1143, *Maßnahmen gegen Wohnungsmangel*, 23 September 1918.

104. *RGBl.* (1920), p. 949, 11 May 1920.

105. Henry Schönewald, *Die Wirkungen der Mieterschutz- und Raumnotgesetzgebung unter besonderer Berücksichtigung der sozialen und wirtschaftlichen Folgen in Hamburg* (Diss., Hamburg, 1922), p. 26.

106. StA.H *Wohnungsamt*, 51, 17 September 1920, H.C. Buehle to *Baurat* Peters.

introduced more out of concern for the home front, than through any desire to bring about a legislative improvement in tenants' rights. In fact rent control is an expedient method of protecting tenants during abnormal conditions such as war, and its application effectively prevents landlords from reaping windfall profits. But it can also discriminate against landlords to the long-term disadvantage of the general housing market, particularly in conditions of inflation such as pertained in postwar Germany.

Little wonder therefore that by 1919 Hamburg landlords were looking back to the prewar era as a lost paradise.[107] During the course of that year, the real value of Hamburg rents fell from a little over 50 percent of their 1914 value to under 10 percent (Table 18). Pressing repair work, delayed because of the war and the rise in the cost of labor and materials, could not be carried out for lack of funds. The cooperative *Produktion*, for example, owned over 900 workers' apartments where the rent had not been raised since 1902; they now cost over 600 marks each per year to maintain, while yielding only 450 marks in rent.[108]

For the Mittelstand the tenant protection and housing shortage legislation very quickly came to symbolize a *Wohnungszwangswirtschaft* (state control of housing) – another offensive feature of the Weimar Republic. The GVH fulminated against rent control as a Socialist plot designed to dispossess them of their properties, but there was little it could do. The changes in the Hamburg housing market were not confined to new regulations; the extensive political leverage that the house owners had enjoyed for so long had vanished overnight with the revolution. In the Citizens' Assembly elections of March 1919, they managed to gain only four seats – a mere 10 percent of their prewar strength.[109] Universal franchise, grumbled the GVH, "had delivered the city into the hands of the working class."[110]

In fact some house owners welcomed the revolution and pointed out that the prewar franchise had not helped them much in their fight against the wartime housing restriction. One particular activist named Carl Fehmerling actually went as far as to propose that house owners form a property owners' council that could deal with the Workers' and Soldiers' Council.[111] However revolutionary fervor

107. "Zwangsweise," *HGZ*, 29 August 1919.
108. "Mieteerhöhung und Sozialdemokratie," *HGZ*, 17 October 1919.
109. Hauschild-Thiessen, *150 Jahre Grundeigentümer-Verein*, p. 261.
110. "Das neue Hamburg," *HGZ*, 21 March 1919.
111. "Öffentliche Grundeigentümer-Versammlung," *HGZ*, 29 November 1918.
See also Hauschild-Thiessen, *150 Jahre Grundeigentümer-Verein*, pp. 258–60.

and house ownership were soon proved to be irreconcilable and radicals such as Fehmerling lost influence with the GVH as the burdens of property in the new state became fully apparent.

In May 1920 another housing shortage law placed further restrictions upon the landlords' freedom of action and more power into the hands of the *MEA*.[112] It was these institutions, composed of local representatives and reflecting local conditions, and not the working class as the GVH seemed to believe, that were deciding cases of conflict in the housing market. The problem was that they were doing so without the benefit of any national judicial structure, and it was the confusion arising out of this situation that led the Reich government to address itself to the problem.

The object was to simplify the law protecting tenants' rights and take the strain out of the relationship between tenant and landlord. In August a memorandum from the Reich Ministry of Labor stated plainly that the aim of any new legislation would be to protect the tenant for as long as the prevailing combination of housing shortage and inflation persisted. As with the control of retail prices, it was argued that a return to free market conditions was impossible as long as the German economy was in an extraordinary condition.[113] In Hamburg the department with responsibility for the *MEA* agreed to the Reich proposals with the important proviso that surcharges to the basic rent be high enough to allow for the rising cost of maintenance that the house owners were forced to bear. Further proposals that tenants' committees be established to determine, with the owners, how these surcharges would be spent were rejected by the Hamburg administration as "housing Bolshevism."[114]

In 1920 the first rent increase since the beginning of the war was granted, but at around 20 percent it was far below what the landlords demanded. The general use of the cost-of-living index by this stage only compounded their anger by showing the enormous gap between rents and other retail prices.

The surcharge question rapidly became a key issue in the housing debate. While the house owners used the deteriorating state of their properties as a propaganda weapon in their battle to get the surcharges granted, the tenants refused to pay them as long as the repair work had not been carried out. In April, for example, the

---

112. *RGBl.* (1920), p. 949, *Wohnungsmangelgesetz*. For details, see Pergande and Pergande, "Die Gesetzgebung," p. 54.
113. StA.H *Senat*, Cl. I, Lit. T, No. 22, Vol. 7, Fasc. 6, Inv. 1, Conv. 1 (hereafter cited as *Senat* Conv. 1), 3 August 1920, Proposal for law to regulate rents.
114. StA.H *Senat*, Conv. 1, Memo from Nöldeke, 22 September 1920.

main tenants' organization in Hamburg, the Zentral-Mieterrat, actually advocated adopting the guidelines of neighboring Prussia, rather than those of the Hamburg *MEA*.[115]

The temporary stabilization of the mark in the summer of 1920 relieved some of the pressure on the landlords, but by the end of the year the real value of rents had sunk once again (Table 18). In December the GVH's chief representative in the Citizens' Assembly called for a 100 percent increase on the prewar level to take effect from the beginning of April 1921. The Hamburg *MEA* admitted that this was the minimum necessary to prevent further decay in the building fabric, but, expressing concern about the ability of the lower-paid to afford the higher rent, settled for a rise of 70 percent.[116]

Even this produced a protest from the Zentral-Mieterrat; in a stormy meeting in January the housing office was accused of working hand-in-hand with the landlords, a rent strike was threatened, and the responsible senator (Nöldeke) was called upon to resign.[117] And the notion that the authorities favored the other side in the housing crisis was not confined to the tenants. Some landlords thought that certain judges in the *MEA* showed prejudice against them in reaching their decisions.[118]

As in any conflict between mutually opposed economic groups, there must have been biased opinions given in the mediation of clashes between landlords and tenants. More important from the point of view of the landlords was the change in the whole climate surrounding housing relations, brought about by the more active intervention of the state. Their old privileged position, untrammeled by legislation or tenants' pressure groups, had vanished forever. In its place was a new egalitarian regime, producing laws in far-off Berlin that were to govern their behavior in Hamburg. Whereas before the war their judgment had been trusted in their own field, now they were reduced to the status of another interest group, competing for advantage with an adversary who greatly outnumbered them in a government-controlled market.

This would have been brought home to them in June 1921 when they inadvisedly attacked the law protecting tenants as immoral.[119]

115. StA.H *Senat*, Conv. 1, *Zentral-Mieterrat*, 6 April 1920.
116. *Amtsblatt der Freien und Hansestadt Hamburg* (1920), pp. 1, 529. See also "Neue Richtlinien des Mieteeinigungsamtes," *Hamburger Echo*, 24 December 1920; "Die Frage der Mieteerhöhung," *Hamburger Nachrichten*, 16 January 1921.
117. StA.H *Senat*, Conv. 1, *Zentral-Mieterrat*, 11 January 1921.
118. "Die Vermieter und die neuen Richtlinien," *Neue Hamburger Zeitung*, 5 January 1921.
119. "Wider die guten Sitten," *HGZ*, 24 June 1921.

The Social Democratic *Hamburger Echo* thundered in response:

> Before the tenant protection laws, the landlords always knew how to
> exploit the law to their own advantage. In those days, when one tried to
> prove that an agreement was immoral, their lawyers argued that morals
> had nothing to do with the law. Now suddenly they want morals in the
> law and they condemn tenants for doing exactly what they used to do!

The newspaper advised them to accept that the golden days were
over and they could no longer hold tenants at their mercy.[120]

120. "Die 'reingefallenen' Grundeigentümer," *Hamburger Echo*, 30 June 1921.

5

Into the Abyss, 1921–1922

> Nine thousand marks to the dollar.
> The daily rate of exchange shows the
> progress of our decline like the tem-
> perature chart of a very sick patient.
> —Count Harry Kessler, diary entry,
> 7 November 1922[1]

In May 1921 the long-awaited announcement on war reparations came from the Entente: Germany was to pay a total of 132 billion gold marks – a financial burden for generations to come. Even if there had been unanimous agreement in Germany on the need to meet the reparations target, it would still have been an extraordinary accomplishment for the nation to pay the annual payments without the aid of a major foreign loan. As it was, there was anything but agreement. Fehrenbach's center-right coalition resigned almost immediately in opposition to the so-called London ultimatum and was replaced by a new government headed by Josef Wirth, who like Fehrenbach was from the left-wing of the Center party. It quickly became known as the fulfillment government, a pejorative reference to its apparent acquiescence to the Allied demand. In fact the policy of fulfillment was never really meant to fulfill the reparations target, but rather to demonstrate the impossibility of Germany's meeting it. Whatever its objective, no sooner was Wirth's government installed than various groups and leaders on the political Right, of whom Karl Helfferich was only the most conspicuous, gathered to attack it.

Besides Wirth himself, the outstanding personality of the new administration was Walter Rathenau, who joined the government

---

1. Count Harry Kessler, *In the Twenties: The Diaries of Harry Kessler* (New York, Engl. trans. 1971), p. 196.

for the first time as minister for reconstruction and in 1922 became foreign minister. As a Jew, his presence further aggravated the anti-Semitic, nationalist Right, but he was not deterred from his support of Wirth's view that further resistance to the Allies held no future for Germany. Instead she should try to reestablish her reputation with her former enemies and work towards a gradual amelioration of the reparation terms. A first step was to make the Erzberger reforms work, but in 1921 the inflation itself was a major obstacle to any kind of fiscal discipline. As fast as taxes were levied, they began to lose their value, and the revenue yield stood in a diminishing proportion to what was needed.[2] In Hamburg the city's budget deficit was partly financed with municipal bonds sold in the United States. American creditors seemed to have a particular faith in the Hamburg economy and speculated on an early revaluation of the mark, thus helping the Senate deal with some of the more pressing items of public expenditure.[3]

The slide into hyperinflation might still have been avoided if it had been possible for Germany to raise a large foreign loan or restrict domestic expenditure enough to produce a balance-of-payments surplus. But the options for cutting expenditure at home were extremely limited, while chances for a loan were blocked by Allied intransigence and J.P. Morgan's banker committee. The latter concluded that no assistance could be arranged for Germany until the reparations schedule itself was reviewed, and with the French government in the hands of the confrontational Poincaré after January 1922, this seemed remote. Then in June Rathenau, who had already received numerous death threats, was assassinated as he drove to his office in Berlin. It was the final stroke needed to precipitate a general crisis of confidence and a flight from the mark.[4] In June 1922 the dollar rate index had stood at 75 (1914 = 1); by August it had reached 270 and Germany was in the grip of hyperinflation.[5] For the next fifteen months it rose with exponential acceleration until in November 1923 it had hit the astronomical figure of 522,286,000,000.

Because Hamburg was so dependent on foreign trade, the collapse of the currency had a deep effect on the local economy.

2. Bresciani-Turroni, *The Economics*, p. 438.
3. Büttner, *Politische Gerechtigkeit*, p. 151.
4. Holtfrerich, *Die deutsche Inflation*, p. 288; Laursen and Pedersen, *The German Inflation*, p. 20.
5. Hyperinflation is defined here, after Cagan, as being present when the rise in retail price index exceeds 50 percent in the course of a single month. Cagan, "Monetary Dynamics," p. 25.

Export merchants benefited from low production costs at home, but importers faced the reverse situation: if they did not convert the proceeds of their sales in the domestic market rapidly into hard currency, they sustained losses. Shipowners were in a strong position, receiving payment in hard currency, but fishermen were not so lucky. They had to sell their catches for marks in the local markets, yet the coal they burned in their trawlers had to be bought for pounds sterling from England. In early 1922 the entire Hamburg fishing fleet was laid up and was only able to continue operations when the fishermen received permission to sell their catches abroad. Amongst the city's industrial manufacturers, those working for export markets prospered for the same reason as the merchants, but a dependence on foreign raw materials was a critical weakness. In general the Hamburg economy benefited more from the inflation than the rest of Germany because the difference between internal and external value of the currency was greater there.[6]

Unemployment was generally low and there was actually a labor shortage in 1921/22. By 1922 the number of workers in Hamburg was 50 percent greater than 1914 thanks to an influx of labor. Strikes were fewer than elsewhere in Germany and the unions managed to achieve above average wage levels. But wages kept up with the inflation only by irregular jumps, and there was a general leveling of differentials within the workforce. Food prices outstripped everything, and pilfering in the docks for foodstuffs like coffee got so serious that the HAPAG began to ship its cargo through Antwerp instead of its home port. Food shortages, as we have seen, had begun in the war, and theft and black market operations became a matter of survival. With the inflation, pilfering assumed the character of an illegal proletarian variant on the general tendency to resort to material assets.[7]

The Artisans and Retailers

With the London ultimatum on reparations in May 1921, the curious plateau in the German inflation came to an end. Hamburg was already the most expensive city in the country, now a chronic fuel shortage added further pressure to the rapidly rising prices. For

6. Büttner, *Politische Gerechtigkeit*, pp. 142–44.
7. Michael Grüttner, "Working-Class Crime and the Labour Movement: Pilfering in the Hamburg Docks, 1888–1923," in Richard J. Evans, ed., *The German Working Class, 1888–1933* (London, 1982), pp. 71–72.

the artisans the lack of fuel was probably a bigger disaster than the inflation, since without heat or power to drive machinery their production came to a standstill. By October coal stocks in Hamburg were so low that the power stations were compelled to cut the electricity supply completely between 4 and 8 P.M.[8]

The shortages in fuel and raw materials, a perennial problem since the war, led indirectly to the new problem of labor shortages. In January 1922 there was a lack of qualified tailors and a dearth of skills in the building industry. Moreover the number of apprentices entering artisan trades was falling sharply, so that in May 1921 the butchers guild had only ninety apprentices to spread amongst a thousand members. Like the bakers, the butchers were reluctant to take on new apprentices as long as the shortages persisted and the outlook looked uncertain.[9]

With the persistence of supply and labor difficulties and the eternal lack of credit, it was proposed in the first half of 1922 that the resources of the Loan Relief Fund be strengthened to assist the artisans.[10] Unlike the bigger industrialists and merchants who managed to gain access to loans at remarkably low rates of interest, artisans had the greatest difficulty raising credit. And this inability to acquire credit for themselves made it naturally hard for them to extend the same facility to their customers, a traditional practice upon which many artisan businesses were built. Tailors, in particular, had to face stiff competition from large retailing concerns with sufficient financial resources to take the credit trade from them altogether.[11]

It is perhaps surprising that at this stage in the inflation cash payment was not demanded immediately upon delivery, since giving credit made less and less sense as the currency depreciation got worse. Both the Chamber of Industry and the Chamber of Retailers felt the inflation actually offered an opportunity to wean the customer off this pernicious habit once and for all, and thus to place Mittelstand enterprises on a more secure footing in the future. Beginning in 1921, the two chambers jointly produced adhesive stickers to be attached to their members' invoices urging prompt payment for goods delivered. But without more drastic sanctions to support them, mere written appeals to the customer's

8. British Consular Report, Hamburg. *PRO FO.371/5976/7514.*
9. "Schlachter-Innung zu Hamburg," *AIGZ*, 21 May 1921; "Geschäfts- und Tätigkeitsbericht," *AIGZ*, 7 January 1922.
10. StA.H *Gewerbekammer*, A. 13, Bd. 2, Protokolle, Handwerkerabteilung, 1 May 1922.
11. "Schneider-Innung," *AIGZ*, 3 June 1922.

good nature were unlikely to have much effect. The practice of giving credit was deeply ingrained amongst both artisans and retailers, and even the bitter experience of the inflation did little to break their attachment to this habitual neighborhood custom.[12]

After June 1922 the inflation assumed such proportions that the tiresome burdens of *Zwangswirtschaft* and the eight-hour day began to fade into insignificance. Suddenly every calculation became more involved, every transaction more difficult, and every purchase and every sale more risky. Questions that the artisan had rarely considered in the past were now daily preoccupations: how much should he pay his journeymen? How high should he set his profit margin? Would it be enough to ensure that he had the means to replace his stock of raw material?

The problem of the replacement cost was faced by everyone in business during the latter phase of the inflation,[13] but it was especially acute for artisans and shopkeepers because, unlike the larger undertakings, they worked on very narrow profit margins and had little or no access to hard assets like foreign currency. Every mistake in anticipating the rise in stock replacement costs meant a drain on their meager capital reserves. The problem was aggravated, from their point of view, by the government's attempt to protect the consumer with price controls. The 1921 *Reichsgericht* decision had forbidden the trader from effectively setting prices according to the replacement cost, and thus every attempt he made to protect himself against the currency depreciation tended to be seen by customers as profiteering.

As pricing became more difficult, the artisan economy deteriorated. By November 1922 there were reports of over 10 percent of independent masters closing their workshops to take jobs as wage laborers.[14] As usual, some branches were more seriously hit than others. Where the artisan faced the fiercest competition from mass-produced goods – in shoemaking and tailoring for example – the crisis was at its worst. In December, as the Chamber of Industry celebrated its fiftieth anniversary, many tailors were working only twenty-four hours per week. Unable to compete with the ready-to-wear garments in the department stores, they were holding down prices in a desperate attempt to gain customers and then

---

12. StA.H *Gewerbekammer*, 0.8, Memo to all guilds, 31 October 1922.
13. HKH 29.J.2.18, 31 July 1922.
14. StA.H *Gewerbekammer*, A. 13, Bd. 2, Protokolle, Handwerkerabteilung, 9 November 1922. This figure applies to the area of the Nordwestdeutschen Handwerkerbund, which included Hamburg; a slightly lower figure may be closer to the number affected in the city itself.

finding themselves without the means to purchase further cloth.[15]

Likewise those trades with special vulnerability to government decree usually suffered more than those that were more independent. The chimney sweeps, for instance, depended largely on a special levy (the *Kehrtaxe*) for their income, which was raised by the local government from house owners. Like all taxes during the inflation, its real value was consistently trailing behind the state of currency depreciation, but worse, the government tended to delay raising the tax until after the journeymen had been awarded a pay raise. By 1922 the chimney sweeps were in great difficulties, and even a four million mark loan from the Loan Relief Fund relieved the situation only temporarily. The only remedy, urged the Chamber of Industry forcefully, was for the Hamburg authorities to change the law to allow increases in the levy to precede wage raises.[16]

A rising crescendo of complaint was also heard from builders at this time, although the claims of the Chamber of Industry that the whole construction industry "would come to a standstill if wage costs and raw material prices continue to rise," were less than convincing. Unlike the chimney sweeps, the building industry was the object of genuine government concern, employing as it did so many workers and having such a direct effect on the welfare of the city population. In October builders were granted a 25 percent wage subsidy, which was actually back dated by one month. This was a major precedent, since Hamburg employers were resolutely refusing to back date workers' wage raises at this time.[17]

Price control affected both artisans and retailers, but the artisans at least had the advantage that they were buying raw materials to which the value of their skilled labor would be added. The retailers had no such flexibility; their price markups were strictly controlled by law. Indeed with the end of the temporary stabilization in 1921, they had every reason to panic. While producers and wholesalers responded to the new bout of inflation with raised prices, calculations in foreign currency, and pricing according to the anticipated costs of production and marketing, the retailers were denied all these remedies by the law.

As autumn approached in 1921, consumers frantically bought goods in an effort to make the most of the depreciating currency and to beat the upward movement in the price of food and other

15. "Zur Lage des Schneidergewerbes," *AIGZ*, 15 December 1922.

16. StA.H *Gewerbekammer*, 0.11, Letter to DHSG, 11 December 1922.

17. "Jahresbericht der Gewerbekammer Hamburg," *AIGZ*, 15 January 1923; StA.H *Gewerbekammer*, 0.8, Rundschreiben Nr. 23, 21 October 1922.

necessities. By October panic buying was reported by all sections of the retail trade in Hamburg. Foreigners were buying fish in the market at prices far beyond the means of the local population and causing understandable resentment.[18] Shoe sales were at fever pitch, with not only foreigners but also Germans buying up shoes to hoard for later use.[19] Many shops were cleared of their stocks in a matter of weeks; normally that would have been cause for satisfaction, but now they were forced to close for lack of supplies, and there was a genuine concern that the latest inflation boom was leading to disaster.

The sharp rise in prices led to renewed accusations of hoarding and profiteering against the retailers. The Chamber of Retailers published righteous denials in the local press and declared that only "unscrupulous elements" would take advantage of the latest currency depreciation, but an ugly atmosphere was developing in the streets. Customers demanded lower prices for shoes, arguing that the cost of leather had fallen in March. Shop owners had difficulty explaining that wholesale prices were changing from day to day and a fall in the cost of raw material six months previously could have no effect on current retail prices. As the distrust between retailer and consumer deepened, an atmosphere of mutual recrimination gripped the marketplace. With the news in November of renewed shop plundering in Berlin, the Hamburg retailers braced themselves for the worst in the coming winter.[20]

Plunder was a frightening, but nonetheless transitory, problem. A more serious predicament was presented by the question of stock replacement. Retailers, and to a certain extent artisans too, were faced after 1921 with the bizarre prospect that every sale they made was another step closer to stock depletion and bankruptcy because the cost of new stock was rising faster than permitted retail prices. In 1922 the demand for the universal adoption of the replacement cost as the retail price became loud and unanimous in Hamburg, yet the government remained opposed. The Reich economics minister (Schmidt) rejected it on the grounds that it implied a return to free market pricing, and this was not feasible until Germany returned to a "normal market situation."[21] The Hamburg

18. *PRO FO.371/7514*, Quarterly Report of the British Consul in Hamburg, 25 January 1922.

19. *Jahresbericht der Detaillistenkammer zu Hamburg für 1921*, p. 10; also "Der Sturm auf die Ladengeschäfte," *Der Einzelhandel*, 1 November 1921.

20. HKH 102.1.A.6.18, Detaillistenkammer Vollversammlung, 12 October 1921, 17 November 1921.

21. "Wucher und Preisbildung im Einzelhandel," *Der Einzelhandel*, 15 December 1921.

administration took its lead from Berlin.

The replacement cost became a public issue in 1922, and even the long-hostile Hamburg press started to show some sympathy for the retailers who were "compelled to sell their goods for prices below their current replacement value."[22] In August and September a debate developed between legal experts at the *PPS* in Hamburg and neighboring Altona. The Altona lawyers felt that, while the antiprofiteering laws should be as accommodating as possible to the retailers, the full replacement cost could not be allowed. As the representatives of a Prussian province, they were reflecting the Berlin view on the matter. In Hamburg, by contrast, the public prosecutor's office was in favor of its immediate introduction.[23]

The difference of judgment that existed between the lawyers of Hamburg and Altona was symptomatic of the confusion of opinions that existed throughout Germany and of the "labyrinth of regulations and instructions" through which even the most able retailer could hardly find his way.[24] By the end of the year there was hardly another domestic issue so disputed as the following question: What is a legitimate retail price and what is profiteering? But with the enormous tangle of red tape that had built up since 1914, there was no longer any authority that could give a clear and unambiguous answer. The *PPS*, which had been set up to implement price control legislation, was on the defensive and unwilling to speculate about the justice of the law. At a national gathering of *PPS* officers in November 1922, the *Wiederbeschaffungspreis* was rejected by delegates from Frankfurt and Munich, who considered that, in view of the "overall prosperity of trade," it was unwise to shift the burden of the inflation one-sidedly onto the consumer. The Hamburg officers were in a dissenting minority when this view carried the day.[25] In Berlin the government adhered to its position, reiterated in a Reichstag session in June, that the *Wiederbeschaffungspreis* was only permissible if it was not "an expression of an emergency situation in the market [*Marktnotlage*]," and despite the patent absurdity of this rule, the government could say with clear con-

---

22. "Die Einzelhandel und die Preisgestaltung," *Hamburger Echo*, 6 September 1922.

23. "Der Wiederbeschaffungspreis als Verkaufspreis," *Hamburger Echo*, 7 September 1922; "Die Preistreiberei-Verordnung und der Einzelhandel," *Hamburger Fremdenblatt*, 7 September 1922; "Der Kleinhandel und die Wucher-Verordnung," *Hamburger Nachrichten*, 7 September 1922.

24. "Kalkulation im Einzelhandel," *Deutsche Allgemeine Zeitung*, 14 September 1922.

25. "Der Kampf gegen die Teuerung," *Hamburger Fremdenblatt*, 23 November 1922.

science in late 1922 that the situation was certainly one of emergency.[26]

For retailers, the choice at the end of 1922 seemed to be: sell at a loss or do not sell at all. Some struck at wholesalers with suicidal gestures, deliberately clearing their stock at prices below the repurchase value in order to place themselves in a position where they could buy nothing further from their suppliers. Whether this lemminglike tactic had any serious effect is unclear; however, the wholesalers did feel sufficiently worried about their customers to issue a joint declaration with retailers and producers calling for the immediate introduction of the *Wiederbeschaffungspreis*.[27]

In December a new *Reichsgericht* decision recognized the right of retailers to take domestic currency depreciation fully into account, but only the inflation in German prices was intended. The collapsing value of the mark abroad, of critical importance to importing wholesalers, remained excluded from retail calculations.

The generally hostile atmosphere between retailers and wholesalers during the inflation was full of contradictions. From the retailers' side, it was the dependent nature of the relationship that produced the bitterness. Yet when opportunities arose to circumvent the wholesalers, they were curiously reticent. For example, indirect Reich taxes such as the sales tax were especially unpopular in Hamburg. The Chamber of Commerce opposed it on the grounds that it endangered the existence of local wholesalers, since it was levied at every stage of distribution and therefore encouraged producers to deal directly with the retailers.[28] The latter should have been delighted at this prospect, but they also opposed the tax because it was proposed that special concessions be made to consumer cooperatives.[29] As was so often the case with the small retailers, their resentment at what they perceived as exploitation by capitalist wholesalers was exceeded by their fear of Socialist cooperatives; at the heart of the matter was the conflict between the time-honored practice of Mittelstand business and the threatening institutions of the working class, and in such a confrontation there

26. "Gestehungs- und Wiederbeschaffungspreis," *Hamburger Fremdenblatt*, 11 August 1922.
27. "Der Wiederbeschaffungspreis – eine Existenzfrage! Eine erneute gemeinsame Forderung von Industrie, Großhandel und Einzelhandel," *Deutscher Großhandel*, 1 October 1922.
28. StA.H *Steuerverwaltung*, I.3.4a. Bd. 1, 29 August 1921.
29. "Ruin des Großhandels und Kleinhandels durch die Gesetzgebung," *Neue Hamburger Zeitung*, 31 December 1921. For a contrary view supporting the Reichstag proposal, see "Die Bevorzugung der Genossenschaften bei der Änderung des Umsatzsteuergesetzes," *Hamburger Echo*, 7 January 1922.

was only one honorable side to be on.

In fact it was only the co-ops and department stores amongst the retailers that were actually paying the sales tax to any meaningful degree, while the small shopkeepers and artisans generally evaded it by being inadequately registered. This produced a reaction amongst consumers who preferred to shop at the larger concerns and calls for action to be taken against offenders.[30] The taxes themselves probably had a symbolic value that was greater than the financial burden they represented. As inflation moved into hyperinflation in 1922, it was increasingly easy for all taxpayers who were not subject to pay-as-you-earn taxes to dispose of their obligations to the state. However what irked the old Mittelstand was the notion that the revenue gathered at their expense was expended on those very things of which they disapproved most in the Weimar Republic: social welfare for the workers and reparations for the former enemy.

The whole sphere of retail distribution almost encapsulates the changed balance of forces within corporatist Germany after 1918. Mittelstand enterprise, accustomed to a small, but nonetheless protected, niche within the economic structure of the Empire, was now threatened by the concessions made to the working class; in short, there was not room enough for everyone. While the workers and the early Weimar governments dedicated to their interests would have been content to see the whole population shopping at consumer cooperatives, the Mittelstand looked to the same governments to safeguard the livelihoods of the small shopkeeper.

Sugar, which was virtually unobtainable in the autumn of 1922, was an oft-quoted example used by critics of the shopkeepers and of the way their unproductive middleman activity forced up the price of a product. Typically it was the *Hamburger Echo* that pointed out that retailers had clamored for the repeal of controls on sugar and had even told housewives that such an annulment would bring about a fall in prices. After the *Zwangswirtschaft* had been removed on sugar production, however, there had been no equivalent improvement in the retail position, and instead producers and wholesalers seemed to be making large profits supplying industrial consumers such as chocolate and marmalade manufacturers. The remedy was simple: consumers should become members of the cooperatives.[31]

30. StA.H *Konsumentenkammer*, I.AI.50, Wirtschafts- und Steuerausschüsse, 13 August 1921.

31. "Kleinhändler und Zuckerpreise," *Hamburger Echo*, 2 September 1922; "Unrationelle Warenverteilung," *Vorwärts*, 26 November 1922.

The White-Collar Workers and Civil Servants

Data on white-collar salary rates in Hamburg during the inflation are few and scattered. Union journals did not publish figures in any systematic way, and official statistics are limited either in scope or time.[32]

While Hamburg employers' records are largely lost, some data is available for the Hamburger Hochbahn AG (HHA). This was a mixed enterprise, running the city's rapid transit railways and trams. It was half owned by the Hamburg state, and thus, after the Citizens' Assembly became fully representative in 1919, the SPD deputies took an active interest in the working conditions of its staff. The major cost item at the HHA was the payroll for its labor force of drivers, conductors, booking clerks, station managers, and unskilled laborers. During the war incomes deteriorated in real terms across the board, but white-collar workers seemed to slip behind their blue-collar colleagues. In Table 12 an index of HHA pay rates for two classes of blue-collar workers and two classes of white-collar workers is given for the years 1914–24. It shows that by the end of the war unskilled workers had advanced further from their (admittedly lower) starting point than white-collar workers. This trend continued throughout the inflation, so that by November 1923 unskilled blue-collar workers had enjoyed real increases of almost twice the amount awarded to class F white-collar workers, that is, 33,333 million compared with 15,046 million. The essential point here is not the absolute figures in marks, but the ratios between the different classes of worker. In November 1923 the class F white-collar worker still earned in the region of 6 billion marks a month, compared to the unskilled worker's 2.6 billion, but the differential between them had been appreciably eroded since 1914, and that was what hurt the status-conscious white-collar employee.

In fact the low earnings of the unskilled blue-collar workers and the desire to ensure that they received at least a subsistence minimum resulted in their wages being raised at a faster rate than those of the higher paid white-collar employees. This subsistence minimum formed the basis of the HHA negotiating position during the inflation. Equal cost-of-living bonuses were granted to all classes to ensure that this minimum was reached, and it had the inevitable

32. For example, the excellent "Der Wert der Gehälter und Löhne in Hamburg," in *Statistische Mitteilungen über den hamburgischen Staat* (Hamburg, 1922) only goes as far as 1922.

Table 12. Staff Salaries at the HHA, 1914–1924 (Rounded to the Nearest Whole Figure, August 1914 = 1)

| | Blue-collar workers[1] | | White-collar workers | |
	Unskilled[2]	Drivers[3]	Class B[4]	Class F[5]
	Paper marks			
1914				
August	1.0	1.0	1.0	1.0
1918				
November	2.3	1.4	1.3	1.3
1919				
February	3.7	2.3	2.0	
1920				
February	6.4	2.8	3.2	2.3
April	9.6	3.9	4.6	3.5
1921				
January	12.5	7.3		
August	13.3	7.8	6.8	4.9
December	21.3	12.4	9.7	7.3
1922				
February	31.4	17.9	13.9	10.9
June	50.4	29.3	23.4	16.8
September	169.3	101.0	79.5	53.8
November	343.8	206.3	170.7	116.3
1923				
January	900.0	525.1	436.0	296.5
March	3216.0	1907.0	1595.0	1087.0
May	3728.0	2256.0	1899.0	1263.0
June	5777.0	3559.0	2943.0	2050.0
July	18000.0	11634.0	10703.0	7297.0
August	124444.0	76651.0	66999.0	56428.0
September	3600000.0	2200000.0	1900000.0	1600000.0
October (4)	66000000.0	41000000.0	35600000.0	30100000.0
(24)	7222200000.0	4448500000.0	3865800000.0	3260200000.0
November (4)	33333100000.0	20531600000.0	17841700000.0	15046400000.0
	Gold marks			
November (7)	0.9	0.5	0.5	0.5
December (1)	0.8	0.6	0.5	0.5

Table 12. Staff Salaries at the HHA, 1914–1924 (Rounded to the
Nearest Whole Figure, August 1914 = 1)

| | Blue-collar workers[1] | | White-collar workers | |
	Unskilled[2]	Drivers[3]	Class B[4]	Class F[5]
	Gold marks			
1924				
January	0.9	0.7	0.6	0.6
February	0.9	0.7	0.6	0.7
April	1.1	0.8	0.7	0.8
July	1.3	1.0	0.9	1.0

1. Blue-collar labor worked an average of ten hours per day until 1919; white collar employees worked eight hours per day throughout the period.
2. Paid at the rate of 0.45 marks per hour.
3. Paid 155 marks per month.
4. Paid 220 marks per month.
5. Paid 400 marks per month.

Source: Ernst Kipnase, *Die Hamburger Hochbahn AG in verkehrspolitischer und sozial-politischer Beziehung* (Berlin, 1925), pp. 214, 218–19.

effect of reducing differentials between the pay scales. The white-collar workers would have preferred bonuses based upon a percentage of income, but because their *Angestelltenrat* (white-collar council) had less influence at the HHA than the workers' bodies, they had little chance of pushing through such a scheme.[33] The cost of preserving their cherished status was further raised by the fact that while drivers, conductors, and stationmasters received free uniforms, office staff had to buy their own clothing. And given the importance of being well dressed to the average white-collar worker – the very term points to the fact – this would have involved him in considerable extra expenditure.[34]

During the inflation the method of salary payment became as important as the amount. The monthly sum that distinguished white- from blue-collar worker was generally paid in arrears, which was a disadvantage when the mark was losing value on a daily basis towards the end of 1923. Such payment gave the

33. Ernst Kipnase, *Die Hamburger Hochbahn AG in verkehrspolitischer und sozial-politischer Beziehung* (Berlin, 1925), p. 217.
34. For a good discussion of consumer preferences amongst German white-collar workers in this period, see Sandra Coyner, *Class Patterns of Family Income and Expenditure during the Weimar Republic: German White-Collar Workers as the Harbinger of Modern Society* (Diss., Rutgers Univ., 1975).

employer, in effect, interest-free use of the salary for a month, at a time when access to any kind of credit was highly desirable.

In September 1922 the ZdA trade union called for fortnightly payments for all white-collar workers, but this was rejected by the nationalist DHV because of its professional disadvantages (*standes-politische Nachteile*). To give up monthly payments, argued the DHV, would be to surrender the monthly notice to which employees were entitled and to lose the month's pay during the period when a new job was being sought. Of greater significance was the distinction that monthly payment offered white-collar employees, and such concern for status was more common in the nationalist DHV than the Socialist ZdA. In particular it was stressed that the monthly salary was a form of renumeration from which deductions were not made for small absences from work, as was the case with the workers' weekly time wage.[35] A compromise position was eventually found in unofficial midmonthly advances on salary. These had the temporary character of a crisis measure, and as the inflation accelerated, they were made increasingly often. In June fortnightly payment became the norm, in September it was weekly, and in October the white-collar worker – all thoughts of status now forgotten – was being paid twice a week.[36]

Various other schemes for ensuring that pay kept pace with the inflation were proposed by the trade unions and other interested bodies. The most common was the cost-of-living bonus, which originated with the civil servants during the war. The practice spread to the private sector when the employers realized that by paying according to family situation, rather than performance, the salary of an unmarried man could be kept down; at the same time bonuses paid to workers with families could be cut the moment the price index started to fall without the need for further negotiations with the trade unions. In August 1921, for instance, a circular from the Hamburg Wholesalers' Association advised members to pay a once-only bonus to their employees to cover the latest bout of inflation, thereby avoiding the granting of any permanent salary increase. Not surprisingly the unions condemned the practice as an attempt to divide the labor force by setting married men against the unmarried; by hiring the latter only, employers could avoid paying much of the bonus.[37]

Another device for keeping pace with the inflation was the

---

35. "Wochen- oder Monatgehaltszahlungen?"*DKWR* (Hamburg, January 1924).
36. "Tarifverträge für Kaufmannsgehilfen," *DKWR* (Hamburg, December 1924).
37. *DHW*, 14 September 1921; *GDA*, 1 January 1922.

so-called sliding scale, through which salaries could rise and fall with the cost of living but have a real value that, in theory at least, would remain constant. It is possible that the supporters of the sliding scale imagined that its general adoption could bring an end to the strife between the two sides of industry and perhaps survive beyond the inflation to stabilize German labor relations in the future. If this was so, then they overlooked the critical interest that the trade unions had in keeping the process of salary negotiation unencumbered by institutional structures. In the spring of 1921 the sliding scale was rejected by all sides of the white-collar trade union movement as an irrelevant distraction from the main business of improving employees' earnings.[38] The most serious obstacle to the adoption of the sliding scale was the lack of an accurate and generally accepted cost-of-living index. If the scale were fixed to an index that understated the cost of living, then the disadvantage to the salary earner would be perpetuated. The official Reich cost-of-living statistics were greatly criticized for taking untypically low prices, often from housewife organizations that compiled lists of the cheapest buys as a service to the consumer. On occasion municipalities, out of misplaced pride, inadvertently connived at the debasing of the official index by providing data to the Reich statisticians that showed their locality with prices lower than elsewhere.[39]

The problem facing the civil servant in the inflation was similar to that of the white-collar worker at the HHA, the HEW, or Karstadt: the need for prompt and adequate payment sufficient to cover not just the bare necessities, but also those important items of clothing that distinguished the new Mittelstand from the ranks of the working class. By June 1921 civil servant salaries in Hamburg were barely covering the cost of essentials and left nothing over for even minor items of dress such as shirts or collars. Many lower paid grades found their pay insufficient to last the month and requested salary and bonus increases to prevent them getting further into debt.[40] The Civil Service Council chairman, Raue, asked the Senate to seek funds from the Reich and turned to the DBB in Berlin for support.[41]

At this stage and throughout the remaining half of 1921, the

---

38. *Nordwestdeutsche Rundschau* (Organ of the ZdA), 31 March 1921; "Zur Gehaltsfrage in den Tarifverträgen," *DHW*, 10 March 1921.

39. See "Der Kampf um die Kaufkraft," *DHW*, 12 April 1922; *GDA*, 23 April 1922 and 16 June 1922; also Arthur Heichen, *Berliner Tageblatt*, 13 August 1921.

40. StA.H *Beamtenrat*, 100, Behörde für das Versicherungswesen, 7 June 1921.

41. StA.H *Beamtenrat*, 100, 31 May 1921.

DBB was engaged in a major struggle for higher salaries and was debating whether to form a common front with the public service workers in pay negotiations.[42] The chief obstacle to such cooperation was the fact that the workers' wages were fixed by collective agreement, while the civil servants' were determined by the legislative process. In August 1921 the DBB national executive rejected an agreement with the ADGB; instead of encouraging an alliance between wage and salary earners, the inflation had simply revealed the fundamental difference of interest between them.[43]

The breakdown in talks between the two organizations was deplored at the shop floor level in Hamburg. In July the Civil Service Council had received petitions from almost every department urging action on pay policy. The resolution of the teachers at the vocational teaching school (all German teachers were civil servants) was typical in suggesting that their "exploitation" had "led to indebtedness and to all the moral dangers that such a situation holds for the state."[44] This oblique reference to the possibility of corruption was indicative of their desperate position at this stage of the inflation. It is not difficult to imagine the many different ways in which even a junior clerk could exploit his position – for example, in the issuing of one of the host of official permits that were required to continue daily business in the age of the *Zwangswirtschaft*. Not surprisingly, there is little written evidence of such wrongdoing amongst civil servants, but we cannot be sure that it did not exist. Of relevance here is the fact that it seemed inconceivable to them that the government would countenance such a deterioration in morale and allow the standards of the German civil service to fall to the level of those of a banana republic simply in the cause of financial stringency. But the government had more pressing concerns. In May Germany had received the final reparation demand from the Entente, which caused not the least dismay amongst the civil servants themselves. They asked, apparently without irony, how the government could consider paying billions of marks to the enemy and could not find a few million for its own loyal servants.[45]

42. See W. Schröder, "Der Deutsche Beamtenbund und die anderen Gewerkschaften," *Die Gemeinschaft*, 7 July 1921.

43. For a full account of the negotiations between the *DBB* and the *ADGB*, as well as of the battle with the government for higher pay, see Kunz, *Civil Servants*, pp. 236–280.

44. StA.H *Beamtenrat*, 100, 13 July 1921, Beamten- und Angestelltenausschuß der Behörde für das Gewerbe- und Fortbildungsschulwesen zu Hamburg.

45. "Zur Lage der Beamtenschaft," *HBZ*, 2 July 1921.

In August some supplements were granted for local costs, but the DBB's main demand of a guaranteed minimum wage of 8,500 marks per month was rejected by Berlin.[46] In Hamburg an *Existenzkampf* (struggle for existence) was declared, and civil servants appeared in mass meetings like the one called on 2 August 1921, when over ten thousand people gathered near Dammtor station. Stirring resolutions were drafted calling for salary bonuses and solidarity with colleagues in other cities; a particular grievance was the lack of special treatment for civil servants employed in large urban centers where the cost of living was higher than in the country.[47] Their sense of neglect was building towards a crisis: their status was at stake as clothing that had still been presentable in 1919 became humiliatingly threadbare and yet was impossible to replace.[48]

Well informed of the unrest amongst civil servants and probably seeking to exploit the breakdown of the Berlin talks between the DBB and ADGB, the Hamburg Communist party (KPD) invited the civil servants to a mass demonstration with the object of forming a single fighting front of blue- and white-collar workers against the inflation. The Communists believed that the inflation was a capitalist ploy to shift the burden of reparations to the working class. The Civil Service Council, which had been approached along with other trade union representatives in Hamburg, did not share this conviction and refused the invitation on behalf of the civil servants. However the Communists evidently struck a chord with some of them, who, undeterred by the council rejection, attended a number of KPD meetings in the autumn of 1921.[49]

Having failed with their pay claim in August, the DBB tried again in September. Now they used the Communist activity in Hamburg to strengthen their case: without a minimum wage, the lower grades would seek more radical leaders, with all the risks that

46. The supplements amounted to about 20 percent for city dwellers; for details, see *Wirtschaft und Statistik* (1921), pp. 426–9.

47. The conflict between civil servants in urban and rural settings and the demands of the former for renumeration that reflected the higher cost of living in the cities are treated in Andreas Kunz's case study, "Variants of Social Protest in the German Inflation: The Mobilization of Civil Servants in City and Countryside, 1920 to 1924," in *Anpassung*, ed. Feldman et al., pp. 323–54.

48. "Der Existenzkampf," *DB*, 1 August 1921; "Der Notschrei an die Öffentlichkeit," *DB*, 15 August 1921; "In höchster Not," *HBZ*, 6 August 1921.

49. StA.H *Beamtenrat*, 100, Vereinigte Kommunistische Partei Deutschlands, 19 August 1921 – 23 August 1921. Also *Beamtenrat*, 17, Protokolle der Vollsitzungen, Bd. 3, 26 August 1921.

that entailed for the government. The Communist threat may have had some effect because in October a new pay settlement was reached resulting in quite impressive gains for the civil servants. In real terms, the senior ranks reached the highest income for the entire inflation period, while the middle and lower grades also made gains, although the effect of widening differentials made theirs less impressive.

But by November prices had risen by nearly 20 percent and all the gains were practically wiped out. "Most of us are vegetarians," reported *Der Bürobeamte*, "meat is a rarity, there is no margarine, our shoes are torn to pieces, our clothes are shabby, and our debts unspeakable."[50] The more radical elements in the Civil Service Council called for strike action, an unprecedented move for civil servants and one that threatened grave and lasting repercussions. The fact that a strike of civil servants was even being discussed illustrates the desperation that the rank and file felt at their treatment by the government and, perhaps more important, their frustration with the apparent ineffectiveness of their own leadership in the DBB. The talk of a civil service strike persisted throughout the winter of 1921/22 and became a reality when the powerful railwaymen's union, the Reichsgewerkschaft, called its members out in the first week of February 1922. The strike, which was concentrated in western and northern Germany including Hamburg, lasted only five days, and its inconclusive outcome did nothing to strengthen the authority of the DBB. Instead it marked "a turning point in the organizational development of the civil servant movement," and "the zenith of civil servant protest and . . . militancy during the inflation period."[51]

In the meantime the Hamburg administration, moving in tandem with the Reich authorities, resisted all claims for further salary rises while professing regret "that more could not be done for the civil servants." The DBB request for special consideration for the lower grades, presented at the beginning of December, met with little response; in vain the civil servants waited for "action before Christmas."[52] In fact they had to wait until April, when a new agreement was reached. It raised income levels somewhat, but once again the inflation wiped out any benefits within a couple of months.

50. "Die Wirtschaftsbeihilfe," *DB*, 15 November 1921.
51. Kunz, *Civil Servants*, pp. 347–48. For a blow-by-blow account of the strike, ibid., pp. 283–327.
52. "Neuregelung der Beamtenbesoldung," *Hamburger Fremdenblatt*, 3 November 1921; "Die neue Regelung der Beamtenbesoldung," *DB*, 15 December 1921.

In Table 13 figures from the Hamburg State Statistical Office for civil servant salaries from 1920 onwards are based upon the cost-of-living index.[53] The effect of the inflation on the wage and salary differentials is immediately apparent. As with the white-collar workers at the HHA, the higher the initial earnings, the faster the depreciation of their real worth in terms of the cost of living. Thus the higher civil servant who earned the princely sum of 814 marks per month in July 1914 had little over 30 percent of his 1914 purchasing power in January 1921, whereas the construction worker who made 50 pfennigs an hour in 1914 – roughly 125 marks per month – was actually better off, with a 28 percent increase in purchasing power. The reason for this was very largely the growth in wage and salary supplements. Because they were paid according to social need, rather than on the basis of skills or performance, lower paid workers tended to get relatively more than the higher paid. The result was an inverse relationship between the degree of brain work involved in a job and the resistance of earnings in that position to depreciation in the inflation. This feature of the inflation goes some way towards explaining why the new Mittelstand of white-collar workers and civil servants appeared to suffer to a disproportionate degree.

In 1922 the emphasis in pay negotiations amongst the civil servants shifted towards means of payment, rather than the amount. Their renumeration was already composed of salary plus bonuses. Now a wives' allowance was added, and proposals made for a clothes and even a culture supplement – there being no more depressing aspect of his poverty for the civil servant than the fact that he could not even afford to buy a good book.[54]

This new concern with methods of payment led to a revival of interest in the sliding scale. Most civil servants accepted its advantages, but there were disagreements over the basis upon which it could be introduced. What arbitrary living standard should be taken as the starting point? What items should be included in the index of living costs?[55] The discussion remained fairly theoretical as long as the government opposed the scheme. Private business was particularly hostile, and the leading employers' organization con-

---

53. This was the most effective indicator of purchasing power and certainly more useful than the so-called dollar rate, which gauged the mark's value on world markets, but not on the street corner. However there were weaknesses in the way the index was compiled, most notably the absence of clothing in the sample basket of goods, at least before March 1922. Holtfrerich, *Die deutsche Inflation*, p. 236.

54. "Kleider- und Kulturzulage," *DB*, 1 June 1922.

55. "Der Kampf um die gleitende Lohnskala," *DB*, 15 May 1922.

Table 13. Index of Real Earnings of Civil Servants, State Employees, and Skilled and Unskilled Workers in Hamburg, 1920–1925 (1914 = 100)[1]

| | Civil servants | | | | | | Workers[2] | |
	(1)	(2)	(3)	(4)	(5)	(6)	(7)	(8)
1914								
July	100.0	100.0	100.0	100.0	100.0	100.0	100.0	100.0
1920								
January	24.6	38.2	52.5	60.5				
March	**15.9**	**24.8**	**34.3**	**39.5**[3]				
June	34.5	54.8	66.2	81.4				
October	30.5	48.2	58.3	71.9				
December	26.4	41.8	50.5	62.3				
1921								
January	31.4	50.6	61.3	74.8	80.0	99.6	77.3	128.0
March	33.1	52.4	63.7	77.8	82.9	103.1	86.7	134.0
May	37.1	58.8	71.6	87.4	93.2	116.1	97.3	150.0
September	32.4	51.5	62.2	76.6	71.8	103.7	88.0	148.0
October	**51.6**	**65.5**	**71.6**	**91.6**	76.9	95.2	89.3	136.0
December	36.7	46.7	50.9	65.3	65.8	99.3	88.0	140.0
1922								
January	39.3	54.2	64.2	80.8	90.6	96.5	85.3	144.0
March	26.8	36.9	43.6	55.1	71.7	75.6	73.3	114.0
June	29.4	44.8	55.4	69.5	75.7	82.0	76.0	142.0
September	32.6	47.9	56.9	71.3	74.8	85.6	66.7	108.0

	(1)	(2)	(3)	(4)	(5)	(6)	(7)	(8)
November	**17.9**	**26.7**	**29.9**	**37.7**	**44.4**	**57.0**	**50.7**	**74.0**
December	27.2	40.6	46.1	57.5	69.6	85.4	76.0	110.0
1923								
January	29.8	44.8	50.5	63.5	56.9	68.3	60.0	98.0
March	33.4	50.0	56.4	70.6	90.0	113.7	82.7	134.0
June	37.7	56.7	63.7	80.2	76.9	90.7	74.7	116.0
September	**50.9**	**75.7**	**79.4**	**100.0**	**140.8**	**171.4**	**112.0**	**276.0**
November	23.9	35.7	37.7	47.3	85.1	78.1	62.7	102.0
December	39.9	54.8	51.5	64.6	74.4	74.4	60.0	76.0
1924								
January	41.0	56.3	52.7	66.5	76.4	76.5	61.3	
April	52.8	72.2	68.0	88.9	83.4	88.9	66.7	
July	**71.3**	**87.6**	**75.2**	**98.9**	**97.1**	**100.7**	**93.3**	
October	66.1	81.3	69.8	91.8	95.1	93.5	92.0	
1925								
January	70.0	87.1	77.0	101.5	95.0	92.6	85.3	

1. Calculated according to the Hamburg cost-of-living index, income without child benefit.

2. Occupations and salaries in July 1914: (1) higher civil servant, 814.00 marks per month; (2) middle civil servant, 330.00 marks per month; (3) lower civil servant, 201.00 marks per month; (4) state employee, 167.00 marks per month; (5) baker, 36.00 marks per week; (6) docker, 5.40 marks per day; (7) fitter, 0.75 marks per hour; (8) construction worker, 0.50 marks per hour.

3. Bold figures represent peaks and troughs in the five-year trend.

Source: Compiled from the *Hamburger statistische Monatsberichte*, Special Issue 1 (April 1924): 77–80; (May 1924): 97–100; *Statistisches Jahrbuch für die Freie und Hansestadt Hamburg* (1925): 204.

demned it on the grounds that civil servants "comprise such a large proportion of the working population that raising their salaries would affect the whole price structure of the economy."[56] But in the spring and early summer of 1922 the crisis reached new proportions. In an appeal to the Civil Service Council, the civil servants' committee at the magistrate's court spoke of colleagues "without a pfennig . . . living entirely on credit" and demanded payment of their August salaries in the second week of July.[57] The point had been reached at which the speed with which salaries were paid was of greater importance than the amount. Negotiated settlements, now devalued within days of the agreement, were becoming a thing of the past. Instead of seeking the highest award possible, they sought the quickest. Old attitudes were replaced by the universal assumption that prices would rise – the only question being, by how much?

As autumn approached a new problem was added to the civil servants' difficulties as the government ran out of bank notes with which to pay them. In September the shortage was so severe that some individuals were paid a month's salary with a single bank note; there were even cases of several different people being paid together with a single bank note.[58] Alarmed, the Hamburg Senate sought permission from the Reich to print emergency money, in time for the October pay round. On 15 September 1922 Berlin authorized the printing of a billion marks, but this was not enough. In addition to the 400 million required for civil servants' salaries, emergency money was needed urgently by the post office, the railways, and the large private employers like the dockyards and the banks. October came and still the salaries had not been paid in full. The dispute between the civil servants and the Senate became acrimonious, indeed so bitter that the business community grew concerned that Hamburg's overseas credit worthiness might be damaged if it became known that the city was unable to print the necessary number of notes.[59]

It is difficult to judge how far the authorities in Hamburg

56. Deutscher Industrie- und Handelstag, *Mitteilungen der Hamburger Handelskammer*, 12, 17 June 1922, p. 235. See also "Die gleitende Lohnskala,"*Hamburgischer Correspondent*, 21 June 1922.

57. StA.H *Beamtenrat*, 32, Bd. 1, Beamtenausschuß des Amtsgerichts Hamburg, 11 July 1922.

58. "Wieder hamburgisches Notgeld," *Hamburgischer Correspondent*, 16 September 1922.

59. "Bargeldnot und Beamtensorgen," *Hamburgischer Correspondent*, 7 October 1922; also "Folgen der Bargeldnot," *Hamburgischer Correspondent*, 26 October 1920. See also StA.H *Hauptstaatskasse* A.VI.10. Bd. 1, 23–25 September 1922.

exploited the bank note shortage to delay payment of salaries, but intentionally or not, the civil servants were provoked by the emergency money crisis. Tensions arose between departments as some staff was paid before others. In August 1922 a proposal for quarterly salary payments in advance was discussed in a full sitting of the Civil Service Council without any agreement being reached. The teachers were in favor of the proposal, many other departments were against it; the result was that a weak request was formulated to the Senate to grant advance quarterly payments to those who wanted them. The request was denied on the basis of insufficient bank notes, but clearly if the Civil Service Council had made a determined demand, then the Senate would have been compelled to organize the printing of the notes. The main argument against quarterly payments – that the inflation would render them worthless before the three months had elapsed – ignored the considerable advantage of converting a larger quantity of cash into goods at earlier, therefore lower, prices.[60] In general, the response to the bank note shortage was one more example of the Civil Service Council's organizational weakness and ineptitude.

In November civil servant salaries fell to the lowest level since early 1920 (Table 13), only this time it was the clumsiness of the system rather than the obstinacy of government that caused the hardship. Petitions poured into the Civil Service Council, most of them using overworn phrases to describe their desperate situation. Coinciding with their "boundless misery" in Hamburg, a political upheaval took place in Berlin as Wirth's government collapsed; in the ensuing chaos, negotiations with the civil servants were postponed at the very moment when the inflation was assuming alarming proportions. The council was powerless and could only hope that discussions would be resumed as soon as possible.[61]

A 50 percent raise was granted towards the end of November, resulting in a slight improvement in real earnings in December, but once again, the salary was paid too late. The feeling of despair at the end of the year was summed up by the clerks in the youth welfare office, who were "incensed that, despite the dismal experience of the October pay round and despite our hopeless situation, on the last payday we were let down once again."[62] As the year drew to a

---

60. StA.H *Beamtenrat*, 17, Bd. 4, Vollsitzung, 31 August 1922 and 14 September 1922.
61. StA.H *Beamtenrat*, 17, Bd. 4, Vollsitzung, 16 November 1922.
62. StA.H *Beamtenrat*, 17, Bd. 4, Vollsitzung, 23 November 1922; 32. Bd. 14, Behörde für öffentliche Jugendfürsorge, 5 December 1922.

close not only was morale extremely low, but petty rivalries between the civil servants, such as the order in which different departments were paid, were hardening into bitter hostilities.

The House Owners

By mid-1921 the Hamburg house owners had become resigned to the inevitability of the Reich rent law (*Reichsmietengesetz* or *RMG*), a piece of Berlin legislation that would encompass, and hopefully simplify, the whole tangled mess of rules and regulations that had grown up in the housing market since 1914. Their hostility to the new law was clear from the utterances of their leader in the Citizens' Assembly, Johannes Hüne, who characterized it as typical of the "envy [that] dictates state policy."[63] But, aware that they would never defeat it, they concentrated instead on getting the vital maintenance surcharges to the basic rent set as high as possible.

As their main weapon in this battle, they turned to the government's own statistics. The combination of rent control and inflation had produced a quite startling reduction in the proportion of family expenditure devoted to housing, compared to prewar years, and the landlords were at pains to bring this fact to the attention of the authorities by using the cost-of-living index. This showed how other necessities had risen in price a great deal further than rents since the beginning of the war. In June 1921, for example, Hamburg rents had increased by a factor of two since 1914, while prices for food, heat, and light had multiplied by between seven and thirteen times (Table 14).[64]

Towards the end of 1921 the conflict between landlords and tenants intensified. While the landlords, anxious that the long-delayed *RMG* might not bring them the necessary improvements when it was finally enacted in 1922, pressed the Hamburg government to obtain permission from Berlin for an interim rent increase,[65] the tenants lobbied the Reich government, which they seemed to trust more than the one in Hamburg, to stand firm "against landlords and speculators."[66]

63. "Gegen des Reichsmietengesetz," *Hamburger Nachrichten*, 16 June 1921.
64. Similar trends were evident elsewhere in Germany. See for example, the expenditure of a professional Berlin household in Holtfrerich, *Die deutsche Inflation*, p. 258.
65. "Die bevorstehende Erhöhung der Mieten und das Reichsmietengesetz," *Hamburger Nachrichten*, 30 November 1921.
66. See reports of tenants' mass meetings in: "Zu den neuen Richtlinien des Mieteeinigungsamts," *Hamburger Echo*, 5 November 1921; "Der Protest der Mie-

Table 14. Reich Cost-of-Living Index for Hamburg, 1921–1922 (July 1914 = 100)

	Food	Heat	Light	**Rent**	Reich index
1914					
July	100	100	100	**100**	100
1921					
January	1543	1190	745	**173**	1080
February	1406	1155	745	**173**	1001
March	1377	1155	745	**173**	963
April	1350	1155	745	**173**	939
May	1283	1155	745	**200**	908
June	1295	1155	745	**200**	910
July	1337	1378	745	**200**	975
August	1499	1635	824	**200**	1142
September	1597	1670	902	**200**	1156
October	1682	1750	902	**200**	1212
November	2067	1892	981	**200**	1458
December	2445	2265	1059	**200**	1711
1922					
January	2507	2735	1255	**200**	1782
February	2970	2771	1255	**200**	2067
March	3297	3286	1490	**200**	2302
April	4473	4068	1765	**357**	3120
May	4959	5826	2078	**357**	3526
June	5296	5933	2078	**357**	3738
July	6103	6856	2171	**357**	4293
August	7900	8828	3294	**483**	5505

Source: "Der Wert der Gehälter und Löhne in Hamburg," *Statistische Mitteilungen über den hamburgischen Staat*, No. 13 (1922): 36–37.

The landlords knew they had a strong case for a rent increase, but it seemed that many years of accumulated hostility now weighed against them. Despite several approaches from the Hamburg authorities in December 1921, the responsible minister delayed taking any decision.[67] He wished to prevent the states from introducing any new measures that might conflict with the eventual legal form

---

ter," *Hamburger Echo*, 7 November 1921; "An alle Mieter von Groß-Hamburg!" *Hamburger Volkszeitung*, 4 November 1921.

67. StA.H *Senat*, Conv. 1, Reichsarbeitsministerium, 2 December 1921 to 31 December 1921.

of the *RMG*, which was held up in the Reichstag by technical complications.[68] Only in April 1922 were rents raised and, three months later, raised again as the *RMG* came into force in Hamburg (Table 14).

The new law brought some order into German housing regulation by establishing exact instructions for fixing rents. It applied to all buildings constructed before October 1918, which in Hamburg meant over 90 percent of the housing stock. But the bitterness it evoked amongst landlords can hardly be exaggerated. Unable to evict undesirable or impecunious tenants without the permission of the *MEA*, they felt they were no longer "master of the house." In the Citizens' Assembly Hüne condemned the new law as "an attempt to socialize property, the strongest pillar of commerce and the Mittelstand."[69] And it was not merely material losses that affected the landlords, but as was so often the case with Mittelstand groups, a diminution of status. The continuing *Wohnungszwangswirtschaft* meant the loss of a cherished and privileged position in Hamburg, a position that only a full restoration of market forces could bring back.

That the landlords should see the *RMG* in political terms demonstrates both the particularist sentiment of the Hamburg Mittelstand vis-à-vis Prussian Berlin and its faulty perception of its position in the Weimar Republic. The landlords seemed not to have grasped the fact that most legislation in a parliamentary democracy is the product of political compromise. Because the *RMG* was the result of elaborate negotiation in the Reichstag, responsibility for fixing the vital rent surcharges was delegated to state parliaments like the Hamburg Citizens' Assembly; these parliaments, now subject to universal suffrage, were almost inevitably more sympathetic to the majority of tenants than to the minority of landlords.

As the Citizens' Assembly busied itself with the *RMG* in the summer of 1922, the landlords mounted an intensive campaign to get rent surcharges increased. At a meeting a few days before the bill was to become law, the Senate was warned that "further neglect of the maintenance on buildings will lead to their collapse, and if this happens and people are killed, then the Senate will bear the responsibility."[70] As if to drive home the point, the same week the

68. The basis for costing in the *RMG* was agreed upon only after extended negotiations in 1921. For an account of its implementation in Munich, see Geyer, *Wohnungsnot*, pp. 141–44.

69. "Reichsmietengesetz und Grundeigentum," *Hamburger Fremdenblatt*, 8 March 1922.

70. StA.H *Senat*, Conv. 1, GVH to Senate, 24 June 1922.

newspapers reported that building facades had been collapsing in Hamburg and that one or two people had already been injured from falling masonry.[71]

Even the Hamburg building cooperatives were persuaded to join the landlords' campaign. The four main cooperatives, in a petition to the Senate, listed the operating costs of a typical eighty-apartment housing block in Barmbek. The total rent for the month (July 1922), including all the surcharges permitted under the *RMG*, amounted to 95,732 marks. The total costs, including taxation, insurance, maintenance, and repairs, came to 221,995 marks. In other words the total income from the block covered less than half the total expenses involved in running it.[72] The experience of one cooperative in particular, the Bauverein zu Hamburg, is interesting because it acted not only as landlord, but also as builder, and completed 268 apartments in 1922. In the cooperative's annual report, the *Zwangswirtschaft* was roundly condemned and the point made that although new dwellings were not subject to rent control, in practice it was impossible to raise their rents much higher than those for controlled premises; to do so would mean no one would live in them.[73]

The evidence from these cooperatives is important, of course, because they represented not the typical venal landlord, but non-profit-making organizations. And it suggests that, GVH rhetoric notwithstanding, the Hamburg house owners were in serious difficulty in 1922. Further increases in the rent surcharge were granted in September and December, but they were to no avail; at the end of the year, the combination of rent control and inflation had cut the value of the rents to less than 1 percent of their prewar level. By Christmas over a thousand house owners in Hamburg were being supported by public welfare.[74]

71. By the summer of 1922 the general state of repair of Hamburg housing was extremely bad. A combination of many years' neglect and hard frosts in the winter of 1921/22 had turned some of them into a public menace. "Haftbarmachung für Gesimsabstürze," *Hamburger Fremdenblatt*, 26 June 1922.
72. The cooperatives were the Bauverein zu Hamburg, the Produktion, the Allgemeine Deutsche Schiffszimmerer-Genossenschaft, and the Beamten-Wohnungsverein. StA.H *Senat*, Conv. 2. Petition to Senate, 29 July 1922.
73. StA.H *Wohnungsamt*, 111, Geschäftsbericht, 1922, Bauverein zu Hamburg.
74. "Jahresbericht des Hamburger Grundeigentümer-Vereins," *HGZ*, 27 October 1922.

6

Year of Turmoil, 1923

> To sell for money was madness, to
> borrow and pay back later was good
> business. People spent two weeks in
> a first-class Bavarian hotel for the
> price of their dead grandmother's
> gold teeth.
> —Franz Schoenberner[1]

1923 was a dramatic, almost disastrous year for the Weimar Republic. It began with the Franco-Belgian invasion of the Ruhr and
ended with the Hitler *Putsch*, and in between, the inflation reached
its culmination in the chaotic conditions that are captured forever in
the image of people carrying baskets of bank notes to make the
simplest purchase. In fact 1923 was only the terminal crisis in a
decade-long process of monetary degeneration, but it is understandably seen as the definitive year of the German inflation.[2]

The Ruhr invasion in January was certainly instrumental in
starting the final avalanche. Not only did it destroy what confidence remained in the possibility of an orderly return to stabilized
conditions, but the loss in production caused by the ensuing strike
by German workers and by the passive resistance launched in their
support paralyzed the economy.[3] With no other means at its
disposal, the government of Wilhelm Cuno furnished the massive
amounts of aid required with the printing press. As the value of the
money produced diminished by the day and finally by the hour, the
earlier benefits of the inflation to economy disappeared. By

1. Franz Schoenberner, *Confessions of a European Intellectual* (New York, 1946), p.
168.
2. See, for example, the little book by Fritz Ringer, ed., *The German Inflation of
1923* (New York, 1969).
3. Holtfrerich, *Die deutsche Inflation*, pp. 329–30.

November the battered mark had ceased to fulfill any of the functions that economists expect of a national currency, that is, it no longer served as a store of value, a unit of account, or a medium of exchange. When the Reichsbank eventually found itself unable to supply all the bank notes needed for the continuation of business, it was compelled to authorize the printing of emergency money (*Notgeld*) by local authorities, and the whole monetary structure of the Reich collapsed under a tidal wave of worthless paper.[4] The very absurdity of the situation that the inflation created was itself responsible for bringing such conditions to a grinding halt. It should be stressed that it was a political and fiscal necessity, rather than an economic one; industry was already doing much of its trade in foreign exchange and would have been able to continue doing so. The government had reached the point, however, where the advantages of the inflation tax were rapidly disappearing,[5] while for those groups in society who were unable to switch to foreign currency, there was the real prospect of starvation.[6]

That the stabilization took until November was partly the result of delays in deciding which scheme should be adopted and partly because the mark was deliberately allowed to fall in value to a level where it could be expediently stabilized. In any event, the first step was the replacement in August of Cuno with Gustav Stresemann. Cuno had been no match for the seasoned statesmen of postwar Europe, particularly on the reparations question, and he lacked any kind of planned response to the Ruhr invasion other than to allow the sense of national outrage in the country to dictate policy.[7]

Stresemann, by contrast, was a far more experienced politician. He immediately ended the passive resistance and brought in Hans Luther as finance minister. On 5 November 1923 a new currency, the *Rentenmark*, was launched. Although it was not convertible and had the backing of nothing more tangible than the productive wealth of German agriculture and industry, it possessed the vital

---

4. By the end of 1923 there was 7.6 quintillion marks of emergency money in circulation, alongside 497 quintillion from the Reichsbank. In addition there was a further 12 quintillion marks of unsanctioned notes. Karl Elster, *Von Mark zur Reichsmark: Die Geschichte der deutschen Währung in den Jahren 1914 bis 1924* (Jena, 1928), p. 202.

5. Revenues were falling sharply because the government underestimated the degree of devaluation between the time when taxes were levied and when they were collected.

6. Holtfrerich, *Die deutsche Inflation*, pp. 310–11. For an explanation of "inflation as a method of taxation," see Keynes, *Tract*, pp. 37–53.

7. See Hermann Rupieper, "The Cuno Government and Reparations, 1922–1923: Politics and Economics," *Studies in Contemporary History* 1 (The Hague, 1979): 289.

psychological value to gain acceptance with the exhausted German public. Critical to its success was the fact that at the moment of its appearance, all credit to the government ceased and the Reichsbank stopped discounting the treasury bills that had been the basis of the nation's finances since 1914. At last the printing presses were halted. In addition the government cut its budget with the dismissal of a large number of public sector employees.[8]

In Hamburg, as elsewhere in Germany, the disintegrating currency brought the first serious unemployment since the end of the war. In December 1923 the national figure for the jobless amongst trade union members passed the 25 percent mark, and in Hamburg there were over 55,000 unemployed – only a few less than the worst days of 1919. By the end of 1924 the work force in the Hamburg docks had been reduced by 43 percent from the 1922 level, although the situation was not as bad for white-collar workers.[9] Tensions rose on both sides of industry as trade unions accused employers of tax evasion and of laying off workers through the tactic of closing factories, while employers spoke of the "demogogical and hectoring excesses of union representatives."[10] In any event the hyperinflation seriously weakened the trade unions by destroying their financial basis, and many of their activities had to be abandoned and personnel laid off. With unemployment rising, the initiative passed back to the employers. After the revolution union membership in Hamburg had risen swiftly to nearly 270,000 in 1920. Thereafter there was a steady decline and then a drastic loss of membership in 1923. As rank-and-file hostility to the union

8. Luther, Schacht, Helfferich, and Hilferding all made a contribution to the final form of the stabilization, and most of them wrote rather self-serving accounts of their roles. For example, see Hans Luther, *Feste Mark, Solide Wirtschaft: Rückblick auf die Arbeit der Reichsregierung während der Wintermonate 1923/1924* (Berlin, 1924), esp. pp. 5–12. For the version by Schacht, the *Währungskommissar*, see Hjalmar Schacht, *The Stabilization of the Mark* (New York, 1927). A valuable survey is provided in Karl-Bernhard Netzband and Hans-Peter Widmaier, "Währungsprojekte und Regierungsverhandlungen auf dem Wege zur Rentenmark," in Karl Erich Born, ed., *Moderne deutsche Wirtschaftsgeschichte* (Cologne, 1966), pp. 351–69, esp. p. 354, where Helfferich's *Roggenmark* scheme is shown to have influenced plans for the *Rentenmark*. Also useful is Sommariva and Tulio, *German Macroeconomic History*, pp. 125–32.

9. Friedrich Hesse, *Die deutsche Wirtschaftslage von 1914–1923: Krieg, Geldblähe und Wechsellagen* (Jena, 1938), p. 481; Preller, *Sozialpolitik*, pp. 164–69; *Bericht des hamburgischen Gewerbeaufsichtsamts über die Jahre 1923/1924*, pp. 5–13; HKH 63.D.4.11.

10. "Gegen Arbeitslosigkeit und Unternehmerwillkür," *Die freie Gewerkschaft* (Organ of the Hamburg ADGB), 12 September 1923; HKH 12.B.1.21, Blohm and Voss to HKH, 3 September 1923.

leadership grew, the Communists (KPD) took advantage of the situation by penetrating the Socialist ADGB unions.[11]

For those with jobs the situation was little better. As the advancing inflation produced a critical shortage of bank notes, ever larger denominations were required, and banks found themselves unable to keep abreast of demand. Labor disputes increased sharply as employers confessed that they did not have the money to pay wages. In the first week of August, for example, workers at Blohm und Voss shipyards were on strike because they had not been paid in full at the appointed time, and the Beiersdorf chemical plant was threatened with similar action.[12] Even with the arrival of the *Rentenmark* in November, workers' difficulties did not cease, and when the stable currency was not introduced fast enough at the Dynamit explosives factory, the employers there were understandably anxious about the "dangerous degree of unrest" amongst its workforce.[13]

Unrest was a constant condition amongst the Hamburg working class in 1923, as the potent mixture of rising unemployment and hyperinflation sharpened social tensions in the city. During the course of the year there were eighty-eight strikes and ten lockouts involving nearly 3,000 firms and over 100,000 men. The worst individual dispute was the seamen's strike between May and August that paralyzed the fishing industry and enraged the wholesalers. In a letter to the Chamber of Commerce in the third week of July, the fish wholesaler Alfred von Pustau referred to the striking seamen as "traitors."[14] In the shipyards, strikes at the beginning of August led to lockouts at Blohm und Voss, following which the strike was taken up by the dockworkers. On 13 August the Senate declared a state of emergency, and there were serious clashes between workers and the police. In September and October the situation got worse; according to one police spokesman, "Inflation and misery have radicalized the masses to the extent that they believe only the abolition of the capitalist system will bring relief."[15]

It was in this atmosphere that events reached their climax in the short-lived Communist uprising launched in the last week of October. This abortive venture had its origins more in the deliberations of the KPD national leadership than in any spontaneous

11. Büttner, *Politische Gerechtigkeit*, pp. 160–66.
12. HKH 29.J.3.7, 8 August 1923.
13. StA.H *Haupstaatskasse*, A VI 12, Dynamit AG to Finanzdeputation, 19 November 1923.
14. *Gewerbeaufsichtsamt*, 1923/24. p. 6.
15. Quoted in Eva Hupert, "Der 'Hamburger Aufstand' von 1923," in Arno

fusion of passions amongst the Hamburg working class, but it was symbolic of the heightened sense of class struggle that had permeated relations between workers and employers by the end of the year. As the Reich government moved against the Communist administration in Saxony and Thuringia, the KPD national leadership saw the need for armed struggle, but only in Hamburg did an uprising take place. The reasons for this remain somewhat disputed, but it appears that the Hamburg comrades went ahead against the instructions of the party headquarters, which had called off a national rising after losing the support of the SPD delegates at a meeting in Chemnitz on October 21. Their leaders, Ernst Thälmann and Hugo Urbahns, belonged to the left-wing of the party that saw a general revolution as imminent, and they felt they had the full backing of the city's workers – a fatal miscalculation. The fighting was concentrated in the working-class districts of Barmbek and Schiffsbek, but although the police were surprised, many of the targeted police stations were not taken. Realizing that the action was isolated and unsupported, and in the face of the overwhelming superiority of the authorities in numbers and weapons, Thälmann called it off less than twelve hours after it began. The uprising failed because it was ill-prepared and few of the party members had forewarning. Moreover many striking KPD members in the docks and shipyards were not persuaded to participate.[16]

In the aftermath of the uprising a winter of abject misery approached for the unemployed, and many of them were soon to be queuing at the soup kitchens set up by the Workers' and Soldiers' Council for a ten-pfennig meal and a food parcel for their children.[17] In the first week of November bread cost 7.4 billion marks, despite massive state subsidy. Not only welfare cases, but the majority of the city's population was now starving.[18] A new hard currency was available, but it was hardly in circulation before the "hyenas of the

Herzig et al., eds., *Arbeiter in Hamburg*, p. 485.

16. In the suppression of the uprising 17 police were killed and 24 Communists. In addition a further 61 unarmed people were killed in the process of building barricades and 267 wounded – amongst them many women and children. Ibid., pp. 487–89; Klessmann, *Geschichte*, pp. 538–39. For an evocative account of the Hamburg uprising recorded from the side of the insurgents, see Larissa Reissner, *Hamburg at the Barricades*, trans. Richard Chappell (London, 1977), pp. 41–110. For a reliable overview, see Werner T. Angress, *Stillborn Revolution: The Communist Bid for Power in Germany, 1921–1923* (Princeton, 1964), esp. chap. 13.

17. The food kitchens served half a million hot meals and issued 66,000 children's food parcels during the winter of 1923/24, *Gewerbeaufsichtsamt* 1923/24, p. 49.

18. Büttner, *Politische Gerechtigkeit*, p. 157.

money market," as the *Hamburger Echo* called them, were pressing around those workers with jobs or waiting for their wives outside food stores, tempting them with higher offers to hand over their Hamburg gold marks. The banks were also included in the *Echo*'s scorn. The newspaper reported the case of a man who tried to pay his rent (valued at seventy-six billion marks) in gold marks at his bank:

> The messenger came back and told me that I could pay the sum in gold marks, but that it must be written in paper marks on the slip and that the gold marks would be calculated as seventy billion marks. I calculated the gold marks yesterday against the dollar rate as seventy-six billion and today – when the rate is already substantially higher than yesterday – the bank will only give me seventy billion for the gold marks. Isn't that outrageous! But that isn't the worst of it. The bank will take my gold marks in payment, but it will pay [my landlord] only in paper marks, thus defeating the whole point of the exercise.

Currency profiteers, concluded the *Echo*, were more dangerous than putschists and should be dealt with accordingly by the authorities.[19]

The Artisans

The inflation struck hard at the institutional fabric of Mittelstand enterprise. By April 1923 the Chamber of Industry was facing bankruptcy and was forced to cease publication of the *AIGZ*.[20] Requests for help from individual artisans became increasingly fruitless, although the chamber continued to petition the Hamburg government on their behalf. By this stage any kind of financial rescue operation for artisans tended to come too late. A typical case was that of a small builder who asked for 500 million marks at the end of July. His request was lost in the bureaucracy, and by the time it was eventually processed by the Chamber of Industry, the further depreciation of the mark meant that he needed 2 billion marks for the same purpose.[21] Even pressure in June from the artisans' national body, the Reichsverband des Deutschen Hand-werks, brought no change in policy on price control and the

19. "Tages-Bericht – Das Geschäft mit der Goldmark," *Hamburger Echo*, 5 November 1923.
20. It had unpaid bills, chiefly for fuel deliveries, of over ten million marks. StA.H *Finanzdeputation* IIc 1b 1B3, 1 March 1923; StA.H *Gewerbekammer*, A.13, Bd. 2, Protokolle, 3 August 1923.
21. StA.H *Gewerbekammer*, O.11, Pentzin and Naegeler, 6 August 1923.

Zwangswirtschaft, and those who were dependent on raw materials from abroad found themselves in an increasingly impossible situation as they lacked the vital hard currency with which to buy foreign goods.[22]

In August the Chamber of Industry accepted a state loan for one hundred trillion marks "to help those artisans who, because of the inflation, are no longer able to pay their workers' wages and would otherwise be forced to dismiss them from work." Not for the first time, the private sector in Hamburg had successfully used the threat of increased unemployment to extract funds from the government, but then in August 1923 one hundred trillion marks was hardly sufficient to protect 8,000 workers from redundancy for a single week.[23]

With the mark now virtually valueless, producers, wholesalers, and other larger concerns in Hamburg switched to working in foreign exchange. The use of foreign currency in domestic transactions had actually been forbidden in 1922 by legislation,[24] which had brought a storm of protest from city merchants and dire warnings that Hamburg's vital overseas trade would be crippled by such a restriction. However the storm blew over when it was discovered that the Chamber of Commerce's right to issue certificates for trade in foreign currency was practiced with great liberality. The head of the chamber's banking section, the ubiquitous Max Warburg, took the view that the only control necessary on their distribution was the threat of their withdrawal in cases of abuse.[25]

Artisans and retailers would have dearly liked to participate, but the indulgence of Hamburg's premier business institution did not include them.[26] In theory the Chamber of Retailers was also allowed to issue the coveted foreign exchange certificates, but since retailers' applications required the prior approval of the treasury, and

22. StA.H *Gewerbekammer*, A.13, Bd. 2, Protokolle, Handwerkerabteilung, 1 June 1923.

23. The credit was only good for four weeks and restricted to those artisans with definite orders on their books. StA.H *Finanzdeputation*, IIc,1b.1B3, 27 August 1923.

24. Verordnung gegen die Spekulation in ausländischen Zahlungsmittel, 12 October 1922, HKH 29.K.1.2a. Bd. 1.

25. HKH 29.K.2.5, Letter 4 July 1923. See also Böhm, *Handelskammer*, pp. 229–30.

26. Holtfrerich somewhat exaggerates the degree to which German trade and industry had switched to using foreign exchange before the official stabilization, *Die deutsche Inflation*, p. 330. The Hamburg retailers were certainly excluded from legal participation in this alternative economy.

that was rarely forthcoming, its power in this respect, as in so many others, was strictly limited.[27]

It must be recognized of course that many retailers and artisans ignored the regulations and demanded payment, illegally, in foreign currency. According to one anonymous shopper who provided evidence to the Chamber of Commerce in September 1923, every shop he had visited in the search for a fur coat had sought payment in foreign exchange. In particular, loopholes in the law for foreign customers were exploited to the full, so that any customer who could present himself as foreign was likely to get special treatment.[28] The continued discrimination against the retail trade brought the usual protests from the Chamber of Retailers, but they had no appreciable effect. Even days before the stabilization in November, further laws were being enacted to enforce the continued use of paper marks in a city that was otherwise running a de facto dollar economy.[29]

Some artisans, particularly those working with textiles, priced their goods in notional gold marks on separate lists and converted these prices into paper marks according to the rate of exchange at the time of sale. But they were also obliged to reckon invoices from their suppliers in gold, and this could produce some nasty surprises when the time came to pay the bill.[30] An example from one of the most traditional branches of the artisan economy will illustrate the kind of problems faced in the last weeks of the inflation. At the end of September the smithies' guild received a complaint from the Cab Drivers' Association to the effect that they were charging too much for horseshoes since they had switched to gold mark calculation. The smithies replied accordingly:

> Our supply situation is completely at the mercy of the foreign exchange market, for paper mark reckoning is impossible unless you want to go bust. Our suppliers reckon according to the Hamburg daily exchange rate, while our members are compelled by their standard form contracts

27. Many businessmen actually refused to recognize the currency certificates of the Chamber of Retailers. HKH 29.K.2.15. The chief piece of legislation was the Verordnung auf Grund des Notgesetzes, Maßnahmen gegen die Valutaspekulation, *RGBl.* I 1923, p. 27. For the Chamber of Retailers' response, "Devisenordnung und Einzelhandel," *Der Einzelhandel*, 1 June 1923.

28. HKH 29.K.2.9. Letter from the Kommissar für Devisenerfassung, 14 September 1923.

29. For Chamber of Retailers' protests, HKH 102.1.A.6.20 Detaillistenkammer Vollversammlung, 11 July 1923. The last piece of legislation was the Verordnung gegen Devisenspekulation, 10 November 1923, *RGBl.* I 1923, p. 1084.

30. StA.H *Gewerbekammer*, A.12, Bd. 5, Protokolle, Plenarsitzung 16 October 1923.

to reckon on the Berlin rate, which is always lower. Our sacrifice is compounded by the fact that we ask for payment the day after work is completed, while our suppliers, without exception, demand prepayment.[31]

In September 1923 the chairman of the Chamber of Commerce called for a stable currency to be made available to local retailers, adding that if it was not forthcoming from Berlin, then an establishment would be set up in Hamburg to provide it. This materialized towards the end of October in the form of the Hamburger Bank von 1923, but although some retailers and artisans were able to benefit from the new currency it issued, it was hardly a bank for the little man.[32] Set up under Warburg's guiding hand with the participation of over one hundred commercial banks, some of which were American, it succeeded in introducing a stable currency known as the *hamburgische Verrechnungsmark*. It was not a clearing bank in the sense that anyone with a bundle of paper marks could open an account there in gold marks or some other stable unit of currency.[33] Moreover the bank's clientele was essentially limited to a privileged circle of long-established merchants and other bankers who had acquired foreign exchange during the inflation and who now needed a new institution to protect them through the difficult days of the stabilization ahead. By and large artisans and small retailers were once again excluded.[34]

The Hamburger Bank von 1923 symbolized the survival of the city's commercial elite through the rigors of war and inflation. Indeed there is some irony in the fact that it was able to orchestrate Hamburg's monetary salvation in the same moment as the elected (Social Democratic) government was battling Ernst Thälmann and the Hamburg Communists in the October uprising. The long-awaited appearance of the *Rentenmark* on 15 November 1923 was

31. StA.H *Gewerbekammer*, E.11, Vereinigung selbständiger Schmiedemeister von Hamburg, 3 October 1923.
32. See StA.H *Konsumentenkammer*, XB IV 7 Bd. 4, Vorstandssitzung des Wirtschaftsrats, 13 September 1923. HKH 102.1.A.6.20, Besprechung mit dem Vorstand der Hamburger Bank von 1923, 30 October 1923.
33. For a description of the *Hamburger Bank von 1923*, see Gottfried Klein, *Dokumente zur Geschichte der Handelskammer Hamburg* (Hamburg, 1965), pp. 186–87; Brandt, *Hamburgs Finanzen*, pp. 29–31.
34. See "Zum Begriff der Wertbeständigkeit," *Hamburger Fremdenblatt*, 31 October 1923. For restrictions on accounts with the bank, HKH 29.A.2.6.4. It was not just the small retailers and artisans who were omitted from the bank's magic circle; consumer cooperatives like Produktion were also excluded. StA.H *Hauptstaatskasse* A.VI.12. Konsumentenkammer, 17 November 1923.

merely national confirmation of a trend that was already established in Hamburg. And by Christmas, prices in the city were lower than almost anywhere else in the country.[35]

The Retailers

As French and Belgian troops moved into the Ruhr in January 1923, a wave of patriotic indignation temporarily united retailers, consumers, and suppliers, but as in 1914 it was notably short-lived. By the end of the month the mark had fallen against the U.S. dollar from 7,260 to 49,000, and all thoughts of solidarity were forgotten in a battle of survival. In February there was a final attempt at stabilization, as the Reichsbank intervened in the foreign exchange market with the last of its hard currency reserves. As in March 1920, the retailers were caught with overpriced stock. Despite the best efforts of the *PPS* it was a hopeless task to educate suspicious consumers to the fact that short-term fluctuations in the exchange rate could not be immediately transformed into lower retail values. With the local press antagonistic as usual, even the retailers' own employees were distrustful. In March 1923, for instance, the DHV journal called for a boycott of shops charging excessive prices and even proposed setting up a secret monitoring system to catch offenders amongst the retailers.[36]

Also in March the inflation was officially recognized in tax legislation, something of special concern to both retailers and artisans. Supplements were added to the original tax demand if it had been devalued by the currency depreciation at the time of payment. However this innovation only applied to arrears, and the enormous cost of revenue devaluation during the permitted payment time continued to be borne by the Reich.[37] As with so many aspects of the nation's financial life in 1923, the whole mechanism of tax collection in Germany seized up completely during the year. On the one hand, it was necessary to continuously increase the rates to take account of the inflation; on the other hand, anybody who was in a position to do so took advantage of the situation by delaying his tax payments for as long as possible. Interest was charged on unpaid tax, but it was rarely sufficient to encourage punctuality; in August 1923, for example, it amounted to 400 percent for a fifteen-day delay – just about the same rate at which

35. Götz, *Detaillistenkammer*, p. 68.
36. HKH 102.1.A.6.10, Detaillistenkammer, Vollversammlung 14 March 1923.
37. *RGBl.* 1 (1923), p. 198; Elster, *Von der Mark zur Reichsmark*, p. 204.

the mark depreciated against the U.S. dollar in the latter half of that month.[38]

The situation was aggravated by the resentment of blue- and white-collar workers who were taxed at source and who therefore had no opportunity to delay payment. They accused employers of threatening the government with the closure of their factories – and the unemployment of their workers – instead of paying what they owed.[39] While it is true that in some months over 90 percent of tax revenue came from pay-as-you-earn sources, the imbalance should not be generalized. Taken over a longer period, wage and salary earners – who were in any case increasing as a proportion of the working population – were not paying more than their fair share.[40] In their defense, employers claimed that the Reich taxes were immensely complicated. Moreover the district tax office (Landesfinanzamt Unterelbe) showed no consideration for the fact that the necessary forms often arrived days after the stipulated payment date, a result of the huge backlog of work that the office faced. By October the collection of Reich taxes in Hamburg had been suspended; the ludicrous situation had been reached where the cost of reckoning the taxes exceeded the total revenue to be collected.[41]

The inflation not only destroyed tax revenue, it also had a disastrous effect on savings. The futility of placing one's assets on deposit in a savings bank became universally clear when the rate of currency depreciation exceeded in one week what the bank offered in interest for a whole year. Not everyone was affected of course. Industrialists and merchants brought their money to large commercial banks and expected them to protect its real value by judicious speculation in foreign exchange. But for the proverbial little man – that is, the Mittelstand – this avenue was closed. They placed their savings in the savings bank whose statutes forbade the kind of operations that were the key to the larger banks' survival. In particular the requirement that a substantial part of the savings banks' assets be held in the form of mortgages was a singular

38. The dollar quotation for the mark in the *Hamburgischer Correspondent* on 15 August 1923 (the day Stresemann took over the chancellorship) was 2.9 million. Sixteen days later it was 11.6 million. HKH 21.A.2.5–7.

39. The trade unions had greeted the appointment of Hilferding as Stresemann's finance minister and his attempts to catch the recalcitrant capitalist tax dodgers. "Gegen die Steuer- und Betriebssabotage des Unternehmertums," *Hamburger Echo*, 25 August 1923.

40. See Brandt's figures, *Hamburgs Finanzen*, p. 58.

41. StA.H *Steuerverwaltung*, II.A2.a, Landesfinanzamt Unterelbe, 12 October 1923.

Table 15. Trading at the Hamburger Sparkasse von 1827, 1913–1925

Year	Savings books	Deposits	Total savings (in marks)	Average savings per book (in marks)
1913	287,765	618,261	217,261,000	755
1914	304,936	589,270	227,755,000	747
1915	321,109	533,601	210,141,000	654
1916	334,066	548,952	216,287,000	647
1917	354,845	640,870	250,418,000	705
1918	384,638	790,843	327,762,000	852
1919	404,920	669,409	381,623,000	942
1920	419,775	591,654	473,644,000	1,128
1921	428,405	542,970	528,980,000	1,234
1922	428,802	523,098	1,287,573,000	3,002
1923[1]	5,250		250,000	48
1924	23,716		7,600,000	320
1925	51,847		26,000,000	501

1. Annuities deposited in the last weeks of the year.
Source: *Jahresbericht der Hamburger Sparkasse von 1827* (1925).

disadvantage. The result was that the savings banks were powerless to shield customers' savings from the "frightening violence of the inflation."[42]

The scale of this violence is shown in Table 15 in the trading figures of one of the principal Hamburg institutions, the Hamburger Sparkasse von 1827. Although the total amount of savings (in marks) increased between 1918 and 1922, the number of individual deposits declined steadily, and there was no appreciable rise in savings books after 1921. This suggests that the increase in total savings was almost entirely a function of the currency depreciation rather than a greater willingness to save.[43]

Indeed it is somewhat surprising that with the resumption in the inflationary spiral after 1921, there was any willingness to save at all. The 1827er, as it was known, pointed to the lifting in 1919 of the laws guaranteeing bank secrecy as the cause for the fall in

42. Ernst Samhaber, *125 Jahre Hamburger Sparkasse von 1827* (Hamburg, 1952), p. 26; see also Oskar Kaven, *Die Hamburger Sparkasse von 1827 in den Jahren 1892 bis 1925* (Hamburg, 1927), p. 78.
43. HKH 29.H.1.7. *Jahresberichte der Hamburger Sparkasse von 1827* (1921–1925).

savings.[44] "Great sums have been withdrawn from circulation and are not placed with the savings banks," and it warned that "only when this money comes out of concealment and the income opportunities of the savings banks are enlarged will we be able to offer better rates of interest." In the final analysis the suspension of bank secrecy, although it may have been of concern to people wishing to evade taxation, was unlikely to have been a major discouragement to saving by 1922. That year the 1827er paid an interest of 17.8 million marks, or 1.4 percent of the total it had on deposit, a miserable figure when one considers that the dollar rate for the German mark depreciated during that year somewhere in the order of 4,000 percent (Table 12).[45]

More remarkable than the destruction of savings by the inflation was the willingness of people to continue saving in spite of it. While the fall in deposits between 1919 and 1922 is noteworthy, it is surely extraordinary that over a half million deposits were still made in each of those four years; compelling testimony to the deep-rooted nature of the savings ethic in German society, particularly amongst the savings banks' chief clientele in the Mittelstand.

The White-Collar Workers

The practice of saving was a defining feature that propagandists tried hard to establish for the Mittelstand. For white-collar employees it was publicized as a characteristic that set them apart from the workers; they saved in order to better themselves. However saving was not a wholly inelastic white-collar attribute, and when the DHV drew attention to the erosion of the savings amongst its members in August 1921, it was using the information to support a pay claim rather than make an ideological point. The fall in savings bank deposits was presented as evidence that white-collar workers were using up their savings to maintain their living standards.[46]

For white-collar workers the busiest employment at this time was probably in the banks. The inflation had made accounting procedures so difficult by June 1923 that the last three digits of any figure – inevitably zeros – were no longer entered in cash books.

---

44. Samhaber, *125 Jahre*, p. 30.
45. HKH 21.A.2.7., 30 March 1921; see also Kaven, *1892 bis 1925*, p. 75.
46. *DHW*, 10 August 1921. Sandra Coyner makes the point that saving amongst white-collar workers in the private sector was relatively elastic, although less so amongst civil servants, in her *Class Patterns of Family Income and Expenditure during the Weimar Republic* (Diss., Rutgers University, 1977), p. 166.

Adding machines and other mechanical calculators were completely defeated by the proliferation of figures, and the reckoning of pfennigs vanished completely.[47] The frenzied conditions produced a tremendous demand for clerks in all the financial and insurance institutions. In August the Hamburg banks had so much work that they were forced to close completely on Tuesdays and Thursdays, an extremely unpopular move that simply made business on the remaining three weekdays even more chaotic. Complaints poured in, with one employer, the Norddeutsche Chemische Werke, reckoning that it was losing 1 percent in revenue by not being able to settle its accounts on two days of the week.[48] By October banks were refusing to handle any sum below the equivalent of two pounds sterling and were rounding up every figure to the nearest million. Small accounts were unceremoniously closed and the balance returned to the holder in the form of a postage stamp. "Customers have to wait three days for their marks, while the banks sell foreign exchange," protested one member to the Chamber of Commerce. "It's a scandal."[49]

The banks were so desperate for staff that practically no qualifications were sought and virtually everyone who applied for a job, got one. It is claimed that bank clerks were better insulated against the vagaries of the inflation because of the ease with which they could speculate in foreign exchange.[50] This may have been true for 1923, but not before. In 1919 GdA members who were working in banks resorted to strike action over a pay claim, and two years later they were threatening to do it again.[51] Reports that bank staff were well-off during the inflation probably stem from the fact that they worked many hours of overtime – the eight hour day restrictions being lifted in the case of banks. Of the 10,412 white-collar workers in Hamburg who worked an average of 352 hours overtime in 1923, over 75 percent were employed in banks.[52]

Determining living standards amongst white-collar workers during 1923 is fraught with dangers, since the only way to judge the real value of salaries is to set them against cost-of-living

---

47. HKH 29.J.2.20, Markt and Co. 29 June 1923.

48. HKH 29.A.4.2.1, Correspondence from the Norddeutsche Bank and Arbeitgeberverband Hamburg und Altona, 21 August 1923, 28 August 1923.

49. HKH 29.A.3.2.7, Bornefeld and Co. 1 October 1923.

50. Carl Dreyfuß, *Beruf und Ideologie der Angestellten* (Munich, 1933), pp. 111–12.

51. *Der Handelstand* (Organ of the '58er Verein), September 1919; *GDA*, 1 November 1921.

52. *Bericht des hamburgischen Gewerbeaufsichtsamts, 1923 und 1924* (Hamburg, 1925). p. 35.

Table 16. Index of HHA Salary Increments and the Cost of Living, 1923 (1913–14 = 1)

	Reich cost-of-living index for Hamburg	Unskilled labor[1]	Drivers[2]	Class B clerks[3]	Class F personnel[4]
1913–14	1.0	1.0	1.0	1.0	1.0
1923					
January	**1052.0**[5]	900.0	525.1	436.0	296.5
March	2419.0	**3216.0**	1907.0	1595.0	1087.0
May	3513.0	**3728.0**	2256.0	1899.0	1263.0
June	**7470.0**	5777.0	3559.0	2943.0	2050.0
July	**27727.0**	18000.0	11634.0	10703.0	7297.0
August	**306340.0**	124444.0	76651.0	66999.0	56428.0
September	**6171703.0**	3600000.0	2200000.0	1900000.0	1600000.0

1. 1914 wage of 0.45 marks per hour.
2. 1914 wage of 155 marks per month.
3. 1914 salary of 220 marks per month.
4. 1914 salary of 400 marks per month.
5. Bold figures show the highest rate of increase.
Source: Wirtschaft und Statistik (1924): 146; see also Table 12.

indexes, and these were never wholly reliable. However it is possible to get a good indication from the HHA salary index and the cost-of-living figures prepared by the Reich statistical office for Hamburg. In Table 16 data from the HHA index for 1923 (Table 12) is presented with the Reich cost-of-living index. The latter had been subject to frequent changes in baseline since its introduction in February 1920, but from the beginning of 1923 the index base was taken to be 1913/14 = 1.

The groups involved are two clerical grades, class B and the higher class F, and two blue-collar positions, unskilled laborers and drivers. The latter are included in the analysis to illustrate the typical manner in which the inflation narrowed wage and salary differentials between skilled and unskilled, blue-collar and white-collar workers. While the cost of living had increased by a factor of over one thousand between the 1913/14 base and January 1923, the salaries and wages of the four groups had risen by progressively lesser degrees ranging from nine hundred for the unskilled laborer to under three hundred for the higher grade white-collar worker. The unskilled laborer's wage had kept up reasonably well with the inflation, even surpassing it briefly in the period of momentary stabilization in the spring of 1923. By contrast the class F personnel, who belonged to the bottom rung of the higher officials' scale (*Oberbeamte*), had lost up to 70 percent of their 1914 purchasing power by January 1923 and hardly improved on their position during the rest of the year.

These tentative results seem to concur with Holtfrerich's conclusion that "the dependent [unselbständig] and professional urban Mittelstand experienced a fundamental deterioration in its standard of living" in the postwar years. "Particularly marked were the real income losses that middle-class families experienced in the periods from the last year of the war until the spring of 1920 and from the beginning of the hyperinflation in mid-1922."[53] However of greater importance than the employee's pay and conditions was whether or not he kept his job, and here it seems the white-collar worker had a genuine advantage over his blue-collar colleague. Hamburg data on the closure of firms between 1921 and 1923 reveals that the latter suffered to a disproportionately greater degree from unemployment during those years. Of sixty-three companies in Hamburg that were compelled to cease trading either through bankruptcy or temporary insolvency, 54 percent of the 8,545 blue-collar workers involved were laid off, while amongst the 946 white-collar employees less than 10 percent lost their positions.[54]

Many employers suspended their business for only a few months during the inflation, and they may have felt that blue-collar workers could be more easily rehired when trading resumed than white-collar employees who had a familiarity with the firm gained over many years of service. In a sense it was the last echo of the old loyalty that had existed between the clerks of the prewar years and their employers. The sharp rise in the number of closures in 1923 brought a corresponding increase in the number of redundancies. For the workers this would have meant a great struggle to provide for the families on their last wage packet, while white-collar employees were largely spared this misfortune.

By the summer of 1923 Hamburg employers were complaining of their workers' demanding salaries in millions, which was a meaningless jibe since a million marks did not buy very much by this stage of the inflation. Local retail prices changed so often that it is difficult to present an accurate picture of white-collar purchasing

53. Holtfrerich, *Die deutsche Inflation*, p. 260.
54. StA.H *Demobilmachungskommissar*, 199, Statistik der Betriebsabbrüche und Stillegungen.

power; moreover the wide discrepancy between the mark's exchange value and its internal purchasing power makes any calculations deceptive. A senior engineer at the HEW, for example, earned 8.4 million marks for the month of July 1923; this sum was hardly worth a single pound sterling, yet it could still have been exchanged at that time for nearly three thousand kilos of brown coal briquettes at Hamburg prices.[55]

As the frequency of pay awards increased in 1923, the pendulum of advantage swung back and forth between employer and employee. But generally the clumsy price-indexing system upon which claims were met was never swift enough, and there were always a vital few days between its publication and the next installment of the employee's salary during which time prices rose further. Only when gold-rate payment took over in October did some stability return, and then it often came at a premium, in retailing, for instance, the DHV was forced to concede a deduction from the employee's salary if it was paid in gold marks.[56]

In the last weeks before the stabilization, U.S. dollars were joined by emergency money as an alternative currency. Most of it was printed locally, but never in large enough quantities to meet demand. Bank note shortages, or course, had been a recurring feature of the inflation, starting in October 1918, when the Hamburg finance deputation had been compelled to print seventy million marks of emergency money. In the last months of 1923, however, the crisis was of epic proportions, and it was aggravated by the total cessation of check and bank transfer traffic. Because of the so-called *Reibungsverluste* – losses sustained because of the currency depreciation between the presentation of a check and the receipt of the money – everybody demanded cash.[57]

The Civil Servants

1923 was no worse for civil servants, from the point of view of living standards, than earlier stages of the inflation. In fact the ten millionfold rise in the Hamburg cost-of-living index during the

55. HKH 24.D.2.2, Die einzelnen monatlichen Kohlenpreise in Hamburg.
56. This was understandable since the retailers themselves were forbidden from using gold prices until November. "Goldgehälter für Kaufmannsgehilfen," *DKWR* (Hamburg, December 1923).
57. Lippmann, *Mein Leben*, p. 318. For the reaction of employers to the bank note shortage, HKH 29.J.3.7. For the efforts of the Hamburg treasury, StA.H *Hauptstaatskasse*, A VI.10. Bd. 2.

year was actually exceeded by the rise in civil servants' real income (Table 13).

At the beginning of the year quarterly payment in advance was introduced for all civil servants in Hamburg. The new system, disputed at such length in the Civil Service Council the previous summer, was now accepted without question. In March, as the Reich government made its last abortive attempt at stabilization, the few weeks of steady exchange rates were used as pretext for rejecting further pay claims that might trigger a new bout of inflation.[58] But as the mark recommenced its fall in May and further concessions on pay became inevitable, civil servants faced new hostility from the general public. Mutual enmities that had smoldered within the fabric of German society since 1914 periodically burst into flame as the inflation gathered pace. With the unfolding disaster of hyperinflation, scapegoats were sought everywhere, and civil servants, like the retailers, were a particularly obvious target for attack. Many Germans saw them as nothing more than a proliferating bureaucracy that was making the government's financial problems worse, and their salaries-in-advance were cited as a possible contributor to the inflation itself. The civil servants naturally rejected any attempt to present their mode of payment as a cause of the inflation; it not only was a source of social distinction, but was now of real practical value and had to be protected at all costs. Their defense consisted of attacks on other groups, particularly those merchants and artisans of the commercial Mittelstand who complained of starvation, but were to be seen "frequenting the best restaurants and attending the theater wearing fine clothes and jewelry."[59]

With the change of government in August, the Reich finance portfolio passed briefly to the Social Democrat Rudolf Hilferding. He made it clear to the states that in view of the grave financial crisis facing the country, all possible savings would have to be made and all possible revenue raised. Hamburg's financial representative to Berlin, Leo Lippmann, explained that the city-state could not meet its obligations, in particular the salaries of civil servants, and needed a greater portion of Reich revenue to survive. At this stage Hamburg was dependent on expensive imported English coal for fuel because the Franco-Belgian occupation had shut off supplies from the Ruhr. But it was difficult to make headway against the competing demands of the other, especially

58. StA.H *Beamtenrat*, 17. Bd. 4, Vollsitzung, 21 March 1923.
59. "Steigende Not!" *DB*, 15 June 1923.

southern, states where the prevailing view seemed to be that civil servants' salary demands should be resisted. Saxony, for instance, complained about the civil servants' quarterly payment in advance and suggested that it encouraged them to speculate on the stock market.[60]

In September 1923 the Civil Service Council received a resolution from colleagues in Cologne calling for joint action against hostile press commentary about civil servants. The government was called upon to tackle what the civil servants considered the real injustices and likely causes of inflation: black marketeers, high industrial profits, and inefficient taxation. It was noted that it was the very people who "benefited from the inflation – merchants, bankers, and farmers – who are now complaining about civil servants' salaries."[61]

The public outburst against the civil servants was a typical and temporary manifestation of inflation hysteria, but it allowed the Reich government to proceed with sweeping staff reductions, thereby combining a financial necessity with the popular will.[62] Proposals had existed to reduce the size of the civil service since 1922, and in Hamburg the probusiness *Hamburgischer Correspondent* had strongly urged cutbacks in the ranks of city officialdom.[63] However it was not until October 1923 that actual legislation was pushed through, and it was between then and April 1924 that large numbers of staff were laid off. Reductions in the Reich civil service amounted to about 16 percent with the level reaching 50 percent among nontenured employees.[64]

Table 17 shows the sudden rise in the number of nontenured employees in the years between 1914 and 1920, which can be explained largely by the growth in government activity in the war and immediate post-War years. The reason why they were chosen to bear the brunt of the staff reductions in 1923 and 1924 was partly their lack of tenure rights and partly the lack of solidarity with the civil servants.[65] The antipathy of the civil servants for the em-

60. StA.H *Senatskommission für die Angelegenheiten der Staatsarbeiter*, II.23.Mb.135, Report by Lippmann, 27 August 1923.

61. "Tagespresse und Beamtenschaft," *DB*, 15 September 1923; StA.H *Beamtenrat*, 3, 4 September 1923.

62. A statistical analysis of the 1923 civil servant redundancies and their accompanying political dimensions are presented in Kunz, *Civil Servants*, on pp. 53–58 and 370–77 respectively.

63. For example, "Lex Diestel: Gedanken zum Hamburger Etat," *Hamburgischer Correspondent*, 21 February 1922.

64. *RGBl.* (1923) I. pp. 999–1010. See also W. Burgdörfer, "Tatsachen und Zahlen zum Behördenabbau," *Allgemeines statistisches Archiv* 14 (1923/1924): 247.

65. For the conflict between tenured and nontenured public employees over the

Table 17. Number of Civil Servants and State Employees in Hamburg, 1914–1924

	Civil servants	State employees	Total
May 1914	13,859	7,144	21,003
May 1920	14,738	14,767	29,505
October 1923	15,190	12,238	27,428
April 1924	13,417	9,464	22,881

Source: Hamburgisches statistisches Jahrbuch (1925): 226–27.

ployees was based apparently upon the perception of them as interlopers, bent on penetrating the ranks of the career civil service. They occupied inferior positions, yet threatened to replace the tenured staff. Moreover the state employees (*Staatsangestellte*) were better organized than the civil servants and portrayed by their leaders as the "enemies of bureaucracy" and the torchbearers of modern methods in public administration.[66] The inflation, by creating a need for savings in the public sector, rendered the two sides irreconcilable. The dismissal of the nontenured staff at the Hamburg district tax office was typical of the way in which their vulnerability was exploited. Despite their acknowledged expertise in taxation procedures, they were replaced by underutilized, but tenured, civil servants from the transport department. The *Correspondent*, which had always been in favor of fewer and more efficient staff in the public service, was disgusted at the move and actually suggested that the director of the tax office favored tenured civil servants over nontenured employees because they were more likely to turn a blind eye to the sloppy management of the city's finances.[67] The split between the civil servants and the nontenured staff was a sad example of how the terminal crisis of the inflation produced schisms within the white-collar labor force, possibly to the ultimate detriment of Weimar democracy.

The last three months before the stabilization were confusing for

---

layoffs, see Andreas Kunz's study, "Stand versus Klasse: Beamtenschaft und Gewerkschaften im Konflikt um den Personalabbau, 1923/1924," *Geschichte und Gesellschaft* 8 (1982): 55–86.

66. Speier, *Die Angestellten*, p. 42.

67. "Massenentlassungen bei den Finanzämtern," *Hamburgischer Correspondent*, 2 August 1923.

all salary earners, but especially for civil servants. With the emphasis entirely on the method of payment, claims for more money were hardly challenged by the government; the question was simply, How could the claim be paid and would it be on time? Bank account holders – common among civil servants – abandoned bank transfers and joined the queues for cash payment, as the traffic between banks took vital days during which salaries were further depreciated. Compensation payments became the norm for staff who did not receive their salaries punctually.[68]

From October 1923 onwards, payment in notional gold marks became general practice in Hamburg's commercial life. Yet while other salary earners received some kind of stable-value currency, civil servants found themselves left behind by developments and were obliged to point out to the Senate that they could not be expected to pay their bills in gold if they were not paid in gold.[69] The most astonishing example of Hamburg emergency money were the tokens issued by the government to its own civil servants, against which local retailers were expected to give credit. The absurdity of asking anyone to give credit in the autumn of 1923 produced sympathy for the retailers even in the Communist press.[70] Only after the stabilization had been set in motion did the civil servants receive an entirely new gold-based salary scale. In real terms it was worth approximately half their prewar earnings, and this gave them cause to worry that their pay would be stabilized at this lower level.[71] However by the second half of 1924, their salaries had risen to a point higher than at any time since 1914 and their decade-long battle with the cost of living seemed to be behind them.

The House Owners

For the house owners, the chaotic year of 1923 marked the nadir for real rental values, but a rapid recovery followed in the last three months as vital rent surcharges were granted more frequently and with less opposition. In February an SPD deputy in the Citizens' Assembly noted that Hamburg had the lowest rents of the seven largest German cities and recommended their immediate increase

68. "Aufwertung verspätet ausgezahlter Bezüge," *DB*, 1 September 1923; StA.H *Beamtenrat*, 77, Aktennotiz, 20 August 1923.
69. StA.H *Beamtenrat*, 19. Bd. 1, Vorstandssitzung, 16 October 1923.
70. "Der Staat hat kein Geld, die Kleinhändler sollen pumpen," *Hamburger Volkszeitung*, 31 July 1923.
71. StA.H *Beamtenrat*, 17. Bd. 4, Vollsitzung, 9 December 1923.

to prevent further deterioration to the city's housing fabric. He suggested that a commission be formed, with the participation of tenants, to determine how high the surcharges could be set. The tenants would not mind paying more as long as they had a share in determining how it was spent. The Socialists, it seems, were at last coming to the landlords' assistance. Indeed so far had concern about deterioration of the city's housing stock progressed in the local community that when a Communist deputy complained that tenants were more important than houses, the whole Citizens' Assembly rose in unison against him.[72]

To match the changing attitude in Hamburg government circles, a new realism was also evident in Berlin, where Cuno was now leading the government. In April the responsible minister told the states that "low surcharges cannot be justified on the grounds that certain groups in the population find it hard to pay their rent. Such cases will simply become factors in wage negotiation, and the welfare service can take care of people in real difficulty. The main thing is that the surcharge level be determined by economic criteria."[73]

After February, when real rent values barely exceeded 0.1 percent of the 1914 level, surcharges were raised monthly, but like nearly every financial contract in Germany at that time, the surcharges were increased neither far nor fast enough. Only in October did the tide turn. As Table 18 shows, that was the beginning of a strong and lasting recovery in real rent values, so much so that when in November the GVH proclaimed, "It is five to twelve and soon the gagged house owners will rebel against the glaring injustice of rent control," their protest already sounded less than convincing.[74] By December rents had risen to 20 percent of prewar values, and they continued to rise throughout 1924, although not with the anticipated rapidity.[75] It was not long before the old stories of profiteering landlords began to reappear in the Hamburg press. In January 1924, for example, a landlord had raised the rent of an attic, renovated with state funds in 1918, from three hundred to seven hundred *Rentenmark* per year; two months later he was

72. "Festsetzung der Mieten," *Hamburger Fremdenblatt*, 8 February 1923.
73. StA.H *Wohnungsamt*, 27. Reichsarbeitsminister, 16 April 1923.
74. "Notschrei der Grundeigentümer!" *HGZ*, 2 November 1923.
75. It was intended that rents regain their 1914 values by October 1924; in fact they did not reach this level until 1927. StA.H *Wohnungsamt*, 17. Reichsfinanzminister 3. Bk.9762, 24 November 1923; also Witt, *Inflation, Wohnungszwangswirtschaft*, pp. 397–98.

Table 18. Nominal and Real Value of Monthly Rents in Hamburg: Index of Increases, 1919–1923 (1914 = 100)[1]

	Paper marks[2]	Gold marks[3]
July 1914	100.00	100.00
January 1919	100.00	52.82
March	100.00	41.65
June	100.00	30.13
September	100.00	19.80
December	100.00	9.96
January 1920	100.00	8.64
March	100.00	4.20
April	120.00	6.96
June	120.00	12.84
September	130.00	11.04
December	130.00	7.92
January 1921	130.00	7.44
March	130.00	9.00
April	165.00	11.04
June	165.00	10.92
September	165.00	8.16
December	165.00	3.60
January 1922	165.00	3.72
March	165.00	3.00
April	255.00	3.60
June	255.00	3.96
September	360.00	1.20
December	1,502.00	0.84
January 1923	1,502.00	0.84
February	1,502.00	0.12
March	9,511.00	1.80
April	12,000.00	2.40
May	15,720.00	2.16
June	22,406.00	1.20
July	51,600.00	1.44
August	199,800.00	0.72
September	3,964,754.00	1.56
October	300,000,000.00	5.16
November	6,063,600,900,000.00	11.88
December	20,024,009,000,000.00	20.05

1. Does not include Housing Subsidy Levy (*Wohnungsbauabgabe*) or surcharges for administration and repairs.

2. Permitted monthly rent of apartment based on notional prewar rate of 8.33 marks (100 marks annually).

3. Gold marks calculated according to the official dollar rate at the beginning of each month.

Source: *Hamburgische statistische Monatsberichte*, Special Issue 3 (June 1924): 118–19.

Table 19. Changes in Land Ownership in Hamburg, 1907–1926 (Voluntary Sales)

1907	2,115	1917	683
1908	1,972	1918	1,692
1909	2,134	1919	4,016
1910	2,112	1920	4,238
1911	1,920	1921	2,432
1912	1,666	1922	3,926
1913	1,405	1923	4,942
1914	1,222	1924	2,375
1915	415	1925	1,911
1916	364	1926	1,276

Source: *Hamburgisches statistisches Jahrbuch* (1928/29): 109.

convicted and given fourteen days imprisonment and a six hundred mark fine by the profiteering court.[76]

One key to understanding the house owners' situation is the movement of house sales. The data in Table 19, covering the twenty-year period from 1907 to 1926, reveal that annual voluntary land sales averaged about two thousand before 1913, but sunk rapidly during the war years. In 1918 there was a recovery, and in 1919 sales rose to unprecedented heights. This suggests that falling rents induced landlords to sell their properties, quite possibly to foreigners who were less interested in income than capital appreciation. The evidence that foreigners were active in the Hamburg housing market in 1919 and 1920 is strong.[77] Because the mark's internal purchasing power at this stage was a great deal more than its external value, foreigners were able to offer temptingly large sums for Hamburg real estate. The GVH warned that German properties would be totally bought up by foreigners, in the same manner as they were buying up German retail goods, unless

76. "Ein wucherischer Hausbesitzer," *Hamburger Fremdenblatt*, 19 March 1924.
77. StA.H *Senat*, Conv.1, Grundbuchamt, Abt.1, 28 February 1920; Senatkommission für die Justizverwaltung, 18 March 1920.

controlling legislation was introduced to stop them.[78]

It is likely that many foreign buyers were speculating on a stabilization of the mark, and their gamble may have appeared successful after March 1920 when it seemed at hand. For the house owners who were selling, the anticipation of a permanent improvement in the economy would have led some to reinvest the proceeds from their sales in the expanding stock market or perhaps into a small business: anything in fact that promised a better income than the rent-controlled housing market. But in 1921 the inflation returned and a pessimistic atmosphere developed prior to the introduction of the *RMG*. Landlords saw little sense now in making paper profits from house sales if the inflation was to continue. In addition the increase in the rate of capital gains tax at this point would have been a further disincentive to sell.[79]

This new caution might have been expected to last until the final stabilization, but in 1922 and particularly in 1923, a new speculative fever gripped the housing market. Properties started to change hands swiftly, and prices rose precipitously, doubling and even tripling in a matter of days.[80] Who the buyers and sellers were in this bubble is difficult to establish, although a new profiteering element was clearly involved because speculation on any future stabilization of the mark was now widespread. The verdict of Eulenburg, for the whole nation, was that the houses went to "potent and highly capitalized people."[81] This broadly defined category may have included members of the Mittelstand, although such a conclusion would have been hotly denied by the GVH. "The fact that properties yield no income because of rent control," argued its main journal, "is of no concern to these new buyers. They make their living from other enterprises and buy houses merely as a haven for their capital. . . . As usual the government seeks to appease the workers [with the *RMG*] and only succeeds in playing into the hands of big capitalists."[82]

With the deterrent of capital gains tax neutralized by the inflation, buyers were able to acquire properties from financially exhausted landlords, sell them again after a minimal refurbishment,

78. "Ausland und Grundeigentum," *HGZ*, 28 November 1919.
79. Lippmann, *Mein Leben*, p. 330.
80. Verein Hamburger Hausmakler, e.V., *Hausmakler und Grundeigentum in Hamburg: Eine Denkschrift zum 50-jährigen Bestehen des Vereins Hamburger Hausmakler* (Hamburg, 1947), p. 44.
81. Eulenburg, "Die sozialen Wirkungen," p. 774.
82. "Grundeigentum und Geldentwertung," *HGZ*, 16 June 1922; also, "Die Belastung des hamburgischen Grundeigentums," *HGZ*, 23 June 1923.

and invest the paper profits in further house purchases. For those house owners who were also retailers, selling on the boom market of 1922/23 may have been the only way to stay in business. With price control cutting their earnings and the main credit institutions closed to them, realizing their assets was the only means of raising the cash needed to buy more stock.[83]

The high housing sales figures for 1922 and 1923 would also suggest that some properties were changing hands several times in the course of the year. But even allowing for this possibility, it is obvious that many embittered landlords parted company with their houses because of rent control. Despite the legal clarification provided by the *RMG*, they still spent long hours at the *MEA* resolving differences with individual tenants and often emerged feeling cheated by the system and the inflation. Their properties, once the foundation of a prosperous existence and an influential position in Hamburg society, were now nothing but a crippling burden.

83. Hauschild-Thiessen, *150 Jahre*, p. 269.

7

Aftermath, 1924–1925

> I have become a philosopher; that is
> the only way of preserving one's
> pleasure in life, one's appetite and
> sense of humour – some of the few
> things that are not taxed. The In-
> flation was such a disaster that now
> one has managed through a few des-
> perate somersaults to attain some
> respite . . . we shall probably not
> again fall into that catastrophe. There
> will nonetheless still be considerable
> convalescent pains before we even
> approximately manage to put our
> economic house in order.
> —Max M. Warburg, December 1923[1]

In November 1918 the future of capitalism in Germany did not appear promising. Workers' and Soldiers' Councils appeared to have
assumed power, and a socialist society seemed to be in the making.
But as has so often been the case, capitalism proved to be resistant
to revolutionary upheaval. Instead of the dictatorship of the proletariat, the Germans got Berlin-style parliamentarianism, behind
which the old conservative elite had merely retreated for a while.

The inflation that raged with varying intensity for Weimar's first
five years effectively concealed the limits to the redistribution of
wealth within German society. As long as they were making
profits from the inflation, industrialists were quite willing to meet
the trade unions' claims for higher wages and allow the workers to
think that the revolution had brought lasting economic benefits.

---

1. Warburg to Carl H. Henriques, 30 December 1923. Quoted in E. Rosenbaum
and A.J. Sherman, *M.M. Warburg & Co., 1798–1938: Merchant Bankers of Hamburg*
(London, 1979), p. 132.

The stabilization was to bring them sharply down to earth. By 1924, if not late 1923, it was clear that big business was the principal winner in the inflation. Industries that had been threatened with nationalization in 1919 and 1920 were now safe in private hands and actually being courted by a government anxious to increase production. The much detested eight-hour day was suspended, and rising unemployment gave further strength to the factory owner's arm. Although another decade of battles with organized labor remained, the bourgeois counterrevolution had already triumphed. What is more, the stabilization marked another shift in the corporatist power structure. From 1924 and at least until the return of the Social Democrats to power in 1928, the Weimar governments promoted the interests of industry at the expense not only of the Mittelstand, but also of the working class, and it was upon the workers' shoulders that the main burden of reparations fell now that stabilized monetary conditions were restored.[2]

Since Gustav Stresemann's administration had collapsed in November 1923, Wilhelm Marx now led the government, with Stresemann's finance minister, Hans Luther, continuing in office. It was Luther who now moved to the center of the stage, forcing through the Reichstag in the spring of 1924 a major program of tax increases and spending cuts in the form of emergency decrees.[3] The framework of the stabilization was in place, but the cost of cementing it was to be heavy. Unemployment, which had risen sharply even before the end of 1923, remained high throughout 1924. Bankruptcies, which had become rare occurrences during the inflation, returned in epidemic proportions as Luther's credit squeeze was applied as part of the stabilization plan. And creditors, expecting restitution for their staggering losses, were left almost empty-handed. They were rarely offered more than 15 percent of the prewar value of their losses by the government, which as the greatest single debtor in the land, had little to gain by helping them. Their treatment was considered scandalously unjust in many quarters and was soon to become a major political issue.[4]

2. This view is strongly represented in Claus-Dieter Krohn, *Stabilisierung und ökonomische Interessen: Die Finanzpolitik des Deutschen Reichs, 1923–1927* (Düsseldorf, 1974), but also is in evidence in Maier, *Recasting* and Feldman, *Iron and Steel.*

3. The use of emergency powers was provided for in Article 48 of the Weimar constitution. For Luther's account, see *Feste Mark*, pp. 5–12.

4. Holtfrerich, *Die deutsche Inflation*, p. 317.

Artisans and Retailers

As the figures in Table 5 confirm, the number of artisans in Hamburg declined between 1907 and 1925. Some would have been shaken out by the rigors of the inflation and the severe credit restrictions of the stabilization period, but the trend to fewer small enterprises was already strong before 1914, and it is improbable that this could have been reversed even in the absence of the war and inflation. Moreover certain trades were already threatened by the headlong modernization of the economy before 1914; the skills of smithies and shoemakers, for example, were bound to become increasingly redundant in the twentieth century. By contrast those trades that had grown with the development of industrial society, such as printing, photography, hairdressing, and electrical repair work, were expanding even during the inflation, according to both the 1925 census figures and the 1930 survey report (*Enquete Bericht*) on the Hamburg artisan economy.[5] One can conclude, therefore, that the inflation did not bring about any wholesale destruction of the artisan community, but rather accelerated the decline of those crafts that were already at risk in the modern world.

For the remaining crafts, the stabilized conditions of the mid-1920s were to offer satisfactory prospects. According to one estimate there was a steady growth in artisan sales in Germany from RM 13.2 billion in 1924 to RM 20.7 billion in 1928.[6] Of course there was a certain degree of price inflation during these four years, and these figures may overstate the recovery to some degree, but nonetheless they indicate a definite upward trend. Another gauge of Mittelstand welfare, the rate of saving, also suggests fairly swift improvement in 1924. As we have seen, the inflation wiped out savings to an extraordinary degree, but the urge to save money was seemingly fundamental, and even more extraordinary was the speed with which it was resumed after the stabilization. In Table 15 the records of the 1827er show that even in the last weeks of 1923 deposits at the savings bank were being built up in *Rentenmark*, and in 1924 there was a "spectacular recovery with many small sums coming from the broadest sections of the community."[7] If the savings bank deposit rate is taken as a barometer of small business

5. *Enquete Bericht*, pp. 20, 79 passim.
6. Based on an estimation of total sales in thirty artisan branches. G. Kaiser, "Umsatzentwicklung, Umsatz je Person und Umschlagsgeschwindigkeit in Handwerk und Kleingewerbe (1924–1928)," *Das Deutsche Handwerksblatt* 2 (1930): 28.
7. *Jahresbericht*, 1924. Other savings banks, including that of the Produktion cooperative, also reported a strong savings revival. Lippmann, *Mein Leben*, p. 370.

Aftermath, 1924–1925

Table 20. Bankruptcy Statistics in Hamburg and Germany, 1913–1924

	Hamburg		Germany	
	Total	Index	Total	Index
1913	311	100	12,756	100
1920	127	41	2,124	17
1921	232	74	4,074	32
1922	129	41	1,703	13
1923	54	17	505	4
1924	315	101	7,842	61

Source: Compiled from *Vierteljahrshefte zur Statistik des Deutschen Reichs, 1913–1924*, 34, p. 1 (1925). Hamburg's bankruptcy trend is noticeably shallower than at the national level. Various explanations can be offered for this peculiarity, but the key probably lies in the preponderance of trade and transport in the local economy, which made it more susceptible to the negative influence of extraneous factors such as the goodwill of foreign trading partners.

activity, then the figures at the 1827er suggest that there were strong signs of life soon after the inflation.

But while the survival of the savings ethic is an encouraging sign, it should not be allowed to obscure the fact that 1924 and 1925 were hard years for both artisans and retailers. Just as savings had dried up during the inflation, so had debts and bankruptcies. As long as the currency was depreciating, the acquittal of debts was especially easy – a fact borne out by the temporary rise in bankruptcies in 1921 at the time when the mark's exchange rate was making a short-term recovery. (Table 20).

With the introduction of stable currency in November 1923, however, the number of bankruptcies rose swiftly, and the auction rooms of the Hamburg bailiffs were full of the goods of debtors subject to compulsory sale of assets.[8] By 1925 most of the more ill-founded companies of the inflation period were liquidated, a necessary "cleansing process" as the bailiff's office described it. Unfortunately a number of older firms also succumbed in these credit-starved times, and amongst them would have been many Mittelstand enterprises. Moreover even if they had survived the swath that the wave of bankruptcies cut through the ranks of

8. Whereas in 1923 a mere 41,655 compulsory sales were carried out, in 1925 the figure had risen to 203,688 (in 1914 there had been 96,019). StA.H *Gerichtsvollzieherwesen*, 25. Jahresberichte 1926, 1928.

business, their position would have been weakened by the bankruptcy of customers and suppliers.

A more significant variable from the political, as well as the economic, viewpoint was the manner in which they had held their assets during the inflation. If they had held bank savings or mortgages, then, as we shall see below, they faced major losses because of the low level of debt revaluation granted in the stabilization.[9] For those whose bank deposits had been destroyed, the Hamburg savings banks treated their disgruntled customers rather better than elsewhere in Germany, but this did not amount to a great deal. Since neither the 1827er nor the other main savings bank, the Neue Sparkasse von 1864, were community institutions such as existed in Prussia or Bavaria, they received no assistance from the state for claims made against them in 1924. It was therefore all the more surprising that these commercial undertakings offered restitution for lost savings at an average of 25 percent of 1913 values, which was a considerably higher revaluation than in other parts of the country.[10]

The information on bankruptcy and savings is suggestive rather than conclusive. It confirms that the first months after the stabilization were hard for small enterprises like artisans and retailers, but it also indicates that basic behavior patterns were intact. People still saved money despite the horrendous experience of the inflation. If major changes had taken place, they were not to be found in the field of business practice or individual action, but rather in the manner in which groups organized themselves.

A striking example was the move towards stricter organization amongst the artisans during the inflation period. If guild membership can be taken as a sign of organization, then the figures in Table 6 speak for themselves. In 1914 there were thirty-three guilds in Hamburg, in 1919 there were thirty-four, and seven years later in 1926 there were forty-six guilds with a total membership of 18,234 – a rise in members of 40 percent over 1919. Also noticeable is the fact that of the forty-six guilds in 1926, no less than thirty-seven were compulsory guilds, a very much higher proportion than before the war. And this trend to greater guild membership was not simply limited to Hamburg. In the years from 1919 and 1926,

9. Before the war, investment in mortgages had been a popular form of saving in Hamburg; indeed liquid capital was placed in mortgages probably to a greater extent than anywhere else in Germany. Besides small savers, mortgages were also a common form of temporary refuge for businessmen because of the ease with which money could be withdrawn from them. Lippmann, *Mein Leben*, p. 266.

10. Ibid., pp. 366–67.

the number of guild members increased by 28 percent in Berlin, by 37 percent in Frankfurt, by 43 percent in Cologne, by 42 percent in Munich, and by 17 percent in Leipzig.[11]

The impression gained from these figures is of German artisans closing ranks in time of crisis with the time-honored formula of institutional restriction. It may have been a negative response within the context of the inflation, when the key to survival lay in flexibility rather than rigidity, but it shows that artisans, despite their professional adaptation to the modern industrialized economy, still held a strong ideological preference for a corporatist solution to their economic problems. In other words, instead of adopting a market-oriented, every-man-for-himself approach, which might have increased the chances of survival for the individual craftsman, the artisans relied on their traditional strength, their guilds, to ensure the survival of their estate (*Stand*). It was this cohesiveness and attachment to status that had made them targets for exploitation by conservatives in the Empire and that would make them similarly attractive to the Nazis during the Weimar Republic. But this should not be interpreted as meaning that they were politically naive. As the author of a recent study of Hamburg artisans in the depression years has put it, "artisans comprised a corporate status community which not only provided them with remarkable social continuity but also with the political strength and confidence to stand their ground against all comers."[12]

By comparison with the artisans, the retailers were a disorganized and disputatious bunch. If they suffered a greater loss of numbers during the inflation period, then it should be remembered that theirs was always a more precarious existence in the first place. In fact the chronic overcrowding in German retailing that had been widespread in the prewar years was partly overcome by the inflation and the harsh conditions of the stabilization.[13] In Hamburg the shopkeepers had only the ineffectual Chamber of Retailers to protect their interests, and it was totally lacking in the influence

11. The shift from free to compulsory guilds was just as marked as the rise in overall numbers. In particular, many previously unorganized single masters joined compulsory guilds, and female participation rose too. *Enquete Bericht*, p. 393; StA.H *Aufsichtsbehörde für die Innungen*, A.3, Bd. 2, Report to Senatskommission für Landesstatistik, 13 March 1926.
12. Frank Domurad, "The Politics of Corporatism: Hamburg Handicraft in the late Weimar Republic, 1927–1933," in *Social Change and Political Development in Weimar Germany*, ed. Richard Bessel and E.J. Feuchtwanger (London, 1981), pp. 174–75.
13. Tobis, *Mittelstandsproblem der Nachkriegszeit*, pp. 58–59.

necessary to tackle the most onerous problem of price control. Politically impotent and divided amongst themselves, they spent most of their energies composing petitions to the government and letters to the press. While they were occasionally the recipients of direct financial aid,[14] in general there were few gestures of assistance from the state.

On the contrary the state was the chief source of their difficulties, for it was the whole legal straitjacket of price control and antiprofiteering legislation, introduced during the war and applied with such relentless vigor until after the stabilization, that made their lives so unrewarding. Living on a knife's edge between bankruptcy and the profiteering courts, the retailers were never able to adapt fully to the inflation's dynamics, as were their suppliers, and they reached a stage where they were actually loathe to sell anything because their stock was the only safe repository for their capital. The entire structure of regulation built up around the *PPS* created an atmosphere of mutual animosity between retailers and their customers, exacerbated by righteous indignation on the one hand and occasional plunder on the other. "The retailers were peculiarly disadvantaged," notes Feldman, "by the fact that it was at their shops and stalls that the consumers directly confronted the shortages and rising prices and periodically responded by breaking store windows, overturning stalls and plundering. Manifestly, the authorities did not approve of such outbursts, but the incredibly complex and confusing antiprofiteering regulations . . . served as the legal counterpart of the public proclivity to take its frustrations out on the retailers."[15]

It was not a preindustrial mentality, but prejudicial legislation that hampered the shopkeeper in his response to the inflation. Indeed if anything demonstrated the old Mittelstand's loss of position within the corporatist consensus that was formed after 1918, it was the rigorous application of economic controls. It was these controls, rather than the inflation itself, that brought impoverishment and ruin and started the old Mittelstand on a political migration to the Right. In the final analysis retailers paid the price for their chosen position in the economy. As provisioners to the population, they were called upon to cushion the consumer from the worst effects of the endless price increases. For the government

---

14. In August 1923 2.5 trillion marks was made available for distribution to the most desperate cases through the Chamber of Retailers. HKH 102.1.A.6.20, *Detail-listenkammer*, Vollversammlung, 21 August 1923, 28 September 1923.

15. Feldman, "A Problem of Modernization?" p. 6.

the alternative of an uncontrolled retail sector, with the additional wage pressure and the consequences which that would have for its relations with big employers, was not a serious option. Under the circumstances, it chose the easier target.

Perhaps the most curious aspect of the old Mittelstand's response to the inflation was the lack of any effective cooperation between artisans and retailers. Admittedly it is hard to imagine what form this would have taken, given the impotence of the retailers' chamber and the traditionally inward-looking concerns of the guilds. But bearing in mind the fact that both sides at least paid lip service to the idea of Mittelstand enterprise and used this concept frequently in their publicity, it is odd that relations between the Chamber of Industry and the Chamber of Retailers were not closer. Instead of uniting to tackle the government on price control and the *Zwangs-wirtschaft*, the two chambers were beset with repeated instances of petty rivalry born out of their competition for funds and members in a city where the real power did not belong to either of them, but to the Chamber of Commerce. A typical point of conflict, for example, occurred in 1922 and involved artisans selling manufactured goods along with their own wares. This was a purely retailing function, argued the Chamber of Retailers, and placed the artisan in direct competition with other shopkeepers; it was only fair that such artisans also join the retailers' chamber and pay its dues.[16]

It was characteristic that the inflation exposed many hidden differences between the two groups and intensified them to the point of mutual friction. Far from closing the ranks of the Mittelstand, it often forced them further apart. Artisans had always shopped in department stores like other consumers, much to the disgust of the small retailers; the inflation made it even more logical to do so. The desire for lower prices simply outweighed any loyalty they might have felt to the neighborhood shopkeeper and, in so doing, revealed the extreme fragility of the Mittelstand alliance.

White-Collar Workers and Civil Servants

It has been an aim of this study to demonstrate that in the case of many Germans of the Mittelstand, the ramifications of the First World War and the following revolution became so intertwined with the more specific phenomena of the inflation in the years from 1914 to 1923 that it is often impossible for the historian to dis-

16. StA.H *Gewerbekammer*, A.12, Bd. 5, Vollsitzung, 17 February 1922.

tinguish the consequences of one from the other.[17] We can be sure however that for certain groups relative impoverishment and loss of status began in the war years; what followed after 1918 was simply an extension or deepening of their misery. This applies to a degree to the old Mittelstand of artisans and retailers, but much more so to white-collar workers and civil servants.

Any verdict on the trends in their living standards must take into account the imperfect nature of the available statistical data, but nonetheless some patterns are discernible. The figures in Table 13, for example, support the conclusion that for Hamburg civil servants, earnings began to slip during the war. The higher grades, which had lost over 75 percent of their 1914 purchasing power by January 1920, already faced the prospect of lower differential margins and a generally depressed standard of living before the hyperinflation began. Certainly clothes, which they could not afford to replace, would have become more worn with the passage of years, but otherwise their average income, seen on an annual basis, did not deteriorate any further from the position it had reached at the end of 1919. Indeed the statistical evidence indicates that their real income was actually rising in 1923, at least until September when the sheer logistics of keeping abreast with the spiraling prices was beyond all wage and salary earners.

A similar trend, although less extreme, emerges from the data on the other Hamburg civil servant grades and from the white-collar workers at the HEW and HHA. Does this mean that the new Mittelstand suffered more from the war than from the postwar inflation? Such a conclusion would be simplistic. Instead there was a cumulative process of decline, a continuation of adverse conditions after the initial shock of the war years. Some trades were hit worse than others. Shop assistants, for example, were affected badly because their employers faced enormous difficulties. Bank clerks, by comparison, benefited from the extra work that the inflation produced, but paid a heavy price in redundancy after the stabilization. Indeed there would appear to be a pattern: those businesses that had profited from the inflation were the first to suffer when it ended. In Hamburg the numbers employed at the six main banks fell from 8,445 in January 1924 to 4,216 in December

---

17. This point is made by Werner Abelshauser, "Inflation und Stabilisierung. Zum Problem ihrer makroökonomischen Auswirkungen auf die Rekonstruktion der deutschen Wirtschaft nach dem Weltkrieg," in Feldman and Büsch, eds., *Historische Prozesse*, pp. 161–74.

1924.[18] At the private Warburg Bank, for instance, "liberation from Lilliputian accounts, from scribbling zeros" may have been a relief for the management, but it meant redundancies for 177 out of the 535 staff members employed there at the end of 1923.[19]

Broadly speaking, white-collar workers were better protected against unemployment than their blue-collar colleagues. Certainly the records of the Hamburg demobilization commissar show that white-collar workers fared better during the worst period of layoffs in 1923. This had probably less to do with the growing strength of their organizations than with the legacy of obligation left over from prewar days and still perpetuated between many employers and their employees. Whatever the cause, it is a fact that white-collar workers were afforded separate treatment and were less vulnerable to layoff. And this was important because at a time when their income was undoubtedly being proletarized, both by the reduction in real earnings and the erosion of differentials between higher and lower paid positions, the white-collar workers could still reassure themselves of their superior status with the comforting thought that at least the boss would do his best to protect their jobs.

As regards white-collar organization, the inflation forced old associations like the DHV to mature into trade unions. But it was the struggle to feed himself and his family, not the appeal of any ideology, that made the white-collar worker appreciate the superiority of collective action over a personal arrangement with the boss. And where the organization adopted rigorous trade union tactics while retaining a middle-class approach to the wider issues of the white-collar movement, it made itself ultimately more appealing to the average employee.

This goes a long way to explaining the long-term success of the DHV in the Weimar Republic, compared to the left-wing Afa-Bund. The DHV successfully exploited the white-collar fear of cultural proletarianization, by linking the inflation to social impoverishment. It was the DHV's real accomplishment that as the achievements of the revolution became discredited amongst white-collar workers towards the end of the inflation, it was able to convince them that they could gain all the advantages of trade union negotiating power without the necessity of becoming Socialists. It did this primarily by stressing the national rather than the class perspective. This not only appealed to the inflated self-esteem

18. *Bericht des hamburgischen Gewerbeaufsichtsamts, 1923 und 1924* (Hamburg, 1925), p. 8.
19. Rosenbaum and Sherman, *M.M. Warburg*, p. 134.

of the white-collar worker, but allowed the union to identify culturally with a traditional German bourgeois doctrine while acting in proletarian fashion on bread-and-butter issues like wages. Not surprisingly it had difficulty reconciling these divergent streams, but occasionally a suitable opportunity presented itself for pressing the case for improving the conditions of its members while lecturing the rest of the community on patriotic themes. In the summer of 1922, for example, when internal prices in Germany were approaching world levels, the DHV claimed that its members were entitled to the same rate of pay as their English or American colleagues, carefully adding that living standards could only reflect the "productive activity of the country as a whole." As long as German production lay below that of other countries, cautioned the union's journal, salaries and profits should be restrained accordingly.[20]

The lifestyles and political affiliations of blue- and white-collar workers may have begun a process of convergence during the war, their differences temporarily submerged beneath a new class identity, as Jürgen Kocka suggests, but in the postwar inflation those differences reappeared with undiminished force. The loss of white-collar earning power produced not solidarity with the workers, but resentment against them, particularly as the new Republic appeared to have been founded for their exclusive benefit.

Nowhere was this clearer than with the civil servants. After 1918 they sought to come to terms with the Republic yet retain their privileges and special status. It was a hard act to perform, but one that was central to the philosophy of the civil servants' chief national body, the DBB. The determination of this organization to ensure the continuation after 1918 of the civil servants' "well-earned rights" is certain testimony to this fact.[21] For this organization the old authoritarian Empire was gone, but the class society of the workers was equally redundant; instead Germany was moving towards a new national consensus, "a secular process of social convergence within the population."[22] It was seeking, in effect, a corporatist solution, which would give the civil service neither an alliance with the trade unions nor connivance with the govern-

---

20. "Der Kampf um die Kaufkraft," *DHW*, 12 April 1922.
21. The DBB actually succeeded in getting the protection of civil servants' rights and privileges written into the Weimar constitution. See Kunz, *Civil Servants*, pp. 156–58.
22. Jane Caplan, "Speaking the Right Language: The Nazi Party and the Civil Service Vote in the Weimar Republic," in *The Formation of the Nazi Constituency*, ed. Thomas Childers (London, 1986), p. 191.

ment, but a secure and respected niche within the national community. It was to remain a distant ideal, although one that was utilized by the Nazis after 1930.[23]

In Hamburg the essential ambiguity of the civil servants' position within the confines of a class society soon became clear in the nature of the Civil Service Council. Initially promising in early 1919, this body proved to be a disappointing instrument for protecting living standards. The early trend towards closer contact between civil servants and other wage and salary earners was reversed after 1921. Had there been a merging of interests between tenured and nontenured staff, the resulting common front might have commanded more respect from the government and perhaps mitigated the severity of the staff cuts which took place in 1923 and 1924. As it was, the chances for such a front were weak, and they foundered on a combination of the civil servants' residual sense of privilege and the special pressures of the inflation. The fact that civil servant salaries were determined by parliamentary committee and not by direct negotiations with the employer made an alignment with other white-collar workers ultimately unattractive. The extra pressure of the staff reduction program made the two sides mutually hostile, instead of ready to close ranks in the face of unemployment.

The House Owners and Mortgages

Nothing illustrates the fault lines in the geology of the modern Mittelstand as well as the complex: house ownership, mortgages, rent control, and inflation. Within the Hamburg Mittelstand there were house owners who benefited from depreciation in the value of their mortgages, and there were house owners who were harmed by the imposition of rent control; often they were the same person, and always it was the inflation that made the critical difference.

The view that the Mittelstand, in so far as it included a large number of mortgagees, could not have had an entirely unfavorable experience of the inflation was long ago expressed by Eulenburg.[24] In fact the rent tax, introduced by the Marx government at the time of the Third Emergency Tax Decree of February 1924, was specifically designed to prevent house owners benefiting from mortgage liquidation during the inflation.[25] But Eulenburg's point is well put

23. Ibid., pp. 192–93.
24. Eulenburg, "Die sozialen Wirkungen," esp. pp. 759–60.
25. The new tax was based on the notion that those owners of old houses who

because the advantage of possessing a debt-free real asset, like a house or block of apartments, in the credit wasteland of the stabilization period far outweighed the burden of any new tax.

However it is by no means clear either that all house owners took advantage of the inflation to liquidate their mortgage or that they indeed retained possession of their property until the stabilization. In Hamburg not all mortgages were repaid before the end of the inflation. At the Hypothekenbank, for example, 4,133 mortgages were on the bank's books at the beginning of January 1923 (value 643 million marks), and twelve months later it still had 2,853 (value 1,752 million marks).[26] In other words, only 31 percent of the outstanding mortgages at the bank were repaid during the hyperinflation year of 1923. Of course this was only a single bank, and the figures refer to only one year. What it does tell us however is that, out of either ignorance or high conscience, not every house owner burdened with a heavy mortgage took the chance offered by the inflation to be rid of it.

One explanation for the less than total mortgage liquidation in Hamburg may lie in the mortgage revaluation campaign that got under way in the winter of 1923/24. For those who expected such a step, repaying their debts in paper marks at this stage made little sense. As it turns out, the rights of mortgagees and creditors fell victim to the larger interest of the government. Although the *Reichsgericht* had actually given a verdict in November 1923 declaring full debt revaluation to be justified,[27] the government viewed any undertaking to mortgage creditors as a precedent that would open the floodgates to a multitude of claimants. With the inflation it had "eliminated its domestic debts overnight and abandoned those of its citizens who held liquid assets in the form of savings,

---

had profited from the inflation should now pay towards the establishment of new homes. *RGBl.* 1 (1924), p. 74; also Pergande and Pergande, "Die Gesetzgebung," p. 87; Silverman, "Pledge Unredeemed," p. 123.

26. During the course of the year a further twenty mortgages had been granted (current price value 1,308 million marks), while 1,300 mortgages were repaid (book value 199 million marks). HKH 29.A.2.7.15. Jahresbericht der Hypothekenbank in Hamburg für 1923.

27. It has been suggested that the court's judgement in favor of revaluation was influenced by the fact that most judges were themselves dispossessed creditors; see Michael L. Hughes, "Economic Interest, Social Attitudes, and Creditor Ideology: Popular Responses to Inflation," in Feldman et al., eds., *Zwischenbilanz*, pp. 390–92. For the role of the *Reichsgericht* in the debt revaluation issue and its successful attempt to establish its right to judicial review under the Weimar constitution, see Hughes, *Paying*, pp. 159–62.

pensions, insurance, bonds, and mortgages."[28] It was not about to endanger this valuable bonus and saddle the German economy with an additional burden at the precise moment when it sought to recover some stability.[29] Reduced to its essence, a full mortgage revaluation would have shifted the losses of the war and inflation from creditors to consumers, taxpayers, and tenants, and this would have been political suicide for any government in 1924. Not surprisingly the government was determined, as one Berlin newspaper put it, "to nip the *Reichsgericht* decision in the bud."[30]

In Hamburg the reaction to the revaluation question was mixed. While the legitimacy of the creditors' claims was never challenged, it seems that justice gave way to pragmatism as the end of 1923 drew near and the prospect of a lasting stabilization occupied everyone's attention. The house owners, while recognizing the mortgager's right to compensation, felt that revaluation should be decided on the individual merits of the case. Thus widows and pensioners should get more than the rich capitalists and savings banks that had uncharitably foreclosed on the hard-pressed landlords during the war.[31] Whatever the circumstances, however, it was generally accepted that the best the mortgagers could hope for was a token revaluation in the order of 10–20 percent of 1914 values. As Leo Lippmann put it, the house owners "got away with it fairly lightly."[32]

Any analysis, such as Eulenburg's, that places the house owners amongst the winners assumes that they refrained from selling their houses before the stabilization, and this assumption cannot be

28. Gerald D. Feldman, "Weimar from Inflation to Depression: Experiment or Gamble?" in Feldman, ed., *Die Nachwirkungen*, p. 388.

29. For the divisions within the cabinet over the revaluation issue, see Krohn, *Stabilisierung*, pp. 44–49. For the legal and political implications of revaluation, see Hughes, "Economic Interest," in Feldman et al., eds., *Zwischenbilanz*, pp. 385–408; and David Southern, "The Impact of Inflation: Inflation the Courts, and Revaluation," in Bessel and Feuchtwanger, eds., *Social Change*, pp. 55–76.

30. "Eine Verordnung gegen die Hypothekenaufwertung?" *Berliner Tageblatt*, 12 December 1923. Leo Lippmann told Hans Luther, who was firmly against any kind of revaluation, that the government's plan amounted to legalized dispossession and was probably contrary to the constitution. StA.H *Finanzdeputation*, IIA.1x.IA, Senatskomm. f.d. Reichs- u. auswärtigen Angelegenheiten, 30 November 1923.

31. This was Eddelbüttel's suggestion at a meeting of the GVH in January 1924. "Mitglieder-Versammlung," *HGZ*, 25 January 1924.

32. At the time of the introduction of the rent tax in February 1924, legislation was put in hand to revalue mortgage claims up to 15 percent of their prewar value. Lippmann, *Mein Leben*, p. 360. For general press commentary on mortgage revaluation in Hamburg, see "Hypothekenaufwertung," *Hamburger Nachrichten*, 19 December 1923; "Das geplante Verbot der Hypothekenaufwertung," *Hamburger Fremdenblatt*, 22 December 1923.

made. For those house owners who lived exclusively from rental income, the combination of inflation and rent control between 1914 and 1923 meant that they had precious little income to keep either their houses or themselves together.[33] As we have seen, many found the strain too great and sold their properties, particularly during the speculative boom of 1922/23. Unless it was quickly reinvested in some other form of material assets, the basketful of paper marks they received would have offered poor protection in the remaining months of hyperinflation and been totally worthless with the arrival of stabilized conditions in 1924. Briefly stated then, the complex of house ownership, mortgages, rent control, and inflation can be reduced to the formula: mortgagers suffered from inflation, while house owners/mortgagees suffered from rent control.

Rent control struck at the heart of Mittelstand beliefs by making private property difficult to retain. In 1923, one Hamburg house owner lamented that it took the entire month's takings from all the apartments in both his houses to replace a single broken toilet seat![34] This prompts the question of whether rent control was a legislative weapon in the class war of the early Weimar Republic. It certainly facilitated the dispossession of those small property owners who had no means of support other than the revenue from rented accommodations. But the answer to the question must surely be no. There was no serious plan to socialize small property after 1918, and if that had ever been a government objective, there were obviously more direct ways to go about it than by driving urban landlords into bankruptcy.

Rather, the legislation should be seen in the context of the times. For while price control was justified only with difficulty after the end of the war, rent control was broadly accepted as inevitable, given the chronic housing shortage and the need to avoid any further suffering for the returning veterans. Furthermore once the task of determining a fair rent was assigned to the *MEA*, the outcome was fairly predictable. They tended to represent the interests of tenants, and however divergent their political and other interests might be, tenants were obviously united in seeking low rents. There was a strong feeling that property ownership carried responsibility as well as advantages and that profits from rents should not be added to the capital gains that any house owner would make in the course of time.

33. Witt, "Inflation, *Wohnungszwangswirtschaft*," p. 395.
34. "Notschrei der Grundeigentümer!" *HGZ*, 2 November 1923.

It is worth stressing when considering the plight of the landlords, caught between the Scylla of rent control and the Charybdis of inflation, that whatever gains were made at their expense by the tenants were not retained. The inflation was a great leveler, and no one group held the advantage for long. Thus the benefits of low rents were swiftly neutralized by the inflationary rise in the prices for other necessities, and the tenants were no better off. In fact the inflation actually radicalized the tenant movement, the evidence for which is clear from the frequency of tenants' protests during the period and the militant activity of the Hamburg *Zentral-Mieterrat* (central tenants' council).[35] Moreover it should be remembered that because tenants were often wage earners, rent control was universally exploited by their employers, who were able to hold down wages by arguing in pay negotiations that their workers were being lodged practically rent-free. Where the employers were manufacturers, it resulted in lower production costs and ultimately lower export prices, so that the real beneficiary of the landlord's sacrifice was the German exporter.[36] Where the employer was the state itself, then the whole legislative basis of the rent control program appears disingenuous, in so far as the state saved on the salaries of its own employees.

In the final analysis it is difficult to prove any political ill will against house owners on the part of the government, although rents presented an easy target in its battle to hold down consumer prices. Tenants, after all, comprised the vast majority of voters, including those from the Mittelstand, while landlords were a relatively unpopular minority. Here again one sees the inherent divisions within the Mittelstand. It is tempting, for example, to consider the problems of retailers and house owners to be identical, and certainly the thrust of the retailers' attack on price control and their battles with the *PPS* resembled the house owners' own campaign against rent control and the *MEA*. But their views diverged in vital respects. In Hamburg some retailers were landlords, owning the building in which their shop formed the ground floor; but many more were tenants, and gradually their leaders in the Chamber of Retailers came to appreciate the fact. Their position changed quite noticeably from one of Mittelstand solidarity to one

35. The same interpretation is offered by Geyer for Munich in his "Wohnungszwangswirtschaft," in Feldman et al., eds., *Die Anpassung*, p. 146.
36. See Robert Kuczinski, "Postwar Labor Conditions in Germany," in US Bureau of Statistics, *Bulletin 380* (Washington D.C., 1925), p. 46. The point is also made by Herbert Anker in *Die Wohnungszwangswirtschaft und ihre volkswirtschaftliche Bedeutung* (Diss., Berlin, 1927), pp. 25–31.

of narrower self-interest. Whereas in October 1920 the Chamber of Retailers offered the opinion that "dwellings are to landlords as . . . goods are to retailers" and offered support in the campaign against rent control, in June 1922 it deplored the high level of rent surcharges anticipated in the *RMG*, arguing that rents were now higher than many small shopkeepers could afford.[37] It was not so much that retailers had changed from free marketeers to advocates of regulation in the space of two years, but rather the pressure of the inflation had driven another wedge between the building blocks of any potential Mittelstand coalition.

The Political Perspective

What were the political consequences of the inflation? Professor Robbins was certainly oversimplifying the matter when he said that Hitler was its foster child, but his comment does serve as a point of departure for considering the inflation's fallout on the Weimar party system. In May 1924 there was the so-called "inflation election" for the Reichstag. Since it was the year of the stabilization, carried out with all the hardships caused by low revaluation of inflation debts, tight credit for business, and new taxes for all, it might more appropriately have been called the "stabilization election"; but the losers of the inflation did have their first opportunity in four years to register their discontent through the ballot box, and the results are interesting for the commentary they make on the entire Weimar party system.

On the Right both the nationalist DNVP and the *völkisch* bloc (the Nazis) made impressive gains, while major losses were suffered by the liberal center represented by the DDP and the DVP.[38] The inflation, particularly after 1922, had ruined the finances and traumatized the supporters of both parties, while the harsh stabilization regime of 1924 delivered them further blows through their association with the government.[39] The support for the Nazis is obviously significant, but since they were unable to sustain their momentum for the second election in December 1924 and thereafter spent the period until 1930 in the political wilderness, the

37. StA.H *Senat*, Conv. 1, Detaillistenkammer, 21 October 1920; Conv. 2, DHSG, 21 June 1922.
38. The Nazis gained 6.5 percent of the popular vote and the DNVP 19.5 percent, while the DDP slipped from 8.3 percent to 5.7 percent and the DVP from 13.9 percent to 9.2 percent.
39. Jones, *German Liberalism*, p. 165.

immediate advantage that they gained from the inflation was demonstrably short-term. Even the DNVP, which increased its vote further in the December election, soon lost ground, forfeiting the backing of the inflation losers by reneging on revaluation promises and participating in the 1925 coalition.[40]

This is not to argue that the Right were not the beneficiaries of the stabilization's inequities, but rather they benefited in an indirect way. What both Childers and Jones have shown in their studies of the Weimar parties and voting patterns is that the political middle ground that the Mittelstand should have represented fragmented in the mid-1920s into special interest groups. These small parties were dedicated to the single issue of achieving restitution for expropriated savers and mortgagers, but their general effect was far more profound. They were the sign of a fundamental legitimacy crisis in the Weimar system and a lack of confidence on the part of the Mittelstand in the established parties of the center that had originated with the inflation and had been vastly increased by the manner in which the stabilization had been carried out.[41]

This fragmentation of Mittelstand electoral loyalties and the mushrooming of special interest parties in 1924 were certainly a "manifestation of anti-system sentiment," as Childers has called it,[42] but they were also indicative of how the Mittelstand perceived the entire political process. Following in the tradition of German party politics from the Empire onwards, it approached the Weimar system in contractual fashion. With sympathy for neither the workings of a parliamentary democracy nor the integrative policies of the established parties, the Mittelstand's method amounted to little more than political barter: its votes in return for specific economic objectives.

Artisans, retailers, and house owners lost interest in supporting the main bourgeois parties because their chief constituency appeared to lie beyond the ranks of the Mittelstand, with either big business (DVP) or the large estate owners (DNVP). In Hamburg the manner in which artisans and retailers had been denied access to

---

40. See Childers, *Nazi Voter*, chap. 2.
41. Larry E. Jones, "In the Shadow of Stabilization: German Liberalism and the Legitimacy Crisis of the Weimar Party System," in Feldman, ed., *Nachwirkungen*, p. 21. See also Thomas Childers, "Inflation and Electoral Politics in Germany, 1919–1929," in Schmukler and Marcus, eds., *Inflation through the Ages*, pp. 373–85; "Interest and Ideology: Anti-System Politics in the Era of Stabilization, 1924–1928," in Feldman, ed., *Nachwirkungen*, pp. 1–20; *The Nazi Voter*, esp. chap. 2; Hughes, *Paying*, pp. 163–65.
42. Childers, "Interest and Ideology," p. 4.

foreign exchange by banks who reserved this precious hard currency for their more influential customers most likely strengthened their bitterness against the city's ruling elite, which in its Weimar existence was most closely associated with Stresemann's DVP. Chamber of Commerce leaders Max Warburg and F.H. Witthöfft both gravitated towards the DVP after 1918 and were probably the two most important businessmen in the Hamburg branch of the party. Their political instincts sprang from their business sense: radical politics of the Right or Left were dangerous and to be avoided at all costs, but the reality of postwar Germany had to be accepted and concessions made to the new democracy, so long as this did not involve any kind of bureaucratic interference in the economy.[43]

While there may have been some common ground between the small artisan masters, shopkeepers, and landlords struggling with the effects of rent control on the one hand, and the clublike capitalism of the Chamber of Commerce leadership on the other, they were clearly worlds apart in their basic philosophy. While the former needed protection from the market and redress of specific grievances, the latter sought the right channels through which to exercise its existing power. It could live with any political system as long as its economic power base remained undisturbed, whereas the Mittelstand needed a specific political arrangement to maintain its economic existence.

The Mittelstand might have thought it had the solution with the appearance of the Wirtschaftspartei in 1925. This was an attempt by house owners to forge their own party in alliance with retailers and artisans, taking as a combined target Marxism and capitalism. Other small parties dedicated to single issues like debt revalorization (for example, the Aufwertungs- und Aufbaupartei) were similarly anticapitalist and antisystem in their pursuit of Mittelstand inflation victims. This meant that they all called for an end to the *Zwangswirtschaft*, but they were equally hostile to a free market economy. They wanted the bureaucratic restrictions on their earning power replaced with the ordered, protective structure of the corporate state.[44]

---

43. See the useful section on these two figures in Büttner, *Hamburg in der Staats- und Wirtschaftskrise*, pp. 360–68.
44. Childers, *Interest and Ideology*, pp. 14–15; *Nazi Voter*, p. 263. For a history of the *Wirtschaftspartei*, see Martin Schumacher, *Mittelstandsfront und Republik, 1919–1933: Die Wirtschaftspartei – Reichspartei des deutschen Mittelstandes* (Düsseldorf, 1972); also his "Hausbesitz, Mittelstand und Wirtschaftspartei in der Weimarer Republik," in Mommsen et al., eds., *Industrielles System*, pp. 823–35.

It is possible to see the activity of these special interest parties as evidence of a belated Mittelstand participation in the Weimar political process, but this would be wrong. Single issues springing from grievances about the inflation could never be the basis for effective involvement. Moreover they were not even effective in uniting the Mittelstand, for while a large number of creditors were in its ranks, not every member of the Mittelstand acted foremost as a creditor; he might instead have given priority to his interest as house owner with a liquidated mortgage or even to his role as taxpayer and consumer. If credit revaluation was a Mittelstand issue, then it had no more value as a unifying factor in the Weimar Republic than Mittelstandspolitik had in the Empire. The special interest parties all suffered electoral failure and proved their uselessness as a means to achieving political influence, but in doing so, they also deprived the liberal parties of much-needed support, a deficiency that eventually proved fatal when those parties were confronted with the Nazi challenge after 1928. The inflation and stabilization in 1924 had started a process of fragmentation in the Weimar party system that could not be stopped and that indirectly helped the Nazis to power.[45]

What of the new Mittelstand? According to Childers, the long-term appeal of the Nazi party for white-collar workers remained "far weaker than traditionally assumed."[46] Certainly the inflation and stabilization produced a less confrontational stance amongst white-collar voters than it did amongst the dispossessed of the old Mittelstand, since they had fewer specific grievances. The erosion of salary differentials during the inflation produced hostility amongst the higher paid, but these inequities were eliminated to a large degree with the reestablishment of stable monetary values after 1924. Likewise the high unemployment amongst white-collar workers in the immediate aftermath of the inflation was not a lasting problem, despite the concerns of the DHV.[47] Of greater significance was the split in the ranks of the organized white-collar force between the left-leaning AfA-Bund on the one hand and the nationalist DHV and liberal GdA on the other. While the former accepted a class-based analysis of society and saw its interests as identical with those of the blue-collar worker, the latter emphasized the social and economic distinctions between the two groups of

45. Jones, *German Liberalism*, p. 4 and *In the Shadow of Stabilization*, pp. 29–31; Childers, *Interest and Ideology*, p. 18 and *Inflation and Electoral Politics*, pp. 380–82.
46. Childers, *Nazi Voter*, p. 264.
47. For example, "Beamtenabbau und Wirtschaft," *DHW*, Beilage, Nr.4, May 1924.

labor. However despite the opportunity for exploitation offered by
the anti-Semitic and antifeminist DHV position, the Nazis appear
to have made remarkably little headway in gaining the nationalist
white-collar vote, with the DNVP instead being the chief beneficiary of their discontent.[48]

With the civil servants the Nazis had greater success. Capitalizing
on the redundancies of 1923/24 and the lower real earnings and
frustrated career ambitions of those civil servants who survived the
stabilization with their jobs, the Nazi approach to the state's employees was more specifically targeted and "more fruitful."[49]
Originally civil servants had supported the DDP and DVP, indeed
they "had traditionally been the backbone of political liberalism in
Germany."[50] But the association of these parties with the disastrous
policies (for the civil servants) of the early Weimar coalitions,
culminating in the staff cuts, cost them dearly in civil servant votes
in 1924. The decade of crisis from 1914 to 1924 had transformed the
civil servant outlook from one of strong identification with the
state as master to a more ubiquitous contractual relationship with
the state as employer. In practice this meant a political migration by
the civil servants to those parties that promised them the most –
even if those parties, like the Nazis, were amongst the Republic's
greatest critics and enemies. As with the appeal to the artisans, the
Nazi pledge to protect the civil servants was an attractive corporatist theme for a group assailed by threats to their economic and
social position in German society.

The Mittelstand and the Corporatist Economy

According to the conventional wisdom, the inflation brought the
Mittelstand impoverishment, loss of status, and political alienation.
This study of Hamburg has shown that there is truth to this view,
but that it is by no means the whole truth. Like everything else
about the Mittelstand, its experience of the years between the
outbreak of war in 1914 and the stabilization of the mark in 1924
was highly diversified. Not only did the behavior of the occupations studied here vary widely, but their interests were often
contradictory. Artisans and retailers argued about the limits to the
authority of their respective chambers; civil servants traded solidarity with their white-collar colleagues for status and security

48. Childers, *Nazi Voter*, pp. 90–91.
49. Ibid., pp. 97–98.
50. Kunz, *Civil Servants*, p. 26.

during the 1923 redundancy program; white-collar workers drew nearer the workers with the buildup of their trade unions but could never bring themselves to sacrifice their feelings of superiority and fashion a true alliance with them; and the house owners, while professing staunch Mittelstand virtues, found themselves at odds with practically everyone else as landlords and were even inconsistent with themselves – opposing rent control as losers of the inflation, yet also opposing mortgage revaluation because they were its winners.

Many of these groups exhibited a particular nostalgia for the special position in society that they imagined they had enjoyed before the war. The GVH leader Hüne, for example, tried to evoke an image of a unified Mittelstand impoverished by Socialists and the *Zwangswirtschaft* but failed, not only because the inflation imposed strains that deepened rather than bridged the existing divisions, but because these divisions were probably irreconcilable in the first place. And herein lies the paradox of the Mittelstand aspiration: because it was an ideological construct, it held the promise of being a vehicle for political action; but as a creation of the corporatist Wilhemine era, it was only successful in defending a static socioeconomic structure. When those conditions changed in 1919 to the more fluid, confrontational order of a party system, its ideology proved inadequate as a basis for effective participation.

It has been pointed out that the Weimar parliamentary system never really functioned in the role of providing representation for the major economic interest groups of the time.[51] Within a corporatist framework, however, the participating factions can bypass the parliamentary route entirely in the exercise of political power; the problem for the Mittelstand after 1918 was not that it had no parties to represent it, rather that it was shut out of the economic power structure. For Theodor Geiger and other more modern commentators, this was a consequence of the refusal of its constituent groups to accept their position within a class society.[52] In a sense this argument is impossible to refute; if white-collar workers and civil servants had meekly joined the ranks of the workers and voted for the SPD, while artisans and retailers had accepted their position as employers and supported the DVP, the more familiar balance of a parliamentary democracy would have emerged, and Weimar

51. Feldman, "A Problem of Modernization?" p. 23.
52. In Geiger's essentially Marxist analysis, the old Mittelstand would either be transformed into capitalist enterprise or go under. The new Mittelstand would be assimilated into the proletariat. See his "Panik im Mittelstand," pp. 637–54.

might even have survived the upheaval of the depression. But as Geiger himself recognized, even the affliction of "false consciousness" made no difference to the Mittelstand's reality, and a third of the German people continued to see themselves as belonging to it up until 1933.[53]

All the groups studied here – whether salary earners or independents – shared a tendency to see themselves in terms of status rather than as a part of an economic class, and for this reason a class analysis of their position is not very helpful. They were not small-scale capitalists using corporatist propaganda to conceal their true nature.[54] Instead it must be accepted that their belief in clearly defined and permanent economic *Stände* (estates) was genuine and was seen as an advance in a class system that had brought only conflict in society. Likewise their distrust of parliamentary democracy stemmed from their perception of it as a mirror image of the amoral forces of the marketplace – survival of the fittest in an economic jungle where no rules applied. Corporatism, by comparison, with its rigid system of stratification and clearly defined roles for all, would bring peace and harmony.

The problem for the Mittelstand was that it was not included amongst the strata of Weimar corporatism, and the explanation for this lies in its inherent diversity. For while there can be little doubt that the experience of economic decline during the inflation and the specter of the workers' revolution in 1918 forced the Mittelstand to organize itself, what emerged was far too heterogeneous to serve as a lever of political power; indeed the Mittelstand's approach to organization was a reflection of its internal variety.[55] While Hamburg artisans reached back into their medieval past and supported the compulsory guilds in increasing numbers, white-collar workers advanced wholeheartedly into the twentieth century and forged fully fledged trade unions from their prewar associations. Hamburg house owners seeking a defense against rent control and inflation flocked to the GVH – an institutional relic that, having lost its political influence in the 1918 revolution, now served them

53. Ibid., pp. 641–42.

54. As Winkler seems to argue in *Mittelstand*, p. 120. Kocka, in reducing all social conflict to the level of class struggle, also follows this line of analysis in *Facing Total War*.

55. Adolf Günther, "Die Folgen des Krieges für Einkommen und Lebenshaltung der mittleren Volksschichten Deutschlands," in Meerwarth, Günther, and Zimmermann, eds., *Die Einwirkungen des Krieges auf Bevölkerungsbewegung, Einkommen und Lebenshaltung in Deutschland* (Stuttgart, 1932), p. 271.

poorly.[56] What these organizations all had in common was a fundamental lack of political power, without which it was impossible for
them to protect their members from the consequences of economic
upheaval.[57]

Eulenburg described the prewar German economy in terms of a
"democratic capitalism," meaning that capital was in the hands of
many small rentiers. The war and particularly the inflation changed
that, as money capital was destroyed and its owners expropriated.[58]
Holtfrerich has pictured this process as a reshuffling of the cards of
economic influence that had been held since the foundation of the
Empire half a century before. As everyone started afresh, with the
slate of debts and credit wiped clean, "the capitalist gamble for
power, profit, and property could start again – if not from the
beginning, on account of the fact that real values in property were
retained, then at least with different starting conditions [*Ausgangs-
bedingungen*]."[59]

What emerged was an economy in which capital was far more
concentrated, but this does not mean that Mittelstand enterprise
was extinguished; rather, the inflation caused an eclipse in Mittelstand independence. Thereafter artisans were more reliant on their
suppliers, retailers on big industry, and the white-collar workers on
their employers. Of course these groups responded with varying
degrees of success by trying to organize themselves better, and the
efforts of the guilds and white-collar trade unions are evidence of
this, but in retrospect it is clear that they were only trailing in the
footsteps of the working class. By attacking its independence, the
inflation had crippled the Mittelstand's ideological nature, the very
basis of its separate existence in an otherwise class-bound society.
Without that independence it could be ignored by the powers
maneuvering for position within Weimar's reformed corporatist
framework.

56. Between October 1919 and October 1921 GVH membership rose from 9,478
to 10,524. Revealingly, there was a sharp fall in 1924 after the inflation to 8,340.
"100 Jahre Grundeigentümer-Verein in Hamburg," *HGZ*, Beilage, Nr.31. 29 July
1932, p. 27.
57. Abelshauser, "The First Post-Liberal Nation," pp. 300–1.
58. Eulenburg, "Die sozialen Wirkungen," pp. 756–57.
59. Holtfrerich, *Die deutsche Inflation*, pp. 276–77.

Sources and Bibliography

1. Archival Material

Staatsarchiv Hamburg

Aufsichtsbehörde für die Innungen
Beamtenrat
Buchhändlerverband
Demobilmachungskommissar
Deputation für Handel, Schiffahrt und Gewerbe
Finanzdeputation
Gewerbekammer
Hauptstaatskasse
Konsumentenkammer
Senat
Senatskommission für die Angelegenheiten der Staatsarbeiter
Steuerverwaltung
Wohnungsamt

Handelskammer Hamburg

(12)	Industrie und Handwerk
(21)	Steuerwesen
(24)	Statistik
(29)	Bank-, Geld- und Kreditwesen
(59)	Wohnungs- und Siedlungswesen
(63)	Tarifverträge
(77)	Außenhandelspolitik
(80)	Organisation der gewerblichen Wirtschaft
(102)	Detaillistenkammer
(V)	Vereine und Verbände

Hamburgische Electricitäts-Werke AG

Salary and Bonus Records, 1913–1919

Public Record Office, London

Quarterly Consular Reports on Economic Conditions in Hamburg, 1921–1922.

2. Official Publications and Statistics

Arbeit und Wohlfahrt (Blätter der hamburgischen Behörden Wohlfahrtsamt und Arbeitsamt).

Enquete Bericht: Verhandlung und Berichte des Unterausschusses für Gewerbe, Industrie, Handel und Handwerk III, Das deutsche Handwerk, Der deutsche Wohnungsbau (Berlin, 1930–31).

Hamburgische Gesetze und Verordnungen, ed. Albert Wulff, 3d ed., rev. M. Leo.

Reichsarbeitsblatt.

Stenographische Berichte aus der Sitzung der Bürgerschaft (Hamburg).

Statistik des Deutschen Reichs, vols. 202–23, 401–19.

Statistisches Jahrbuch für das Deutsche Reich, 1914 passim.

Einzelschriften zur Statistik des Deutschen Reichs, 14, 16, 24.

Vierteljahreshefte zur Statistik des Deutschen Reichs, 23–34.

Wirtschaft und Statistik, 1921–1925.

Statistik des hamburgischen Staates, 25, 29, 34, 49.

Statistische Mitteilungen über den hamburgischen Staat, 2, 4, 12, 13, 20.

Hamburger statistische Monatsberichte (Aus Hamburgs Verwaltung und Wirtschaft), 1924–1928.

Statistisches Jahrbuch für die Freie und Hansestadt Hamburg, 1925.

Bericht über die medizinische Statistik des hamburgischen Staates bis zum Jahre 1927 (Hamburg, 1927).

3. Reports and Memoranda

Bau-Verein zu Hamburg, Geschäftsberichte, 1922, 1923.

Grundeigentümer-Verein zu Hamburg, Jahresberichte, 1914–1924.

Hamburger Sparkasse von 1827, Jahresberichte, 1921, 1922, 1923, 1924, 1925.

Hypothekenbank in Hamburg, Jahresbericht, 1923.

Konsum-, Bau- und Sparverein Produktion GmbH, Hamburg, Geschäftsberichte, 1920, 1921.

Verein Hamburger Hausmakler, e.V., Denkschrift zum 50-jährigen Bestehen des VHH, "Hausmakler und Grundeigentum in Hamburg" (Hamburg, 1947).

Detaillistenkammer Hamburg, Jahresberichte, 1919–1921, 1923.

Gewerbekammer Hamburg, Jahresbericht, 1913.

Handelskammer Hamburg, Jahresberichte, 1918, 1919. Mitteilungen, Nr.1 (1921).

Deputation für Handel, Schiffahrt und Gewerbe, Jahresbericht, 1925.

Gerichtsvollzieheramt, Jahresbericht, 1926.

Gewerbeaufsichtsamt, Jahresberichte, 1922–1924.

Hamburger Beleihungskasse für Hypotheken, Geschäftsberichte, 1924–25.

AfA-Bund, Angestellten Bewegung 1921–1925, (Berlin, 1925)

Verband der Vereine creditreform e.V., Jahresberichte, 1914–1923.
Deutscher Industrie- und Handelstag, Kleinhandelsausschuß, Berichte, 1916–1917, 1919–1922.

4. Periodicals

Allgemeine Industrie- und Gewerbezeitung, Organ of the Hamburg Gewerbe-kammer.
Der Bureaubeamte, Organ of the Gewerkschaft der Bürobeamten des ham-burgischen Staates, e.V.
Der Einzelhandel, Organ of the Hamburg Detaillistenkammer, incl. Nr.13 (1931), W. Siegmund, "Die Struktur des Einzelhandels in Hamburg nach der Umsatzsteuerstatistik."
Hamburger Grundeigentümer Zeitung, Organ of the Grundeigentümer-Verein zu Hamburg.
Hamburgische Beamtenzeitung.
Deutsche Handels-Wacht, Organ of the Deutschnationale Handlungs-gehilfen-Verband.
Der Handelstand, Organ of the Hamburg GdA.
GDA, Organ of the national GdA.
Nordwestdeutsche Rundschau, Organ of the ZdA.
Nordwestdeutsche Handwerkszeitung.
Deutscher Großhandel.

5. Newspapers

Hamburger Anzeiger
Hamburgischer Correspondent
Hamburger Echo
Hamburger Fremdenblatt
Hamburger Nachrichten
Hamburger Volkszeitung

6. Books and Articles

Abel, Theodore. *Why Hitler Came into Power*. Cambridge, Mass., 1986.
Abel, W., ed. *Handwerksgeschichte in neuer Sicht*. Göttingen, 1978.
Abelshauser, Werner. "The First Post-Liberal Nation: Stages in the Devel-opment of Modern Corporatism in Germany." *European History Quar-terly* n.s. 3, 14 (July 1984): 285–317.
Achner, Leonhard. "Die Lebenshaltung des Mittelstandes in der Vor-kriegszeit und Gegenwart." *Allgemeines Statistisches Archiv* 15 (Munich, 1926): 355–79.
Allen, William S., ed. *The Infancy of Nazism: The Memoirs of Ex-Gauleiter Albert Krebs, 1923–1933*. New York, 1976.

Angell, James W. *The Recovery of Germany.* New Haven, 1929.

Angel-Volkov, Shulamit. "The Decline of the German Handicrafts – Another Reappraisal." *Vierteljahrschrift für Sozial- und Wirtschaftsgeschichte* 61 (1974): 165–84.

Anker, Herbert. *Die Wohnungszwangswirtschaft und ihre volkswirtschaftliche Bedeutung.* Diss., Berlin, 1927.

Baasch, Ernst. *Geschichte Hamburgs, 1814–1918.* 2 vols. Gotha-Stuttgart, 1925.

Bach, G.L., and Albert Ando. "The Redistributional Effects of Inflation." *Review of Economics and Statistics* 39 (1957): 1–13.

Balderston, T. "War Finance and Inflation in Britain and Germany, 1914–1918." *Economic History Review* (May 1989): 222–44.

Bessel, Richard, and E.J. Feuchtwanger, eds. *Social Change and Political Development in Weimar Germany.* London, 1981.

Blackbourn, David. *Class, Religion and Local Politics in Wilhemine Germany: The Centre Party in Württemberg before 1914.* New Haven, 1980.

———. "The Mittelstand in German Society and Politics, 1871–1914." *Social History* 4 (1977): 409–33.

Böhm, Ekkehard. *Anwalt der Handels- und Gewerbefreiheit. Beiträge zur Geschichte der Handelskammer Hamburg.* Hamburg, 1981.

Bolland, Jürgen. *Die hamburgische Bürgerschaft in alter und neuer Zeit.* Hamburg, 1959.

Bonn, Moritz J. *So macht man Geschichte. Bilanz eines Lebens.* Munich, 1953.

Borchardt, Knut. *Strukturwirkungen des Inflationsprozesses.* Berlin, 1972.

Brandt, Jürgen. *Hamburgs Finanzen von 1914 bis 1924.* Diss., Hamburg, 1924.

Brauer, Theodor. "Das soziale System des Kapitalismus: Mittelstandspolitik." In *Grundriß der Sozialökonomie,* sec. 9, pt. 2. Tübingen, 1927, pp. 370–410.

Brenke, Carl. *Die Finanzierung des Handwerksbetriebes.* Stuttgart, 1936.

Bresciani-Turroni, C. *The Economics of Inflation: A Study of Currency Depreciation in Post-War Germany.* London, 1937.

Broeker, Paul. *Die Arbeitnehmerbewegung.* DHV, Hamburg, 1919.

Bronfenbrenner, Martin. "Inflation and Deflation." In *International Encyclopedia of the Social Sciences,* vol. 7. New York, 1968.

Bry, Gerhard. *Wages in Germany, 1871–1945.* Princeton, 1960.

Burgdörfer, F. "Tatsachen und Zahlen zum Behördenabbau." *Allgemeines statistisches Archiv* 14 (1923/24): 245–55.

Büttner, Ursula. *Hamburg in der Staats- und Wirtschaftskrise, 1928–1931.* Hamburg, 1982.

———. *Politische Gerechtigkeit und sozialer Geist. Hamburg zur Zeit der Weimarer Republik.* Hamburg, 1985.

Cagan, Philip. "The Monetary Dynamics of Hyperinflation." In *Studies in the Quantity Theory of Money,* edited by Milton Friedman. Chicago, 1956.

Caplan, Jane. "The Imaginary Universality of Particular Interests: The 'Tradition' of the Civil Service in German History." *Social History* 4 (1979): 299–327.

Cecil, Lamar. *Albert Ballin: Business and Politics in Imperial Germany, 1888–1918.* Princeton, 1967.

Childers, Thomas. *The Nazi Voter: The Social Foundations of Fascism in Germany, 1919–1933.* Chapel Hill, 1983.

———, ed. *The Formation of the Nazi Constituency.* London, 1986.

Colm, Gerhard. "War Finance." In *Encyclopaedia of the Social Sciences*, vol. 15. New York, 1935.

Comfort, Richard A. *Revolutionary Hamburg: Labor Politics in the Early Weimar Republic.* Stanford, 1966.

Coyner, Sandra. "Class Consciousness and Consumption: The New Middle Class during the Weimar Republic." *Journal of Social History* 10 (1976/77): 314–16.

———. *Class Patterns of Family Income and Expenditure during the Weimar Republic.* Diss., Rutgers University, 1975.

Crew, David F. *Town in the Ruhr: A Social History of Bochum, 1860–1914.* New York, 1979.

Croner, Fritz. *Soziologie der Angestellten.* Cologne, 1962.

Crossick, Geoffrey, and Heinz-Gerhard Haupt, eds. *Shopkeepers and Master Artisans in Nineteenth Century Europe.* London, 1984.

Crüger, Hans. "Konsumvereine." In *Handwörterbuch der Staatswissenschaft*, vol. 5. Jena, 1923.

Czada, Peter. "Ursachen und Folgen der großen Inflation." In *Finanz- und wirtschaftspolitische Fragen der Zwischenweltkriegszeit*, edited by Harold Winkel. Berlin, 1973.

Dahrendorf, Ralf. *Society and Democracy in Germany.* London, 1968.

Dreyfuß, Carl. *Beruf und Ideologie der Angestellten.* Munich, 1933.

Elster, Karl. *Von der Mark zur Reichsmark: Die Geschichte der deutschen Währung in den Jahren 1914 bis 1924.* Jena, 1928.

Epstein, Klaus. *Matthias Erzberger and the Dilemma of German Democracy.* Princeton, 1959.

Eulenburg, Franz. "Die sozialen Wirkungen der Währungsverhältnisse." *Jahrbuch für Nationalökonomie und Statistik*, 122 (1924): 748–94.

Evans, Richard J. *Death in Hamburg: Society and Politics in the Cholera Years, 1830–1910.* Oxford, 1987.

———. "'Red Wednesday' in Hamburg: Social Democrats, Police, and Lumpenproletariat in the Suffrage Disturbances of 17 January 1906." *Social History* 4 (1979): 1–31.

———. *Rethinking German History: Nineteenth Century Germany and the Origins of the Third Reich.* London, 1987.

Fehrman, Eberhard, and Ulrike Metzner. *Angestellte und Gewerkschaften: Ein historischer Abriß.* Cologne, 1981.

Feldman, Gerald D. *Army, Industry, and Labor in Germany, 1914–1918.*

Princeton, 1966.

——. "The Economic and Social Problems of the German Demobilisation, 1918–1919." *Journal of Modern History* 47 (1975): 1–22.

——. *Iron and Steel in the German Inflation, 1916–1923.* Princeton, 1977.

——. "The Weimar Republic: A Problem of Modernization?" *Archiv für Sozialgeschichte* 26 (1986): 1–26.

——, ed. *Die Nachwirkungen der Inflation auf die deutsche Geschichte, 1924–1933.* Munich, 1985.

Feldman, Gerald D., and Otto Büsch, eds. *Historische Prozesse der deutschen Inflation, 1914–1924.* Berlin, 1978.

Feldman, Gerald D., Carl-Ludwig Holtfrerich, Gerhard A. Ritter, and Peter-Christian Witt, eds. *Die Anpassung an die Inflation.* Berlin and New York, 1986.

——, eds. *Die Erfahrung der Inflation im internationalen Zusammenhang und Vergleich.* Berlin and New York, 1984.

——, eds. *Die deutsche Inflation: Eine Zwischenbilanz.* Berlin, 1982.

Fischer, Wolfram, ed. *Quellen zur Geschichte des deutschen Handwerks.* Göttingen, 1957.

——. *Wirtschaft und Gesellschaft im Zeitalter der Industrialisierung.* Göttingen, 1972.

Geiger, Theodor. "Panik im Mittelstand." *Die Arbeit* 7 (1930): 637–54.

——. *Die soziale Schichtung des deutschen Volkes.* Stuttgart, 1932.

Geithe, Hans. *Wirkungen der Lebensmittelzwangswirtschaft der Kriegs- und Nachkriegszeit auf den Lebensmitteleinzelhandel.* Berlin, 1926.

Gellately, Robert. *The Politics of Economic Despair: Shopkeepers and German Politics, 1890–1914.* London, 1974.

Gerloff, Wilhelm, ed. *Die Beamtenbesoldung im modernen Staat.* Schriften des Vereins für Sozialpolitik, 184/1. Leipzig and Munich, 1932.

Götz, Heinz. *Die Detaillistenkammer Hamburg, 1904–1929.* Hamburg, 1929.

Graham, Frank D. *Exchange, Prices, and Production in Hyperinflation: Germany, 1920–1923.* Princeton, 1931.

Grünberg, Emil. *Der Mittelstand in der kapitalistischen Gesellschaft.* Leipzig, 1932.

Grüttner, Michael. *Arbeitswelt an der Wasserkante: Sozialgeschichte der Hamburger Hafenarbeiter, 1886–1914.* Göttingen, 1984.

——. "Working-Class Crime and the Labour Movement: Pilfering in the Hamburg Docks, 1888–1923." In *The German Working Class, 1888–1933*, edited by Richard J. Evans. London, 1982.

Günther, Adolf. "Die Folgen des Krieges für Einkommen und Lebenshaltung der mittleren Volksschichten Deutschlands." In *Die Einwirkungen des Krieges auf Bevölkerungsbewegung, Einkommen und Lebenshaltung in Deutschland*, edited by Rudolf Meerwarth et al. Stuttgart, 1932.

——. *Die Lebenshaltung des Mittelstands.* Schriften des Vereins für Sozialpolitik, 146/2. Leipzig and Berlin, 1920.

Gut, Albert, ed. *Der Wohnungsbau in Deutschland nach dem Weltkrieg.*

Munich, 1928.

Hamel, Iris. *Völkischer Verband und nationale Gewerkschaft: Der Deutschnationale Handlungsgehilfen-Verband, 1893–1933.* Frankfurt a.M., 1967.

Hamerow, Theodore S. *Restoration, Revolution, Reaction: Economics and Politics in Germany, 1815–1871.* Princeton, 1958.

Harms, Bernard, ed. *Strukturwandlungen der deutschen Volkswirtschaft.* 2d ed. Berlin, 1929.

Hartfiel, Günther. *Angestellte und Angestelltengewerkschaften in Deutschland.* Berlin, 1961.

Haupt, Heinz-Gerhard. "Kleinhändler und Arbeiter in Bremen zwischen 1890 und 1914." *Archiv für Sozialgeschichte* 12 (1982): 95–132.

Hauschild-Thiessen, R. *150 Jahre Grundeigentümer-Verein in Hamburg von 1832, e.V: Ein Beitrag zur Geschichte der Freien und Hansestadt Hamburg.* Hamburg, 1982.

Heiden, Konrad. *Der Führer: Hitler's Rise to Power.* Boston, 1944.

Henningsen, J. *Steuer- und Wirtschaftsfragen in der Hamburger Bürgerschaft nach dem Umsturz.* Hamburg, 1924.

Herf, Jeffrey. *Reactionary Modernism: Technology, Culture, and Politics in Weimar and the Third Reich.* Cambridge, 1984.

Herzig, Arno, Dieter Langewiesche, and Arnold Sywottek, eds. *Arbeiter in Hamburg: Unterschichten, Arbeiter und Arbeiterbewegung seit dem ausgehenden 18. Jahrhundert.* Hamburg, 1983.

Hesse, Friedrich. *Die deutsche Wirtschaftslage von 1914–1923: Krieg, Geldblähe und Wechsellagen.* Jena, 1938.

Hintze, Otto. *Beamtentum und Bürokratie.* Edited by Kersten Krüger. Göttingen, 1981.

Hirsch, Fred, and John H. Goldthorpe, eds. *The Political Economy of Inflation.* London, 1978.

Hirsch, Julius. "Der moderne Detailhandel." in *Grundriß der Sozialökonomie,* sec. 5, pt. 2. Tübingen, 1925.

Hoebel, Heinrich. *Das organisierte Arbeitgebertum in Hamburg-Altona.* Diss., Hamburg, 1923.

Hoffmann, W.G., and J.H. Müller. *Das deutsche Volkseinkommen, 1851–1957.* Tübingen, 1959.

Holtfrerich, Carl-Ludwig. *Die deutsche Inflation, 1914–1923: Ursachen und Folgen in internationaler Perspektive.* Berlin, 1980.

Hughes, Michael L. *Paying for the German Inflation.* Chapel Hill, 1988.

Ipsen, Hans-Peter. *Hamburgs Verfassung und Verwaltung.* Hamburg, 1956.

Jaeger, Franz. *Die Einwirkungen der Kriegs- und Nachkriegszeit auf den Einzelhandel.* Hamburg, 1922.

James, Harold. *The German Slump: Politics and Economics, 1924–1936.* Oxford, 1986.

Jantzen, Günther. *Hamburgs Ausfuhrhandel im 20. Jahrhundert.* Hamburg, 1953.

Jochmann, Werner, and Hans-Dieter Loose, eds. *Hamburg. Geschichte der*

Stadt Hamburg und ihrer Bewohner. Vol. 1. Hamburg, 1982.

Jones, Larry E. "'The Dying Middle': Weimar Germany and the Fragmentation of Bourgeois Politics." *Central European History* 5 (1972): 23–54.

———. *German Liberalism and the Dissolution of the Weimar Party System, 1918–1933.* Chapel Hill, 1988.

———. "Inflation, Revaluation and the Crisis of Middle-Class Politics: A Study in the Dissolution of the German Party System, 1923–1928." *Central European History* 12 (1979): 143–68.

Kaelble, Hartmut. "Social Stratification in Germany in the 19th and 20th Centuries: A Survey of Research since 1945." *Journal of Social History* 10 (1976/7): 144–61.

Kaiser, G. "Umsatzentwicklung, Umsatz je Person und Umschlagsgeschwindigkeit in Handwerk und Kleingewerbe (1924–1928)." *Das Deutsche Handwerksblatt* 2 (1930): 28.

Kaufmann, Heinrich. *Kurzer Abriß der Geschichte des Zentralverbandes deutscher Konsumvereine.* Hamburg, 1928.

Kaven, Oskar. *Die Hamburger Sparkasse von 1827, 1892–1925.* Hamburg, 1927.

Kersten, Dietrich. *Die Kriegsziele der Hamburger Kaufmannschaft im Ersten Weltkrieg.* Diss., Hamburg, 1963.

Kessler, Harry. *In the Twenties: The Diaries of Harry Kessler.* New York, English translation 1971.

Keynes, J. Maynard. *A Tract on Monetary Reform.* London, 1923.

Kipnase, Ernst. *Die Hamburger Hochbahn AG in verkehrspolitischer und sozialpolitischer Beziehung.* Berlin, 1925.

Klein, Gottfried. *Dokumente zur Geschichte der Handelskammer Hamburg.* Hamburg, 1965.

Klessman, Eckart. *Geschichte der Stadt Hamburg.* Hamburg, 1981.

Kocka, Jürgen. *Die Angestellten in der deutschen Geschichte, 1850–1980.* Göttingen, 1981.

———. *Facing Total War: German Society, 1914–1918.* Cambridge, Mass., 1984.

———. "The First World War and the *Mittelstand*: German Artisans and White-Collar Workers." *Journal of Contemporary History* 8 (1973).

———. *White-Collar Workers in America, 1890–1940: A Social and Political History in International Perspective.* Translated by Maura Kealey. London and Beverly Hills, 1980.

———, ed. *Bürger und Bürgerlichkeit im 19. Jahrhundert.* Göttingen, 1987.

Koeppe, H. "Besoldung und Besoldungspolitik." In *Handwörterbuch der Staatswissenschaft,* vol. 2. Jena, 1924.

Koshar, Rudy. *Social Life, Local Politics, and Nazism: Marburg, 1880–1935.* Chapel Hill, 1986.

Krohn, Claus-Dieter. "Helfferich contra Hilferding: Konservative Geldpolitik und die sozialen Folgen der deutschen Inflation 1918–1923."

Vierteljahrschrift für Sozial- und Wirtschaftsgeschichte 62 (1975): 62–92.

——. *Stabilisierung und ökonomische Interessen: Die Finanzpolitik des Deutschen Reichs, 1923–1927.* Düsseldorf, 1974.

Kuczinski, Robert. "Postwar Labor Conditions in Germany." In US Bureau of Statistics. *Bulletin 380.* Washington, D.C., 1925.

Kunz, Andreas. *Civil Servants and the Politics of Inflation in Germany, 1914–1924.* Berlin and New York, 1986.

——. "Stand versus Klasse: Beamtenschaft und Gewerkschaften im Konflikt um den Personalabbau, 1923/1924." *Geschichte und Gesellschaft* 8 (1982): 55–86.

Lampe, Adolf. *Der Einzelhandel in der Volkswirtschaft.* Berlin, 1930.

Laufenberg, Heinrich. *Die Hamburger Revolution.* Hamburg, 1919.

Laursen, Karsten, and Jorgen Pedersen. *The German Inflation, 1918–1923.* Amsterdam, 1964.

Lebovics, Herman. *Social Conservatism and the Middle Classes in Germany, 1914–1933.* Princeton, 1969.

Lederer, Emil. *Die Privatangestellten in der modernen Wirtschaftsentwicklung.* Tübingen, 1912.

——. "Privatbeamtenbewegung." *Archiv für Sozialwissenschaft und Sozialpolitik* 31 (1919): 215ff.

Lederer, Emil, and Jacob Marschak. "Der neue Mittelstand." In *Grundriß der Sozialökonomie,* sec. 9, pt. 1. Tübingen, 1926, pp. 120–42.

Lippmann, Leo. *Mein Leben und meine amtliche Tätigkeit.* Hamburg, 1964.

Lorenz, Gustav. *Die Wohnungsproduktion und ihre Regelung in dem letzten Jahrzehnt, 1914–1924.* Diss., Würzburg, 1927.

Luth, Erich, and Hans-Dieter Loose. *Bürgermeister Carl Petersen, 1868–1933.* Hamburg, 1971.

Luther, Hans. *Feste Mark, Solide Wirtschaft: Rückblick auf die Arbeit der Reichsregierung während der Wintermonate 1923/1924.* Berlin, 1924.

Maier, Charles S. *Recasting Bourgeois Europe.* Princeton, 1975.

Marx, Karl, and Friedrich Engels. *The Communist Manifesto.* Penguin edition, 1967.

Mendel, Max, and Josef Rieger. *Die "Produktion" in Hamburg, 1899–1924: Geschichte einer genossenschaftlichen Verbrauchervereinigung von Gründung bis zum 25. Geschäftsschluß.* Hamburg, 1924.

Meyer, Heinrich. *Hamburg als Güterumschlagsplatz vor und nach dem Krieg.* Hamburg, 1930.

Mommsen, Hans, Dietmar Petzina, and Bernd Weisbrod, eds. *Industrielles System und politische Entwicklung in der Weimarer Republik.* Düsseldorf, 1974.

Moore, Barrington, Jr. *Social Origins of Dictatorship and Democracy.* Harmondsworth, 1973.

Moulton, H.G. "Economic Conditions in Europe." *American Economic Review* 13 (1923): 50–64.

Needleman, Lionel. *The Economics of Housing.* London, 1965.

Netzband, Karl B., and Hans P. Widmaier. "Währungsprojekte und Regierungsverhandlungen auf dem Wege zur Rentenmark." In *Moderne deutsche Wirtschaftsgeschichte*, edited by Karl Erich Born, 351–69. Cologne, 1966.

Niehusen, Peter. *Die Hamburger Kaufmannschaft und ihre Haltung zur Exportförderung in der Wiederaufbauphase des deutschen Außenhandels vom 1918–1929*. Diss., Hamburg, 1980.

Nipperdey, Thomas. *Nachdenken über die deutsche Geschichte*: Essays. Munich, 1986.

Nocken, Ulrich. "Corporatism and Pluralism in Modern German History." In *Industrielle Gesellschaft und politisches System*, edited by Dirk Stegmann, Bernd-Jürgen Wendt, and Peter-Christian Witt. Bonn, 1978.

Nurkse, Ragnar. *The Course and Control of Inflation: A Review of Monetary Experience in Europe after World War 1*. League of Nations, 1946.

Nussbaum, Manfred. "Unternehmenskonzentration und Investstrategie nach dem Ersten Weltkrieg." *Jahrbuch für Wirtschaftsgeschichte*, 15/2 (1974): 42–59.

O'Swald, Alfred. "Der Handel," in *Hamburg in seiner politischen, wirtschaftlichen und kulturellen Bedeutung*, edited by Deutsche Auslandsarbeitergemeinschaft. Hamburg, 1921.

Patch, William L. *Christian Trade Unions in the Weimar Republic: The Failure of Corporate Pluralism*. New Haven, 1985.

Pentzlin, Heinz. *Hjalmar Schacht: Leben und Wirken einer umstrittenen Persönlichkeit*. Berlin, 1980.

Pergande, Hans-Günther, and Jürgen Pergande. "Die Gesetzgebung auf dem Gebiete des Wohnungswesen und des Städtebaues." In *Deutsche Bau- und Bodenbank AG, 1923–1973*. Bonn, 1973.

Pesl, L.D. "Mittelstandsfragen," *Grundriß der Sozialökonomie*, sec. 9, pt. 1. Tübingen, 1926, pp. 70–120.

Petzina, Dietmar. *Die deutsche Wirtschaft in der Zwischenkriegszeit*. Wiesbaden, 1977.

———. "Gewerkschaften und Monopolfrage vor und während der Weimar Republik." *Archiv für Sozialgeschichte* 20 (1980): 195–217.

Preller, Ludwig. *Sozialpolitik in der Weimarer Republik*. Düsseldorf, 1949.

Priamus, H.J. *Angestellte und Demokratie: Die nationalliberale Angestelltenbewegung in der Weimarer Republik*. Stuttgart, 1979.

Reincke, Heinrich. *Hamburg: Ein kurzer Abriß der Stadtgeschichte von den Anfängen bis zur Gegenwart*. Bremen, 1925.

Ringer, Fritz. *The German Inflation of 1923*. New York, 1969.

———. *The Decline of the German Mandarins: The German Academic Community, 1890–1933*. Cambridge, Mass., 1969.

Roesler, K. *Die Finanzpolitik des Deutschen Reichs im Ersten Weltkrieg*. Berlin, 1967.

Rosenbaum, E., and A.J. Sherman. *M.M. Warburg & Co., 1798–1938: Merchant Bankers of Hamburg*. London, 1979.

Rosenberg, Arthur. *Geschichte der Weimarer Republik.* 19th ed. Frankfurt a.M., 1978.

——. *Imperial Germany: The Birth of the German Republic, 1871–1918.* Boston, 1964.

Ross, Frank A. "The Passing of the German Middle Class." *American Journal of Sociology* 29 (1924): 530–41.

Rupieper, Hermann J. "The Cuno Government and Reparations, 1922–1923: Politics and Economics." In *Studies in Contemporary History,* vol. 1. The Hague, 1979.

Saldern, Adelheid von. *Mittelstand im "Dritten Reich": Handwerker-Einzelhändler-Bauern.* Frankfurt a.M., 1979.

Samhaber, Ernst. *125 Jahre Hamburger Sparkasse von 1827.* Hamburg, 1952.

Schacht, Hjalmar. *The Stabilization of the Mark.* New York, 1927.

Schmidthuysen, Fritz. *Die Deckung der Wohnungsbauabgabe in Deutschland bis zur Stabilisierung.* Würzburg, 1928.

Schmoller, Gustav. *Was verstehen wir unter dem Mittelstand?* Göttingen, 1897.

Schmukler, Nathan and Edward Marcus, eds. *Inflation through the Ages: Economic, Social, Psychological, and Historical Aspects.* New York, 1983.

Schoenberner, Franz. *Confessions of a European Intellectual.* New York, 1946.

Schönewald, Henry. *Die Wirkungen der Mieterschutz- und Raumnotgesetzgebung unter besonderer Berücksichtigung der sozialen und wirtschaftlichen Folgen in Hamburg.* Diss., Hamburg, 1922.

Schraeder, Bernard H. *Die Entwicklungstendenzen der deutschen Warenhauskonzerne.* Würzburg, 1930.

Schramm, Percy. *Hamburg, Deutschland und die Welt.* Munich, 1943.

——. *Hamburg – Ein Sonderfall in der Geschichte Deutschlands.* Hamburg, 1964.

Schumacher, Martin. *Mittelstandsfront und Republik, 1919–1933: Die Wirtschaftspartei – Reichspartei des deutschen Mittelstandes.* Düsseldorf, 1972.

Sheehan, James J. *German Liberalism in the Nineteenth Century.* Chicago, 1978.

Silverman, Dan P. "A Pledge Unredeemed: The Housing Crisis in Weimar Germany." *Central European History* 3 (1970): 112–39.

Singer, Kurt. *Staat und Wirtschaft seit dem Waffenstillstand.* Jena, 1924.

Sinz, Herbert. *Das Handwerk: Geschichte, Bedeutung und Zukunft.* Düsseldorf, 1977.

Smith, Woodruff D. *The German Colonial Empire.* Chapel Hill, 1978.

Sommariva, Andrea, and Giuseppe Tullio. *German Macroeconomic History, 1880–1979: A Study of the Effects of Economic Policy on Inflation, Currency Depreciation, and Growth.* New York, 1987.

Speier, Hans. *Die Angestellten vor dem Nationalsozialismus: Ein Beitrag zum Verständnis der deutschen Sozialstruktur, 1918–1933.* Göttingen, 1977.

Stachura, Peter D., ed. *The Nazi Machtergreifung.* London, 1983.

Stucken, Rudolf. *Deutsche Geld- und Kreditpolitik 1914, bis 1953.* Tübingen, 1953.

Suhr, Otto. "Die Angestellten in der deutschen Wirtschaft." In *Angestellte und Arbeiter*, an AfA-Bund publication. Berlin, 1928.

Tobis, Hans. *Das Mittelstandsproblem der Nachkriegszeit und seine statistische Erfassung.* Diss., Grimmen, 1930.

Ullrich, Volker. *Kriegsalltag: Hamburg im Ersten Weltkrieg.* Cologne, 1982.

——. *Die Hamburger Arbeiterbewegung vom Vorabend des Ersten Weltkrieges bis zur Revolution, 1918/19.* Hamburg, 1976.

Walker, Mack. *German Home Towns: Community, States, and General Estate, 1648–1871.* Ithaca, N.Y., 1971.

Warburg, Max. *Aus meinen Aufzeichnungen.* New York, 1952.

Wehler, Hans-Ulrich. *Das Deutsche Kaiserreich, 1871–1918.* Göttingen, 1973.

——. *The German Empire, 1871–1918.* Translated by Kim Traynor. Leamington Spa, 1985.

Wein, J. *Die Verbandsbildung im Einzelhandel.* Berlin, 1968.

Wendemuth, Ludwig, and Boettcher, Walter. *The Port of Hamburg.* Hamburg, 1927.

Wernet, W. *Handwerkspolitik.* Göttingen, 1952.

Wernicke, J. *Kapitalismus und Mittelstandspolitik.* 2d ed. Jena, 1922.

Williamson, J.G. *Karl Helfferich, 1872–1924: Economist, Financier, Politician.* Princeton, 1971.

Winkler, Heinrich A. "Extremismus der Mitte? Sozialgeschichtliche Aspekte der nationalsozialistichen Machtergreifung." *Vierteljahrshefte für Zeitgeschichte* 20 (1972): 175–91.

——. "From Social Protectionism to National Socialism: The German Small-Business Movement in Comparative Perspective." *Journal of Modern History* 48/1 (1976): 1–18.

——. *Mittelstand, Demokratie und Nationalsozialismus: Die politische Entwicklung von Handwerk und Kleinhandel in der Weimarer Republik.* Cologne, 1972.

——, ed. *Organisierter Kapitalismus: Voraussetzungen und Anfragen,* Kritische Studien zur Geschichtswissenschaft, vol. 9. Göttingen, 1974.

Wischermann, Clemens. *Wohnen in Hamburg vor dem Ersten Weltkrieg.* Münster, 1983.

Wiskemann, Erwin. *Hamburg und die Welthandelspolitik von den Anfängen bis zur Gegenwart.* Hamburg, 1929.

Witt, Peter-Christian. "Inflation, Wohnungszwangswirtschaft und Hauszinssteuer. Zur Regelung von Wohnungsbau und Wohnungsmarkt in der Weimarer Republik." In *Wohnen in Wandel*, edited by Lutz Niethammer. Wuppertal, 1979.

——. "Reichsfinanzminister und Reichsfinanzverwaltung, 1918–1924." *Vierteljahrshefte für Zeitgeschichte*, 23 (1975): 1–61.

Index

Altona, 69, 116
artisans, 11, 39–42, 143, 164, 185
  Chamber of Industry
    (Gewerbekammer), 57, 59, 82–84,
    114, 142
    facing bankruptcy, 141
    joint venture with the Chamber of
      Retailers, 112
  Gewerbefreiheit, 40–41
  guilds, 40–42, 57, 59–60, 82–84
    bakers, 57, 58, 87
    bookbinders, 83
    Bund der Innungen, 85 n. 43
    chimney sweeps, 114
    cobblers, 87
    smithies, 57, 143
    tailors, 58, 59, 82
  Hamburg, 37–38
  journeymen's wages, 86
  Loan Relief Fund for Traders
    (Darlehnshilfskasse für
    Gewerbetreibende), 59, 114
  Nordwestdeutschen
    Handwerkerbund, 85
  Reichsverband des deutschen
    Handwerks, 83, 141

bank note shortage, 130–31, 137, 152
bankruptcy, 151, 163, 165–66
banks, 28, 148
  staff, 149, 170–71. *See also*
    white-collar workers
Brauer, Theodor, 39, 41

Chamber of Commerce
  (Handelskammer), 117, 139, 143
  foreign currency certificate issue,
    142
  influence in Hamburg, 30, 43,

    81–82, 169, 180
  postwar plans, 56, 78–79
civil servants, 45–47, 68–71, 170. *See
  also* white-collar workers
  Civil Service Council (Beamtenrat),
    98–102, 153, 154, 173
    pay demands and, 123–26, 130–31
  Communist party and, 125–26
  Deutscher Beamtenbund (DBB), 71,
    97–98, 124–26, 172
  earnings, 127–29, 131
  social wage, 100–101
  supplements and bonuses, 69–70
  state employees (*Staatsangestellte*),
    154–55, 173
  teachers, 124
  unpopularity, 153
Communist party (KPD), 34, 139
  Hamburg uprising (1923), 139–40,
    144
consumer cooperatives, 43, 89, 92,
  117. *See also* retailers
  landlords, 105, 135
  Produktion, 62–63, 135
corporatism, 118, 167–69
  Weimar Republic, 11–12, 17, 184–85
  Wilhelmine Empire, 8–12
cost-of-living, 55, 66
  index, 106, 123, 127, 132–33,
    149–50, 152
  supplements, 56, 69–70, 100, 102,
    119. *See also* civil servants

Eddelbüttel, Friedrich, 72
eight-hour day, 85, 89, 113. *See also*
  revolution
Erzberger, Matthias, 22–24, 53, 77,
  110. *See also* taxation
Eulenburg, Franz, 18, 173, 175, 185

First World War, 27, 45, 63, 169
  financing, 52–54
foreign currency, 142–43
foreigners, 115, 143, 159–60

Geiger, Theodor, 6–7, 183–84
German Democratic party (DDP), 12, 81, 178, 182
German National People's party (DNVP), 12, 78, 85, 178–79, 182
German People's party (DVP), 81, 85, 178–79, 182, 183
gold marks, use of, 140–41, 144, 152, 156

Hamburg
  Citizens' Assembly (Bürgerschaft), 80–81, 107, 134, 156–57
    pre-1914, 31–34, 44, 51
  demography, 34–35
  economy, 26–30
    docks, 51, 54, 138
    shipyards, 28, 55–56, 139
  housing, 49–51. See also house owners
    Alley Quarters, 32, 35, 51
  political structure, 30–34. See also Social Democratic party
  Prussia, relationship with, 26–27, 46, 78, 134
  Senate, 73, 81–82, 99, 131, 134
    pre-1914, 30, 43
  trade and transport, 26, 35–38, 78–79, 110–11
  Workers' and Soldiers' Council, 79–81, 82, 99, 140
Hamburger Bank von 1923, 144
Hamburger Echo, 33, 108, 118, 141
Hamburger Hochbahn AG (HHA), 119–21, 123, 150–51
Hamburgische Electricitäts-Werke (HEW), 66–67, 152
Hamburgischer Correspondent, 154–55
Hamburg Wholesalers' Association, 122
Helfferich, Karl, 14, 52–54, 109
house owners, 49–51, 71–74
  compulsory billeting, 104
  deterioration of buildings, 73
  Grundeigentümer-Verein, 49–51, 72, 105–7, 135, 159–60
  hostility to SPD, 50
  house sales, 159–61
  mortgages, 173–76, 181
    Hypothekenbank, 174

mortgage revaluation, 174–75
Hüne, Johannes, 132, 134, 183

Independent Social Democratic party (USPD), 56, 80
inflation, 76, 79, 127, 141, 162, 169
  attitude of governments to, 14–16
  causes, 13–14, 52–54
  hyperinflation, 14, 138, 151, 153, 176
  redistributive effects, 14–15
  theory, 13–16

Kapp *Putsch*, 75, 76, 96–97, 102

Laufenberg, Heinrich, 80
Lippmann, Leo, 29, 103, 153, 175

Melle, Werner von, 81
Mittelstand, 2–8, 10–13, 55, 60, 74
  corporatist economy and, 118, 163, 168, 182–85
  definition of, 6–7
    new, 32, 123, 127, 170, 181
    old, 118, 168–69
  "destruction of," 19, 60, 182
  enterprise, 43, 83, 112, 117–18, 141
  housing, 51, 104–5, 134, 160, 173, 177–78
  Mittelstand policy (*Mittelstandspolitik*), 7–8, 11, 41, 181
  Weimar politics and, 179–80

Nazi party (NSDAP), 95, 178, 181–82. *See also* Weimar party system
  appeal to Mittelstand, 2–5, 12–13, 167
  connection with inflation, 4–5

O'Swald, Alfred, 56

preindustrial mentality, 2–4
price control, 61–64, 113–14, 176
price control offices (*PPS*), 61–62, 93–94, 116, 145, 168
prices, 61, 87, 90–92

Reich rent law (*RMG*), 132–34, 160–61, 178
Reichsbank, 18, 52, 138, 145
Reichsgericht, 93, 113, 117, 174–75
Reichstag, 31, 34, 92, 95, 116, 178
Relief Fund for Retailers and Traders, 58

Index

rent arbitration offices (*MEA*), 72, 106–7, 134, 176–77
rent control, 88, 105–7, 176–78
Rentenmark, 137, 139, 144, 157, 164. *See also* stabilization
rent values, 157–58
reparations, 18, 109–10
retailers, 42–44, 161
  Chamber of Retailers (Detaillistenkammer), 89, 112, 177
    lack of effectiveness, 43, 90, 142–43, 167, 169
    price controls and, 61–62
  consumer cooperatives and department stores, 43, 90
  Karstadt, 96
  plunder, 55, 115
  profiteering courts, 64, 88, 168
  replacement cost price (*Wiederbeschaffungspreis*), 115–17
  Retail Employers' Association, 90, 95
revolution, 79–81

saving habit, 15, 146–48, 164–65. *See also* Mittelstand
savers, 19
savings banks (*Sparkassen*), 146–48, 164, 166
Schramm, Percy, 78
shortages
  credit, 112
  fuel, 112, 153
  raw material, 87, 104, 112
Social Democratic party (SPD)
  Hamburg, 73
    First World War, 56
    post-1918, 80–82, 93, 100
    pre-1914, 31, 33–34, 50
    reformist character of local party, 34, 81–82
  national, 7, 85, 163, 183
stabilization, 137–38, 153, 155–56, 163–68, 178
  debt revaluation and, 20, 163
  temporary (1920), 17, 23, 76, 111, 165
Stresemann, Gustav, 137, 163

taxation, 21–24
  capital gains tax, 160
  collection difficulties, 145–46
  Erzberger's reforms, 22–24, 77

Hamburg, 29, 31, 77–78, 84, 117
  inflation and, 23–24
  luxury tax, 84
  sales tax, 118
  Third Emergency Tax Decree (1924), 173
tenants, 71–72, 105–7, 176–77

unemployment, 111, 138, 163, 181
  as alternative to inflation, 16, 17

Warburg, Max, 31, 80, 142, 144, 180
Weimar party system, 12–13, 20, 178–85 passim
white-collar workers, 44–45, 64–68, 170–71
  Allgemeiner freier Angestellten-Bund (AfA-Bund), 95, 96–97, 181
  civil servants, relations with, 99
  Deutschnationale Handlungsgehilfenverband (DHV), 64–65, 99, 148, 152
    antifeminism, 68, 182
    attachment to status, 122
    industrial action, 97
    nationalist outlook, 48–49, 95, 171–72, 181
  Gewerkschaftsbund der Angestellten (GdA), 94, 181
  Hamburg, 35–39
  Hamburg 58er Verein, 48, 94
  living standards, 149–51
  salary rates, 64–67, 119–21, 150–51
    method of payment, 121, 123
    wage differentials, 15, 67, 119, 121, 150
  status consciousness, 68, 119
  unemployment amongst, 151, 171
  Zentralverband der Angestellten (ZdA), 122
Witthoefft, F.H., 81, 180

Zentralarbeitsgemeinschaft, 11, 17, 94
Zwangswirtschaft, 12, 124, 169. *See also* price and rent control
  local controls
    agriculture, 92, 118
    artisans, 84, 87, 113, 142
    housing, 105, 135
    national economy, 53, 56, 79, 81, 84, 183